WITHDRAWN

International Tourism
to 1990

International Tourism to 1990

by
Robert Cleverdon
Anthony Edwards

Abt Books
Cambridge, Massachusetts
EIU Special Series 4

Library of Congress Cataloging in Publication Data

Edwards, Anthony David, 1936–
International tourism to 1990.

  (Economist Intelligence Unit special series)
  "Economist Intelligence Unit Ltd."
  Bibliography: p.
  1. Tourist trade. I. Cleverdon, Robert. II. Economist Intelligence Unit
Limited. III. Title, IV. Series.
G155.A1E33   1982   382'.45   82–13847
ISBN 0-89011-582-6

Originally published by The Economist Intelligence
Unit as Special Report Nos. 62 and 60.

Printed in the United States of America

The Authors

Robert Cleverdon is a Senior Consultant in the Strategic Consultancy Department of the EIU. He has been engaged in a wide range of tourism-related assignments, involving extensive over-sea travel, and is a regular contributor to the EIU's International Tourism Quarterly.

Anthony Edwards operates a small consultancy organisation, Anthony Edwards Consultants, a high level independent economic consultant to government and business, specializing in studies on policies and potential for industrial development and tourism. He has traveled widely in the developing world.

Contents

List of Tables

Part 1: International Tourism Development Forecasts to 1990

List of Figures/Charts

Part 1: International Tourism Development Forecasts to 1990

xi

List of Tables

Part 2: The Economic and Social Impact of International Tourism on Developing Countries

List of Figures/Charts

Part 2: The Economic and Social Impact of International Tourism on Developing Countries

Preface

The rapid growth of international tourism over the last ten years has made it second only to oil as an item in world trade. Nonetheless, those countries and industries involved in supplying tourist services often work in ignorance, both of the current tourist market environment and of the size and direction of likely changes in it. This volume draws together two reports, first published by the Economist Intelligence Unit in London, England, both of which provide informed answers to some outstanding questions about international tourism now and for the next decade.

The question underlying the first of these reports is when and in what specific areas the growth of international tourism is likely to flatten out. It is clear that travel abroad cannot continue indefinitely to absorb a rising proportion of personal incomes or annual leave periods. Those involved in providing facilities, transportation and other tourist services need to understand how the pattern of international tourism will change, in order to adjust to lower growth rates in some instances and to focus more attention on markets that have grown less rapidly and thus have some potential for further growth. The report provides a comprehensive picture of current trends in international tourism and forecasts travel expenditures to 1990 for each of the six countries that provide most of the tourist business.

Tourism as a means of economic development has been the subject of much contention and often ill-informed discussions in recent years. Many developing countries (LDCs) with rich natural resources eagerly embraced tourism as the panacea for all their economic problems, only to find that net foreign exchange earnings are far lower than anticipated and that tourism brings with it numerous sociocultural problems. Others have become so economically dependent upon tourism that these problems are regarded as no more than minor irritations and a necessary cost of development. The second report in this volume examines the economic and social impacts of international tourism on developing countries and proposes measures to reduce the problems associated with it.

This book should prove to be of unique interest for all those involved in international tourism, including those who arrange or provide transportation, hotel and restaurant facilities and other services to tourists as well as government planners and decisionmakers.

Part One:
International Tourism Development Forecasts to 1990

Introduction

The fundamental question underlying this Special Report is whether, and where, international tourism growth is likely to flatten out in a long term sense. It is clear that travel abroad cannot continue indefinitely to absorb a rising proportion of personal incomes or annual leave periods; and, indeed, increases in the latter are likely to be slow. But how far away is this inevitable flattening off? Is it already starting? Or is it decades, or even further, away? And, how is the pattern of international travel likely to change between trips to bordering countries (still the largest single category in expenditure terms, though of far less significance for the travel industry), other short haul trips and long haul travel?

This Special Report suggests that, worldwide, growth is likely to be a little faster in the 1976 to 1990 period than in 1966 to 1976. However, this is largely due to the changing balance of travel between major origin countries. Those from which travel is likely to grow most rapidly in the future – notably West Germany and Japan – are, relatively speaking, far more important origin countries now than were the most rapidly growing origin countries in 1966.

Travel from an increasing number of countries is, in fact, likely to flatten out substantially in the 1985 to 1990 period – in some cases before then. Those involved in selling facilities and transport predominantly to these countries are likely to need to adjust to sharply lower growth rates in their market environment than they have been used to hitherto. This may imply a need to devote more attention to markets which to date have grown less rapidly and in consequence are further away from the hypothetical ceiling to travel.

Section II discusses types and limits of forecasting procedures, and paints a broad brush picture of the structure and development of world tourism since 1966 in general economic terms.

Section III considers the deficiencies of tourism data, draws up a comprehensive table for use as a data base, showing the 1966 and 1976 structure of world tourism expenditures, and the split of these between cross border, other short haul and long haul trips; the picture which emerges from this table is discussed.

Section IV examines the concept of ceilings to international travel, attempts to define how far major tourist origin countries have got from this ceiling (essentially a sloping one determined by slowly growing annual leave periods), and suggests the maximum tourism growth rates sustainable without coming across ceiling limitations.

Section V seeks to determine for France, West Germany, Japan, the UK and the USA, as major origin countries, the responsiveness of foreign tourism to incomes growth and to changes in the cost of foreign tourism relative to costs for other outlets for consumer spending.

Section VI uses the data base as in Section III and draws upon the work of Section V to derive total forecasts of travel expenditures by country of origin, which are then adjusted for ceiling limitations, as suggested in Section IV.

Section VII breaks down the total travel expenditure forecasts into cross border travel, other short haul travel, and long haul travel.

Appendix 1 presents the data series (derived from official statistics) used for the calculations of Section V.

In terms of method, Section V is thus the key one, as it is here that price and income elasticities and constants (i e the underlying rate of travel growth irrespective of income growth or prices) are calculated for use in Section VI, in conjunction with forecasts of income growth and relative price movements, to forecast total travel by origin country.

Characteristics and Problems

TYPES AND LIMITS OF FORECASTING

The type of forecast is dependent on what it is for

Methods of tourist forecasting inevitably vary considerably according to what a particular forecast is required for. The most appropriate procedures for forecasting one to two years ahead are different from those for five to ten years ahead. For short to medium term forecasts of travel to a particular destination, arrivals figures generally represent a reasonable data base. But because methods of measuring arrivals vary widely, and because they do not distinguish between very different levels of expenditure per day (see Section III), they are useless as a basis for multicountry comparisons, or for long term forecasting. If forecasting travel growth to a particular country, the facilities on offer (or which might be on offer) and the cost of travel to the country, and how these compare with facilities and prices elsewhere, are more important influences than the total growth of world or regional travel; the marketing and promotion of the facilities may also be as important a determinant of travel to a country, at least in the short to medium term, as the facilities themselves. This report is concerned with long term travel on a worldwide basis. In assessing the long term potential for travel to any region, country, or area, it is essential to bear in mind, throughout, the likely pace and pattern of tourist growth globally.

Dangers of disaggregation

It must be emphasised that any locally orientated forecast cannot be simply a disaggregation of global or regional forecasts. To take a hypothetical example: it may be possible to forecast that total UK expenditure on overseas travel will rise to £1,000 mn at 1975 prices by 1985, and be 90 per cent confident that this figure is correct within + or - 10 per cent; it may also be possible to forecast that the share within this of long haul travel for coastal resort holidays in tropical areas will be 10 per cent, with similar confidence limits. It is pointless then to attempt to break this down further into shares for the Caribbean, East Africa, etc, let alone into localities within these regions. The relative share of, say, the Caribbean within the total depends on how its facilities compare with those in East Africa and other areas; or how effectively each is promoted and marketed; and on how prices compare. A purely economic approach could not arrive at more than a rough guess at the Caribbean share of the tropical coastal resort holiday market from the UK. If the guess were 50 per cent with the (90 per cent) confidence limits at 40 per cent and 60 per cent, such travel to the Caribbean from the UK could be anywhere between £33 mn and £73 mn at 1975 prices by 1985. For such problems, global forecasts can only set the essential framework; considerable detailed marketing assessment work has to be done.

Straight line projections

The simplest economic forecasting procedure is a simple projection of past trends. This is normally done by fitting a straight line to past data by the least squares method. Though there are other procedures, this is perhaps the most straightforward way of establishing trends; it largely eliminates the distortions to growth rates which are achieved by convenient choices of base and final years for data comparisons. Any more elaborate forecasting method is of little value unless it can be shown (by reference to past data) that it is likely to achieve an appreciably more reliable result than could simple straight line projections. In the context of travel, however, even purely linear procedures present difficulties, largely because of the lack of data on the volume of travel collected on a consistent basis for all major tourist origin (or even destination) countries over a sufficient period of time. Such data problems complicate the forecaster's task, and make the end product liable to be rather less accurate than would normally be possible for a better documented sector.

Models impracticable at present

To improve on straight line projections, it is necessary to consider what the forces are which create travel growth. In principle, if sufficient forces can be identified, if their relative degrees of importance and how they interrelate can be established, and if numerical values for the past and for the future can be attached to each, a forecasting model can be devised. It is in fact fairly easy to establish what the forces bearing on tourist demand are, and to devise a hypothetical model using these. The problems are to measure these variables and to determine how a change in each will affect travel demand. Main variables which might feature in a model to forecast total foreign travel from a particular origin country are:

- a. population growth and structure;
- b. income growth, or preferably the growth in that proportion of personal incomes (discretionary incomes) from which foreign travel expenditure comes;
- c. income distribution between socio-economic groups;
- d. the general rate of domestic inflation;
- e. changes in the relative prices of major items on which discretionary incomes may be spent;
- f. changes in periods of annual leave entitlement;
- g. the facilities for tourism domestically and their price;
- h. the facilities for and price of holidays abroad;
- i. new attractions for tourists, at home and abroad;
- j. promotion and marketing of tourism at home;
- k. promotion and marketing of tourism abroad;
- l. government restrictions on travel or travel expenditure;
- m. social and other forces affecting consumer preferences and priorities for spending discretionary incomes;
- n. weather at home and abroad.

6

The information actually to construct and operate a model, even a simple one using only a few of the above variables, simply does not exist. How, for instance, can one measure the effectiveness of the total overseas travel promotional effort by the trade, let alone decide its importance as a determinant of travel compared with other variables? The IUOTO pilot study on Long Term Forecasts, published in 1971, confirmed that a model building approach was not then practicable; improvements in data since then have done little to improve the situation.

Importance of income growth –

However, it is generally supposed, and numerous studies have confirmed this, that personal disposable income growth (or still better, if it can be isolated, discretionary income growth) is an important determinant of travel demand. It can be demonstrated that, historically, a growth of 1 per cent in incomes tends to be accompanied by a growth of rather over 1 per cent in travel; although a causal link cannot be proven, it is a reasonable supposition which statistical evidence would support. Section V of this report attempts to measure income elasticity of travel demand (or the response of travel to changes in incomes).

– and relative price movements

Another element which can, with difficulty, be measured and which it is reasonable to presume has a significant influence on foreign travel is how the growth of the cost of travel abroad compares with the development of consumer prices generally, or of domestic travel costs. One would expect people to travel abroad less when foreign travel rises more rapidly in price than other outlets for discretionary incomes, and particularly than domestic travel. Considerable attention has been devoted to price elasticity of demand in relation to price changes for particular modes of transport (e g air and rail fares, motor fuel usage), but not in relation to overseas travel generally. This is probably not because it is felt to be unimportant but because of the lack of adequate and accessible data on what the price changes have been. A crude method for assessing relative price movements has been devised and employed here (see Section V).

Other variables and the possibility of a ceiling to foreign travel

Other variables can be treated as residuals, combining together to form a constant, or underlying, rate of growth independent of income or price movements. Yet, composed as it is of a whole variety of elements, it would be surprising if this constant were not in fact a changing function, as some of its components increase in importance and others recede. The data do not permit one to measure with any reliability what sort of curve the constant may represent, and how long term such changes are. However, it is obvious that many of the other variables embraced by this constant are of far greater importance in relation to particular market segments than to the totality of travel. While, for instance, there can be little doubt that the combined marketing and promotional efforts of the travel trade have a considerable and changing influence on what types of holidays people take, and where, it is far from clear that long term fluctuations in the total promotional effort affect the total long term proportion of consumer incomes in any origin country devoted to combined domestic and foreign travel.

A crucial consideration in the context of long term travel is that an eventual ceiling to total travel demand must exist – people cannot indefinitely continue to spend more and more of their spare time and incomes on travel. This concept is considered in Section IV, and features in the forecasting procedure employed in this report.

SOME CHARACTERISTICS OF WORLD TOURISM

Signs that the long term growth rate of travel is levelling off

Chart B in Section III shows total growth in world tourism over 1963-77 measured at the destination country end in terms of both arrivals and receipts at constant prices. In principle, the amounts involved should match fairly closely data from origin countries on residents returning from trips abroad; and, in practice, the total of expenditure data by origin countries derived as the data base in Section III is close to total receipts (a similar process matching arrivals to departures is not possible).

The chart shows that, after some years of fast growth, travel remained static in 1968 and then resumed rapid expansion for the next five years (a 9 per cent annual growth rate); in 1974 travel fell sharply (particularly on a real receipts basis), picked up only slightly in 1975, since when it has again risen rapidly (again, particularly on a real receipts basis); this recent growth has, however, been slower on an arrivals basis (6.8 per cent per annum) than in the 1968-1973 (inclusive) period, and even on a receipts basis (14.2 per cent per annum) it has been insufficient to bring growth back to the trend established up to 1974.

The implication therefore is that the long term growth of foreign travel is beginning to level off. The whole question of a ceiling to travel is discussed in Section IV. Those involved in the travel trade in most major origin countries have, of course, experienced far more than just signs of travel levelling off in the past few years. But the dynamic trend of travel from, particularly, Japan and Middle Eastern countries since 1973 must be remembered. And there is some evidence that after years of growth the proportion of package holidays (the prime concern of a large part of the travel trade) has fallen; thus in 1973, 63 per cent of Britons taking holidays abroad went on package tours, while by 1977 the proportion had fallen to 59 per cent.

An increasing proportion of travel from secondary and minor origin countries

Chart A shows these trends in travel abroad by West Germans, US citizens, the French, Canadians, and UK citizens (in order of their importance in world travel in expenditure terms). It can be seen that only Canada's trend since 1973 compares favourably with the world average. Of the remaining five of the main ten origin countries, travel from Japan has been buoyant since 1973, Dutch travel has edged upwards, while comparable numbers of traveller data are not available from Austria, Belgium and Mexico. The implication is, of course, that the secondary and minor origin countries are of rising importance.

Chart A

INDICES OF NUMBER OF VISITS ABROAD
FROM MAIN ORIGIN COUNTRIES 1965=100

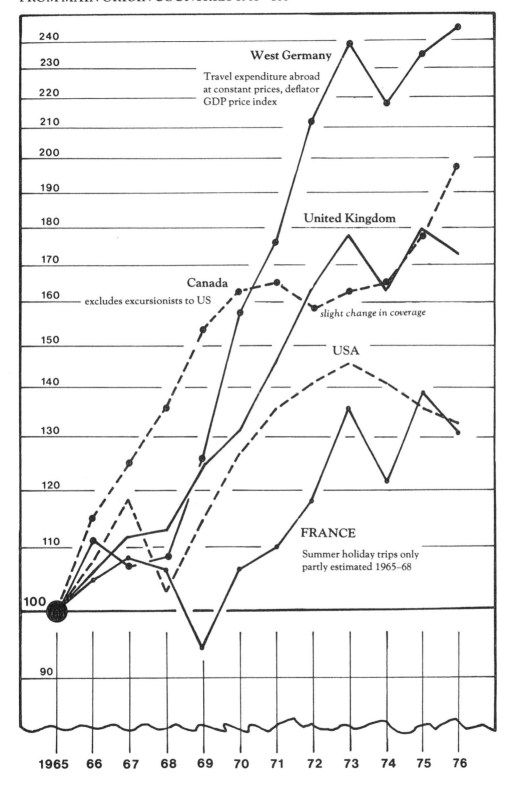

9

The five largest origin countries still account for over half of world tourism

Nonetheless, as the table which follows shows, the really large origin countries still dominate the world travel scene. (Data are drawn from Table 5 in Section III, where the methods of estimation are explained, where necessary, and some comments are included on the trends which emerge.)

Table 1

World Pattern of Expenditure on Foreign Tourism[a] by Country of Origin

	1966 ($ mn)	1976 ($ mn)	1976 ($ per caput)	Foreign tourism as a % of total tourism, foreign & domestic, in 1976[b]
Ten major origin countries				
West Germany	1,573	8,954	143	...
USA	2,657	6,856	32	10
France	1,304	3,434	64	...
Canada	836	2,589	112	73
Netherlands	374	1,886	137	...
Japan	118	1,663	15	...
UK	832	1,799	32	59
Belgium/ Luxemburg	320	1,609	159	...
Mexico	479	1,575	26	...
Austria	171	1,518	201	70
Total	8,664	31,883	52	...
(of which: five largest)	(7,202)	(23,719)	(64)	(...)
Rest of world	3,529	12,016	4	...
World total	12,193	43,899	11	...

Note: See Section III for sources etc.

a Excludes fare payments. b Definitions of domestic tourism vary widely; figures shown include rough estimates of transport costs for both types of tourism.

The most important individual trends are the increasing dominance of West German tourism; only the Netherlands and Belgium of the other main origin countries in 1966 have increased their shares of the world total; the relative importance of US and UK travel has shrunk particularly sharply; Japan, only the 15th most important origin country in 1966, is now sixth; were fares to be included it would be higher still.

Table 2

Expenditure Per Caput on Foreign
Tourism[a] by Major Origin Countries in 1976

($)

	Cross border	Other short haul	Long haul	Total
West Germany	63.7	66.0	13.0	142.7
USA	14.3	3.6	13.8	31.8
France	37.4	2.0	25.0	64.4
Canada	74.8	–	36.9	111.7
Netherlands	48.9	72.2	15.7	136.8
Japan	–	2.2	12.5	14.8
UK	7.0	17.4	7.6	32.0
Belgium/ Luxemburg	80.7[b]	64.0[b]	13.8[b]	158.5
Mexico	23.5[c]	0.1	1.9	25.5[c]
Austria	164.1	17.9	18.9	200.8
Total of above	24.8	13.0	13.6	51.5
Rest of world	1.0[b]	1.1[b]	1.5[b]	3.6
World total	4.7	3.0	3.4	11.0
% of world total from ten major origin countries	(82.7)	(68.4)	(62.4)	(72.6)

Note: See Section III for sources, etc. An element of estimation
is required for most countries for the division of expenditure
between bordering countries (countries with a common border or
divided by a narrow strip of water), other short haul, and long haul.

a Excludes fare payments. b A considerable element of estimation.
c Based on US receipts data. Mexican data suggest far lower
expenditure.

Income groups and tourism

Marketing studies demonstrate that the higher income groups spend more per head
on tourism, both total and foreign, than do the lower income groups. It is not
always so clear, however, that the proportion of incomes devoted to tourism is
significantly higher for the top income groups than for those a little below them in
the income scale. If there is some such levelling off (and adequate evidence on
this is hard to come by), it would not be surprising. For the vast majority of the
top, as well as the lower, income groups there is a limit to the amount of time
which can be devoted to holidays. Nor is there for everyone a continuing appeal
in visiting new and distant locations. The prestige of travel to exotic areas
diminishes as such trips become more common.

These considerations may appear unimportant when such attitudes so far affect
only a small, even minute, proportion of the potential travelling public. For
every member of the upper income groups who may feel he wants to opt out of
what he sees as a status seeking travel rat race, there are many more members
of the middle income groups only too anxious to trade up, and others in the lower
income groups who want to join in. This might imply that any noticeable flattening
of the travel growth curve for such reasons is decades away.

The USA is exceptional in its low level of
spending on foreign tourism relative to domestic

Even among the main origin countries, there are some big variations in expenditure per head of population. The high West European figures, led by Austria (a reflection of an exceptionally high expenditure on cross border trips), are largely, of course, because international travel is easy in a geographically fairly compact area; it is worth noting, however, that the UK lags well behind most other Western European countries. Among important economic powers, Japan and Italy spend on foreign tourism less than half of even the UK figure. The low level of US spending per head, even more marked if income levels are also considered, is essentially a reflection of the wide opportunities for domestic tourism. For only a few countries is there information on domestic tourism expenditure and this information is not strictly comparable with that on foreign. Nonetheless, it is clear that the USA is exceptional in the low relative level of foreign tourism expenditure.

Patterns of travel by distance of trip

As Table 2 shows, the ten major origin countries dominate all three types of travel - to bordering countries, other short haul travel, and long haul - but the longer the trip, the less marked their relative dominance is. While the major origin countries travel roughly as much to bordering countries (in expenditure terms, far more in number of visits) as to other short haul and long haul combined, the travel patterns of Asia, Africa and Latin America are heavily oriented to long haul travel. (Lesser West European and East European origin countries have high proportions of cross border and other short haul travel - affecting the overall rest of world pattern.)

Implications of a possible levelling off in demand in upper incomes groups

However, there are in fact obvious and perhaps rather more immediate implications for the travel trade. The first is that the upper income groups may be few in numbers, but are relatively profitable customers for the trade. Secondly, the promotion of foreign travel in particular has long leaned heavily on a smart, or upper income group, image. Whole areas have become popular destinations for mass travel on the basis of their rich man's image. If other income groups were to get the impression that it was no longer smart to take these types of holiday, consumer resistance to them might spread. New marketing and promotional policies, changing the image of foreign travel, could obviously help to stem any such trend.

New outlets for leisure time and money?

But if some new pattern of spending preferences among the upper income groups is emerging (and the evidence on this is more a matter of impressions than of statistics), then the promotional efforts of the trade can do little more than check it. Historically, plain snobbery and the quest for exclusiveness have long been important influences on the development of new outlets for spare personal funds. The travel trade has been a prime beneficiary of this. It may be that greater egalitarian attitudes in the world today mean that such aspirations are becoming less important as initiators of new spending patterns. Nonetheless, certain possible pointers to future spending are worth noting.

1. There is evidence of a growing disenchantment with foreign travel to conventional holiday areas (such as the Mediterranean and the Caribbean), and specifically with resort areas, among members of upper income groups in their thirties and forties - historically important as initiators of new spending outlets. It is a matter for debate whether such attitudes stem primarily from the contempt bred by familiarity, or from simple snobbery.

2. A growing disenchantment also (spreading wider in age and income bracket terms) with the consumer goods society is affecting spending on, for instance, more expensive cars and other durables; this, together with the disenchantment with travel, means that a significant proportion of the wealthier countries' populations are acquiring resources of money and leisure time for which an outlet needs to be found.

3. One such outlet is the second home which has grown in popularity. This affects travel demand in a number of ways. First, the preference, on the whole, is for second homes which are reasonably accessible for regular visits, particularly weekends - hence generally within easy motoring distance. Second, a significant proportion, often half or more, of annual leave periods is often spent at second homes. Third, the expense of establishing, and improving, second homes as well as a permanent residence reduces, though possibly only temporarily, the funds available for conventional holidays.

4. Another outlet for surplus leisure time and financial resources is in special interest and active holidays. What constitutes these, and what are more or less mainstream, varies over time; in the 1920s and 1930s, for instance, winter sports were distinctively unusual pastimes. Even those parts of the travel trade not themselves interested in catering for fringe groups could well find it worth-while to consider, as long term pointers, the growth in the popularity of expensive, but esoteric, holidays such as visits to China, sailing in the Mediterranean, walking in the Himalayas, riding in Andalucia, and so on.

The Data Base

TOURISM DATA

A great deal more attention in recent years has been devoted to improving data on tourism, both at the national level and internationally (notably through the efforts of and cooperation within the World Tourist Organisation - formerly IUOTO - and the OECD's Tourism Committee). Both in terms of concepts and definitions, and in the practicalities of measuring tourist flows, there are, however, considerable difficulties in producing really reliable and useful data. It remains true that there are far better data on, say, the world cutlery or canned fish industries and on international trade in these items than on tourism, which is of vastly greater economic significance.

Tourism data emphasises arrivals in destination countries -

The main emphasis of the data collected on tourism is on covering all international tourist arrivals, whether at frontiers or at registered tourist accommodation. The former does not usually distinguish between short stay or transit travellers and those spending significant periods in the country concerned; though it is perfectly possible to get details on length of stay at the time of departure, this is rarely recorded by the major destination countries, and when it is recorded it is often not analysed. Arrivals at registered tourist accommodation not only omit those staying with friends and relatives or in other non-registered accommodation (indeed some countries cover only hotel arrivals), but an individual tourist may be counted several times as he moves around the country; moreover, particularly if a tourist tax is payable, hotel keepers, etc, are often far from conscientious in making full returns to the authorities. Data on nights spent in registered accommodation are more useful, but many countries do not collect these. Finally, there is in most countries little information on domestic tourism which can be compared with that on foreign tourism.

Accurate measurement of international tourism clearly requires that all countries measure it at the same point and in the same way, and all carry out the agreed procedures with at least reasonable efficiency. In spite of the efforts of the WTO and the Tourism Committee of OECD, the world is still far from that situation. Resistance to universal adoption of a reliable system is only natural, for two reasons. First, it is rarely the case that the system of checking tourist arrivals was set up specifically for the purposes of collecting tourist data; more often it was set up for the control of aliens, and in many countries this is still regarded as its prime function. Second, the system may well serve the country's own tourist authorities and tourist industry perfectly well, particularly in the comparatively short term context which is often of prime concern (length of stay or the proportion of tourists in non-registered accommodation do not usually fluctuate much from year to year, but over a ten year period major changes in these can be disguised by simple arrivals data). The lack of comparability between frontier arrivals in one country and accommodation arrivals in another is thus of less concern than it is to those seeking to look at the world tourist industry as a whole.

– and data from different destinations cannot be aggregated

The ludicrous results achieved by aggregating arrival figures from different destination countries to arrive at regional and global totals (it is surprising that the WTO does this in its statistics) can readily be perceived from Table 6. This compares UK and US records of countries visited by UK or US residents with the destination country records of arrivals from the UK or the USA. It is not suggested that the UK or US figures are more accurate in respect of any particular destination. They simply measure something different than do arrival figures, but they do so in an identical way for all destinations, and their statistical reliability is within + or - 1 per cent. Variations as between destinations in the differentials between the US and UK figures on the one hand and arrivals figures on the other are consequently a measure of how much different methods of recording arrivals affect the figures.

Differences in data series can be explained

It is easy to understand why, for instance, frontier arrivals of UK or US residents in West Germany should be four to six times greater than tourist arrivals in accommodation (transit traffic, staying with friends and relatives, etc), and also why the UK/US records give lower totals than do the West German records (short stays not separately noted); but this also makes it obvious why one cannot add accommodation arrivals in West Germany to frontier arrivals in Spain (as incidentally does the WTO) in seeking to compile an all European total of US travel by destination. In respect of the US figures, the following striking differences between the data series emerge.

	Average difference (%)	Near standard deviation in differences (%)
Between US data & accommodation arrivals	69	70
Between US data & frontier arrivals	140	245
Between accommodation arrivals & frontier arrivals	110	139

Much the same picture could be presented for the UK. To a large extent the differences can be explained. But it is nonetheless clear that for the purposes of analysing total travel a combination of accommodation arrivals and frontier arrivals is worthless, while neither series is collected by sufficient countries on a comparable basis to be usable as a general data base. Moreover several countries have introduced changes in methods of data collection during the past ten years or so. No doubt the changes have generally been for the better, but they invariably complicate and often invalidate attempts at analysis.

Table 3

Comparison of Origin and Destination Country Data for US and UK Travel in 1976 ('000 travellers)

	US travel			UK travel		
	US data on countries visited by US residents	Destination country data: visits by US residents[f]		UK data on countries visited by UK residents	Destination country data: visits by UK residents[f]	
Country visited		Accommodation arrivals	Frontier arrivals		Accommodation arrivals	Frontier arrivals
W Europe						
Austria	395	515[a]	...	197	384[a]	...
Denmark	214	...	37	109	...	305[d]
France	902	1,107[a]	1,010[d]	2,036	2,518[a]	1,600[d]
West Germany	802	1,232[ae]	5,443	673	624[a]	3,901[a]
Greece	229	419[a]	493[a]	356	482[ae]	434[a]
Ireland	251	...[a]	231[a]	1,304	...[a]	785[a]
Italy	665	1,845[a]	1,664	690	873[a]	1,670
Netherlands	432	443[a]	...	531	451[b]	...
Portugal	57	...[abg]	53	85	82[ab]	123
Spain	309	865[a]	793	2,170	2,507[ab]	2,982
Switzerland	585	930[a]	...[c]	252	447[a]	...
UK	1,386	1,171[ce]	1,490[c]	x	x	x
Others						
Canada	12,317	...	11,642[a]	200	...	369[a]
Mexico	2,581	...	2,715[a]	...	...	3[a]
USA	x	x	x	346	...	539
Australia & New Zealand	...	...	128	63	...	99

a Tourists only. b Hotels only. c Departures. d Tourist stays. e Estimated on basis of ratio of frontier arrivals to accommodation arrivals in 1975. f In practice many hotels, etc, record visitors by nationality, rather than by country of residence. g Includes Canada.

Source: WTO.

17

Chart B

THE GROWTH OF WORLD TOURISM 1963 to 1977

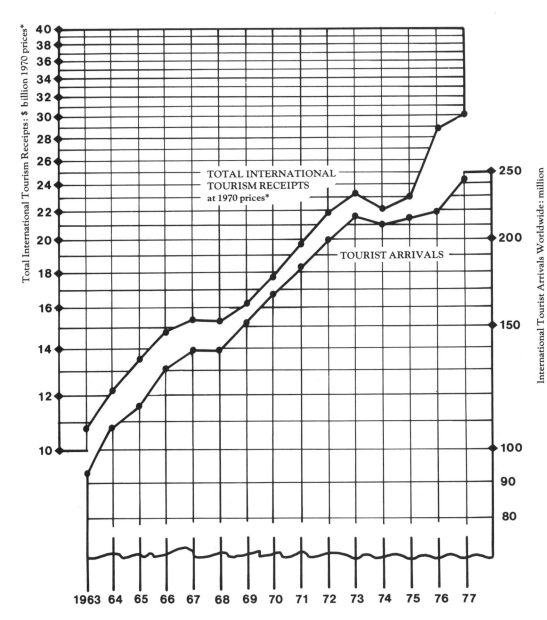

* 1970 prices

Deflator: All OECD Price Index of GDP at purchasers values

Tourism expenditure by country of origin is used as data base

The data used as base in this report (as in its predecessor) relate to tourism expenditure by main origin countries. Since the forces which determine tourism growth (notably incomes growth) can best be analysed at the origin rather than at the destination end, the forecasting procedure has to be based on origins, not on destinations. The data are presented in full in Table 5, and the accompanying text to Section III outlines how they were arrived at. A large number of countries do not compile figures on tourist expenditures abroad, though far more have data on receipts, and consequently a considerable amount of (often fairly crude) estimation has been involved. However, all the major tourist origin countries do publish such expenditure figures, as does a fairly representative cross section of smaller ones; consequently only around 10 per cent of total tourist expenditures have required an important degree of estimation, virtually all the remaining 90 per cent being published in official statistics, and probably in general fairly reliable.

The totals involved do appear to match fairly well IUOTO/WTO data on tourist receipts worldwide (as totalled by the British Tourist Authority in its Digest of Tourist Statistics).

	1966	1976
Worldwide tourist receipts ($ mn)	12,500	43,600
Estimated worldwide tourist expenditures ($ mn)	12,193	43,899

It is also worth noting that if international tourist receipts are deflated by a general OECD price index (of GDP at purchaser values), it matches fairly well with the development of total tourist arrivals worldwide, however measured – implying that whatever the deficiencies of arrivals data as an indicator of the pattern of travel, they give a fair indication of its total growth worldwide. Chart B compares the two series; it can be seen that except in 1976 (when the receipts at constant prices series rose much more rapidly than did the arrivals series) the growth of the two series has been closely in line.

Logarithmatic plotting also makes evident that, in spite of the sharply improved trend since 1975, travel is far from catching up with the trend growth rate established in the years prior to 1973. The implication is that the long term trend òf travel is indeed already flattening off.

TOURIST EXPENDITURE SERIES

Expenditure figures exclude fare costs –

Apart from the lack of data from many, mostly minor, origin countries the use of tourism expenditures by countries of origin as the data base for the derivation of forecasts has two main snags and poses one serious analytical problem. The first major snag is that the figures exclude international fare payments. A limited number of countries have data on fare payments to foreign carriers, ranging (among major origin countries) from around 12 per cent of international tourist expenditure excluding fares in West Germany and the Netherlands, up to 37 per cent for the USA, 46 per cent for Japan, and no less than 86 per cent for Australia.

A world average would probably be around 25-30 per cent (lower than this in Europe, higher elsewhere). Fare payments to domestic carriers (available only for the USA and the UK - 58 per cent and 265 per cent respectively of payments to foreign carriers) would add overall as much as another 40-50 per cent to the total. So travel expenditure including fares appears to be at least two thirds more than expenditure excluding fares. Overall the proportion of expenditure devoted to fare payments seems, however, to have changed only moderately over the past ten years - the increasing trend towards medium and long haul travel, rather than simple cross border and short haul trips, largely compensating for the falling cost of air fares (though not of other fares) relative to tourism prices generally. The implication is that a travel growth rate including fares (were this to be practicable) would typically be similar to one excluding fares. Note though that, since fares for all air carriers are in the long run determined to an important degree by costs in dollar terms (e g for aircraft and fuel), the picture would be slightly different in respect of an origin country whose exchange rate has moved sharply relative to the dollar (e g West Germany on the one hand, or the UK on the other).

– and are often insufficiently broken down by destination

The second snag is that only a handful even of major origin countries give fairly complete breakdowns of expenditures by country of destination, though most give incomplete breakdowns. Such breakdowns are of course of importance in arriving at a division of expenditures between cross border trips, other short haul travel, and long haul travel. To arrive at such breakdowns - as in Table 5 - a considerable degree of estimation has been needed for Belgium, Switzerland, and Spain among the more important origin countries, as well as for most lesser origin countries. It is also worth noting that, hardly unexpectedly, there are big variations in expenditure per day as between destination countries, implying that reliance on numbers of travellers (e g arrivals) data is misleading. Thus the average UK traveller to Austria spent £9.5 per day (excluding fares) in 1976, while the average spent in Australia was only £3.6 a day. Variations reflect not so much relative living costs in different destinations as the proportion of visits which are to friends and relatives.

Methods for adjusting current price data to constant prices

A conceptual problem in using country of origin tourism expenditure data as a base for forecasts arises from the fact that, to get a historical perspective, it is necessary to adjust expenditure data in current prices to a constant price basis - to eliminate inflation. But how in principle should this be done? There are three obvious different methods, the choice between which substantially affects the apparent growth rates of tourism expenditures.

1. Adjusting data on tourist expenditure in dollar terms (into which expenditures are usually converted for inter country comparability even if not originally compiled in dollars) for the decline in the general purchasing power of the dollar, taking into account both the rate of domestic inflation in the USA (as measured for instance by the GDP price index) and the decline of the dollar against other currencies (as measured by perhaps its SDR value). The obvious snag of this easily applied approach is that the relevance of internal inflation in the USA to worldwide travel expenditure by West Germany is not very apparent.

2. Adjusting data on tourist expenditures in national currency terms for domestic inflation (again, as measured   by, say, the GDP price index). This shows how the national resources devoted to international tourism have grown, relative to, for instance, expenditure on housing, or local recreation - obviously relevant in the context of tourism forecasting. But it does not of course indicate how the price of the tourism product, basically a foreign cost, has changed. Nor does it enable one to compare growth rates in tourism for individual origin countries in a way that can be matched to what they spend in destination countries.

3. Adjusting data on tourism expenditures in national currency terms for the price of the tourism product - embracing changes in air fares, in the prices charged by hotels, restaurants and other outlets for tourism spending, and in package tour prices. Such price changes must be expressed in origin country currency terms, thus taking exchange rate changes into account. Conceptually this approach has much to recommend it (though it cannot be used to compare tourism expenditures with other outlets for spending), but there are serious data problems. For few origin countries do the data exist to compile an index of air fares. Only a few destination countries have indices of hotel and restaurant prices (and many other items on which tourists spend money are difficult to identify adequately in the components of retail price indices). Information on the development of prices of individual package tours can, with considerable labour, be derived from tour operators' brochures, but is worthless without comparable information on numbers of people carried at different prices. A reasonably satisfactory alternative (and one used for much of the workings underlying this report) is to use a weighted average of exchange rate adjusted retail price indices in destination countries as a proxy for tourist prices. The evidence is (see Section V) that the development of these is generally not too remote from actual changes in the prices of the services, etc, tourists buy.

In principle method C is best, but there are serious snags in applying it generally

Table 4 illustrates how large the differences between the three methods are for a country whose currency has depreciated sharply and has experienced above average inflation (the UK) and by contrast for a country with considerable currency appreciation and relatively modest inflation (West Germany). For countries in which exchange rates have been roughly held and inflationary trends have been more typical (Sweden and France, for instance) the three different methods of adjustment would show broadly similar results. In principle, the third method (C) is perhaps the most satisfactory. But lack of adequate information on destinations for most minor origin countries and for some major ones makes it difficult to apply on a universal basis (the relative importance of different destinations for each origin country should be reflected in their weightings in an index of tourism product prices). Moreover the absence of adequate information on fares development, though perhaps not too serious for West European countries, or for the USA, Canada and Mexico (travel from all of which is dominated by cross border trips and short haul travel, and representing some 83 per cent of world travel between them), is a real deficiency in the context of those countries from which travel is largely long haul. In the elasticity calculations of Section V, method B or a close approximation to it is generally used.

Table 4

Examples of Using Different Methods to
Adjust Tourism Expenditure to Constant 1966 Prices

Tourism expenditure	UK	West Germany
1966 $ mn current prices	832	1,573
1976 $ mn current prices	1,799	8,954
1976 $ mn constant 1966 prices A	1,254	6,240
1976 $ mn constant 1966 prices B	1,026	3,468
1976 $ mn constant 1966 prices C	840	3,914
Per cent growth per annum in tourism expenditure		
Current prices	8.0	19.0
Constant 1966 prices A	4.2	14.8
Constant 1966 prices B	2.1	8.2
Constant 1966 prices C	0.1	9.5

Notes: Constant 1966 prices A - compensating for loss of
value of dollar (US GDP price index and value of dollar in
SDR terms). Constant 1966 prices B - resource basis (dollar
expenditures converted to national currency at current
exchange rates and adjusted by national GDP price index, then
reconverted to dollars at 1966 exchange rates). Constant 1966
prices C - tourism product price basis (dollar expenditure
converted to national currency and adjusted by exchange rate
adjusted retail price indices for destination countries, then
reconverted to dollars at 1966 exchange rates).

The table on world tourism expenditure

Table 5 shows estimated total world tourist expenditure in 1966 and 1976 by country
and area of origin. For 1976 there are approximate breakdowns of the total
between cross border travel, other short haul travel and long haul (of course a
small proportion of cross border travel is actually long haul). Where data exist
on fare payments and domestic tourism expenditure, these are also shown. The
footnotes to the table are important; they explain where estimates have been
needed and how these have been framed, and main points to be borne in mind in
analysing the data.

Overall, as is suggested by the earlier comparison of these total tourist
expenditures data with worldwide tourism receipts data, the figures are probably
reasonably accurate. This reflects primarily an acceptable degree of reliability
in total tourism expenditure figures for virtually all OECD countries plus several
other major origin countries; as already stated only in respect of about 10 per
cent of the total is there an important degree of estimation (shown in the table as
figures in brackets). However, the following should be noted.

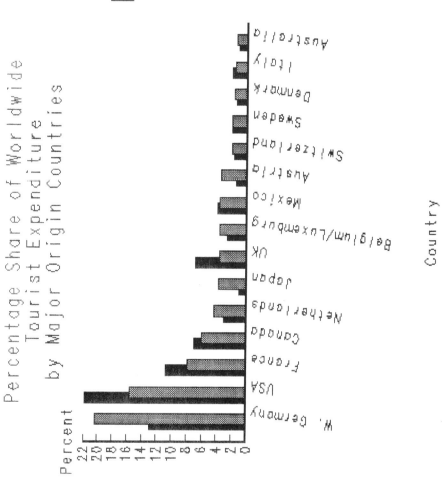

Percentage Share of Worldwide
Tourist Expenditure
by Major Origin Countries

Percent

22 20 18 16 14 12 10 8 6 4 2 0

W. Germany
USA
France
Canada
Netherlands
Japan
UK
Belgium/Luxemburg
Mexico
Austria
Switzerland
Sweden
Denmark
Italy
Australia

Country

1966
1976

Figure 1

1. A rather larger degree of estimation has been needed for the 1976 breakdown of travel between bordering countries, other short haul, and long haul, most notably for the following fairly important origin countries - Belgium/Luxemburg, Switzerland, Spain and Brazil.

2. Nearly all figures for Eastern Europe and for the Middle East have involved a considerable element of estimation. So have the data for a large number of generally very minor origin countries in other Asia, Latin America and Caribbean, and Africa; Argentina and Nigeria are the most important of these. The estimates for Eastern Europe and the Middle East have been derived largely from data on recorded arrivals worldwide from these countries, linked to the few countries in these groups for which expenditure data exist; it is possible to relate these to expenditure per destination country arrival. For minor origin countries in other Asia, Latin America and Caribbean, and Africa, the most usual approach has been to take tourism expenditure figures per head of total population for comparable countries. (For instance there are 27 countries in Africa south of the Sahara, excluding South Africa, for which for at least one year in the mid 1970s data exist on tourism expenditure; these were brought to a common estimated 1976 expenditure and divided by population in that year. The average of rather over $2 per head of population was then applied to the 27 other south of the Sahara countries on which there are no data at all.)

Major trends which emerge

The most obvious point to emerge from the table is the dominance in the world tourist scene of a handful of major origin countries. The five largest origin countries accounted for 54 per cent of world tourist expenditure in 1976 against 59.1 per cent in 1966, and the 15 largest for 81.3 per cent against 79.6 per cent. Thus though the share of the most important origin countries has shrunk somewhat, that of the only slightly less important ones such as Japan, Austria, Belgium and the Netherlands has risen to compensate. The remaining 82 per cent of the world's population account for 19 per cent of world tourism, much the same proportion as ten years earlier.

Percentage Share of Worldwide
Tourist Expenditure by Major Origin Countries

	1966	1976
West Germany	12.9	20.4
USA	21.8	15.6
France	10.7	7.8
Canada	6.9	5.9
Netherlands	3.1	4.3
Japan	1.0	3.8
UK	6.8	3.7
Belgium/Luxemburg	2.6	3.7
Mexico	3.9	3.6
Austria	1.4	3.5
Switzerland	1.8	2.1
Sweden	2.0	2.1
Denmark	1.5	1.7
Italy	2.1	1.6
Australia	1.1	1.5
Total of above	79.6	81.3

($ mn)

Table ... Expenditure on Tourism by Country of Origin

	International tourism expenditure [a]					Growth 1966–76 (% pa)		International fare payments to foreign carriers in 1976	Expenditure in 1976 on domestic tourism [g]
	1966 [e]	1976 Cross border [bc]	Other short haul [bd]	Long haul [bd]	Total [e]	Current prices [f]	Constant prices [f]		
W Europe									
West Germany	1,573	4,000	4,139	815	8,954	17.0	14.0	1,117	..
France	1,304	1,996	108	1,330	3,434	10.0	6.0	..	..
Netherlands	374	675	995	216	1,886	17.5	13.5	230	2,650[i]
UK	832	393	977	429	1,799	8.0	4.0	566	..
Belgium/Luxemburg	320	(819)	(650)	(140)	1,609	17.5	13.5	..	..
Austria	171	1,240	135	143	1,518	24.0	20.0	..	882
Switzerland	224	(375)	(260)	(300)	935	15.5	11.5	276	..
Sweden	242	278	479	160	917	14.0	10.0	..	..
Denmark	184	300	338	110	748	15.0	11.0	..	..
Italy	261	150	162	396	708	10.5	6.5	169	..
Norway	78	259	309	65	633	23.5	19.0	..	1,018[i]
Spain	91	(300)	(69)	(35)	404	16.0	12.0	..	7[j]
Yugoslavia	34	(30)	(25)	(5)	(60)	(-6.0)	(-2.0)	..	..
Finland	77	54	163	100	317	15.0	11.0	28[h]	116[i]
Ireland	85	100	(75)	(60)	(235)	10.5	7.0	(15)[i]	144
Portugal	82	5	100	35	140	5.5	2.0	35	..
Greece	41	5	46	39	90	8.0	4.5	35	..
Others	25	(4)	(9)	(22)	35	3.5	–	..	..
Total	5,998	10,983	9,039	4,400	24,422	15.0	11.0	..	..
E Europe									
East Germany	(100)	(85)	(247)	(1)	(333)	(13.0)	(9.0)	..	..
Czechoslovakia	30	(88)	(95)	(1)	(184)	(20.0)	(15.5)	..	..
Poland	42	(117)	(93)	(3)	213	17.5	13.5	..	..
Hungary	17	(20)	(122)	(2)	144	24.0	19.5	..	..
USSR	(25)	(22)	(52)	(6)	(80)	(12.5)	(8.5)	..	..
Others	(50)	(21)	(13)	(2)	(36)	(-2.5)	(-6.5)	..	..
Total	(264)	(353)	(622)	(15)	(990)	(14.0)	(10.0)	..	..
N America									
USA	2,657	3,094	784	2,978	6,856	10.0	6.0	2,542[k]	98,000[i]
Canada	836	1,734	–	855	2,589	12.0	8.0	576	1,500[i]
Total	3,493	4,828	784	3,833	9,445	10.5	6.5	3,118	99,500
Australasia & Oceania									
Australia	140	–	–	644	644	16.5	12.5	557	..
New Zealand	62	–	–	233	233	14.0	10.0	..	..
Others	(10)	–	(5)	(20)	(25)	(9.5)	(5.5)	..	..
Total	212	–	(5)	897	902	15.5	11.5	..	..
Middle East									
Iran	(55)	(60)	(20)	(170)	(250)	(16.5)	(12.0)	..	..
Turkey	26	(120)	(3)	(85)	208	23.0	18.5	..	..
Saudi Arabia	..	(70)	(30)	(100)	(200)	..	..	..	..
Other Gulf	49	(15)	(50)	(85)	(150)	11.0	7.0	..	..
Israel	..	(-)	(15)	(126)	141	..	..	..	..
Lebanon	..	(75)	(40)	(10)	(125)	(5.0)	(1.5)	..	..
Others	18	(12)	(3)	(45)	(60)	(13.0)	(9.0)	..	..
Total	(364)	(375)	(178)	(611)	(1,164)	(12.5)	(8.5)	..	..
Other Asia									
Japan	188	–	250	1,413	1,663	30.0	25.5	771	..
Hong Kong	..	(74)	(55)	(166)	(295)	..	..	185	..
Thailand	27	(10)	(38)	(144)	192	21.5	17.5	..	..
South Korea	..	–	(23)	(23)	46	..	..	..	..
Singapore	..	(50)	(30)	(70)	(150)	(6.5)	(2.5)	..	..
Malaysia	35	(6)	(30)	(53)	(65)	(6.5)	(2.5)	..	..
India	..	(1)	(6)	(23)	(25)	..	..	..	..
Indonesia	18	(12)	(3)	(45)	(60)	(13.0)	(9.0)	..	..
Bangladesh	–	–	–	(3)	3	x	x	..	..
Pakistan	..	(-)	(1)	(3)	(4)	..	..	..	..
Sri Lanka	..	(1)	(1)	(3)	3	..	..	..	3
Phillippines	53	(-)	(3)	(13)	(15)	(-13.5)	(-17.5)	(3)	..
Others	..	(1)	(1)	(18)	(20)	..	..	..	..
Total	(400)	(155)	(417)	(1,969)	2,541	(20.5)	(16.0)	..	..

Table: International tourism expenditure [a]

	1966 [e]	Cross border [bc]	Other short haul [bd]	Long haul [bd]	Total [e]	Growth 1966-76 (% pa) Current prices	Growth 1966-76 (% pa) Constant prices	International fare payments to foreign carriers in 1976	Expenditure in 1976 on domestic tourism [g]
Latin America & Caribbean									
Mexico	479	1,450 [l]	(5)	(120)	(1,575) [l]	12.5	8.5	...	...
Brazil	43	(150)	(-)	(209)	359	23.5	19.0	111	...
Puerto Rico	94	-	219	20	239	10.0	6.0	130	...
Argentina	35	(45)	(5)	(75)	(125)	(13.5)	(9.5)	...	...
Colombia	54	15	5	98	118	8.0	4.5	...	...
Ecuador	8	(8)	(4)	(30)	42	18.0	14.0	...	...
Panama, Guatemala, El Salvador, Costa Rica	62	(63)	(40)	(110)	213	13.0	9.0	...	...
Other Central America	(25)	(23)	(14)	(38)	(75)	(11.5)	(7.5)	...	...
Other South America	(220)	(70)	(45)	(335)	(450)	(7.5)	(3.5)	...	...
Jamaica	12	(1)	(30)	(30)	61	(17.5)	13.5	18	...
Trinidad & Tobago	13	(3)	(10)	(15)	28	8.0	4.0	12	...
Other Caribbean	(50)	(10)	(70)	(95)	(175)	(13.5)	(9.5)	...	...
Total	1,095	(1,838)	(447)	(1,175)	3,460	(12.0)	(8.0)	...	...
Africa									
South Africa	81	(20)	(10)	(160)	(190)	9.0	5.0	...	...
Nigeria	34	(5)	(10)	(85)	(100)	11.5	7.5	...	...
Libya	27	(10)	(70)	(15)	(95)	13.5	9.5	...	...
Morocco	35	(10)	(70)	(15)	(95)	10.5	6.5	...	...
20 others south of Sahara on which some data available	(120)	(30)	(50)	(230)	(310)	(10.0)	(6.0)	...	...
27 others south of Sahara on which no data	(45)	(10)	(15)	(90)	(115)	(10.0)	(6.0)	...	...
3 other North African (no data)	(25)	(5)	(35)	(30)	(70)	(11.0)	(7.0)	...	...
	(367)	(90)	(260)	(625)	(975)	(10.5)	(6.5)	...	...
Approximate world total	12,193	18,622	11,752	13,525	48,899	13.5	9.5	...	...

Note: Figures in brackets indicate an important element of estimation.

a Excluding international fares. b Few origin countries give complete breakdowns of tourism expenditure by country of destination, so partial estimates have been necessary in most cases. Where a considerable degree of estimation has been necessary, figures are given in brackets, as also for countries where no breakdown is available (that shown being derived generally from destination country data, or by analogy with similar countries). The breakdowns for most African, Latin American and Caribbean, and other Asia countries are particularly rough. c All countries with a common border or divided only by narrow strips of water (e g the English Channel). d Generally travel within the same continent or sub-continent is considered short haul, except where the distance between recorded origins and destinations is such as to make a trip necessarily long haul (over around 1,750 nautical miles). This procedure is reasonably satisfactory for travel from European countries and also for most developing countries, less so for US travel. e For many countries, generally of minor importance as origin countries, there is no recorded information on foreign travel expenditure. For these rough estimates have been framed, and the figures are shown in brackets. For those for which information on number of residents departing for abroad are available, the estimates have been based on an assumed average expenditure level similar to that in similar neighbouring countries. For others even cruder estimates have been based on assumed levels of expenditure per head of total population. For the special case of travel from oil rich Middle Eastern countries, estimates have been based largely on partial information from specific main known major destination countries, but are very approximate. f In constant 1966 dollar terms, adjusted not only for the declining internal US purchasing power of the $ (as measured by GDP price index) but for its decline against other currencies (as expressed in its SDR value). Total deflator over 1966-76 period is thus 1.435. This is of course different both to adjusting tourist expenditures to origin country resources devoted to these (which would necessitate adjusting by each country's exchange rate adjusted GDP price index) or to the real cost to travellers (for which,for each origin country, costs in each destination country have to be considered). g Definitions and coverage vary considerably as between countries (particularly in respect of types of accommodation covered and the inclusion or otherwise of transport costs). h International fare payments included under tourism expenditure. i Including transport costs. j Published figure - looks implausibly low. k US travellers also paid $1,470 mn to US carriers, and UK travellers around $1,500 mn to UK carriers. l Based on US receipts data. Mexican data suggest a far lower expenditure.

Main sources: WTO and IUOTO International Travel Statistics; OECD Tourism Policy and International Tourism in OECD member countries.

Among the major origin countries, the outstanding feature is the growth of West German tourism to over a fifth of the world total. But, of the remaining nine most important tourism countries in 1966, only the Netherlands and Belgium had increased their shares by 1976, with the UK's share showing a particularly sharp fall. Overall, Western Europe as an origin area increased its share of world tourism from 49 per cent in 1966 to 56 per cent ten years later. The rapid growth in Japanese travel boosted other Asia's share, while Australia and New Zealand's share also rose. Most other areas suffered a decline in travel shares, most notably the USA, although there were some quite important individual exceptions – Brazil, some Eastern European countries, Turkey and Thailand. Note, though, that the boom in Middle Eastern travel took off only in the mid 1970s and has only just begun to be reflected in these figures.

The importance of cross border trips

Overall, some 42 per cent of world travel expenditure is on trips to countries sharing a border with the tourist's country of residence, and another 27 per cent is on other short haul trips, leaving 31 per cent for long haul. But this is mainly because of the dominance of cross border and other short haul travel in Europe and cross border travel both ways between the USA and Canada and the USA and Mexico (which accounts for the bulk of the Latin American and Caribbean total). The bulk of travel expenditure by the rest of the world is on long haul trips.

Approximate Percentage Shares of 1976 Travel by Area of Origin

	Cross border	Other short haul	Long haul
Western Europe	45	37	18
Eastern Europe	35	63	2
North America	51	8	41
Australasia & Oceania	–	1	99
Middle East	32	15	53
Other Asia	6	16	78
Latin America & Caribbean	53	13	34
Africa	9	27	64
World	42	37	31

Because airlines, tour operators and travel agents are so little involved in catering for it, there is a tendency among the travel trade to ignore the vast amount of European, North American and Mexican travel which takes the form of cross border trips; this constitutes around 40 per cent of total world travel expenditure. Somewhere between 7.50 and 10 per cent is travel by West Europeans within Western Europe, but not to bordering countries, on do-it-yourself arrangements, again not involving the travel trade (other than hotels, etc), mostly by private motor car; the most important such flow is probably from West Germany to Italy, though West Germans going to Spain, and Dutch and British going to Italy and Spain, are also important.

Wide variations in the relative importance of domestic and foreign tourism

For only a few countries are there data on expenditure on domestic tourism, and definitions used for this do vary considerably. Some only count trips involving one or more nights away from home, or even more narrowly trips involving stays in hotels only. Others cover all trips of more than a certain distance away from home, whether or not a night is involved. Almost all include transport costs (in contrast to data on foreign tourism). Yet such definitional differences probably affect the totals quite modestly - by perhaps + or - 25 per cent. If foreign tourism figures are adjusted to include fare payments to both national and foreign carriers, they can be roughly compared with domestic tourism. This is done below for the more significant tourist countries for which it is possible. It can be seen that the apparent relative importance of domestic and foreign tourism varies widely. At one extreme, in Canada and Austria, foreign tourism is in expenditure terms three times as important as domestic, while at the other extreme, in the USA, it is only one ninth as important.

Relative Importance of Domestic and
Foreign Tourism, Both Including Transport Costs
($ mn)

	Domestic tourism	Foreign tourism	Domestic tourism as a % of all tourism expenditure
UK	2,650	3,865	41
USA	98,000	10,868	90
Canada	1,500	3,500[b]	30
Austria	882	2,075[b]	30
Norway	1,018[b]	750[b]	58
Poland	958[b]	213[a]	82

a Excluding fares. b Fare element in foreign tourism roughly estimated.

A Ceiling to Tourism

Tourism cannot continue rapid growth indefinitely

Throughout the world tourism is absorbing rising proportions of both total consumer incomes and people's time. With marked setbacks occasioned by wars and other major political developments, and less marked ones at times of economic recessions and slumps, this trend has been evident for a long time, possibly indeed since the Renaissance, certainly since the days of the Grand Tour. The last major global setback to tourism was during the second world war, but, with the probable exception of travel from East European countries, the ground lost has of course long been made up many times over.

Obviously, though, no component of consumer incomes can indefinitely rise faster than incomes as a whole. Eventually its growth rate cannot exceed that of incomes generally, and perhaps will even fall as some new outlet for spending either rises in popularity or becomes expensive and to an important extent non-substitutable (it has been suggested that energy may be in this category in, say, 20 years' time). This implies that sooner or later real tourism expenditure, instead of rising at 9.5 per cent per annum as it did between 1966 and 1976 (see Section III), will rise by at most 5 per cent per annum (the World Bank's arguably somewhat optimistic projection of the world GDP growth rate between 1975 and 1985). Similarly, even though a shortage of work opportunities in Western industrial countries is likely to lead to an increase in leisure time, this is not a process which can continue indefinitely. Nor is such extra leisure time necessarily going to be spent mostly, or even largely, on tourism.

A hypothetical growth curve

Chart C illustrates the well known characteristic curve over time of any non-essential element of consumer spending.   Gradual acceleration (as a percentage of total incomes) at A is followed by a quite rapid rise, faster than that in consumer spending generally (B), a levelling off (C) to a peak (D), from which an eventual decline (E) is likely, as other new outlets for non-essential spending become relatively more popular. The whole process from A to E may be spread over a brief period, as with passing fads; over a few decades, as with the cinema; or over centuries – the category into which tourism may well fall. It may be interrupted by wars and political upheavals, and by periods of economic recession or slump. The rate of growth in expenditure on a non-essential in its most rapid phase (B) is usually considerably faster than that in consumer expenditure generally; if it represents only a small part of consumer incomes, it may well grow at several times the pace of expenditure as a whole, but spending on some major element is unlikely to sustain a rise of much more than around 1.5 times the growth rate of the incomes of potential purchasers.

In the context of tourism forecasting, a prime problem is to assess for each major origin country where tourism spending is on this growth curve, how long a period the process from A to E is likely to represent, and how steep the curve will be during its next phases. For most major origin countries it is clear that the A to E process is more than 50 years long, and probably more than 100 years long. It also seems that for most the A phase is past. But is the B phase also past? Will history eventually show that the A phase was a long period of build up, while the B phase lasted only 10-20 years, and the C phase too was relatively shortlived? These are questions underlying long term tourism forecasting.

Chart C

Typical growth curve for
a non-essential element
of consumer expenditure

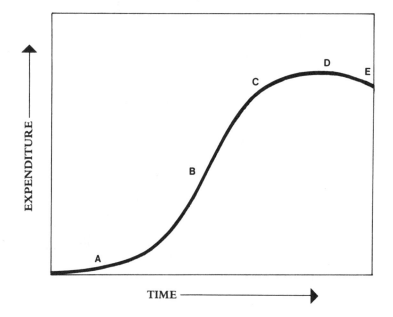

Evidence on existing penetration levels

Table 6 presents available figures on the levels of tourism achieved in 1976 relative to consumer expenditures, and in terms of days spent on tourist trips per head of population. As noted in the footnotes, a substantial element of estimation has been involved in many of the figures, and they should be regarded as no more than orders of magnitude. Information on domestic tourism is poor for most countries and definitions used make it difficult to compare with foreign tourism. Admitting the definitional and data collection problems, the figures on how much people spend in total in time and money on tourism are lamentably inadequate considering how important the sector is in economic terms. Nonetheless some important points do emerge.

Table 6.   Penetration Levels of Foreign and Domestic Tourism in 1976

	1976 expenditure on tourism as a % of all consumer expenditure				Days spent on tourist trips per head of population in 1976		
	International		Domestic (inc transport costs)	Approximate total	International	Domestic	Combined
Ten major origin countries	Exc fares	Inc rough estimate of fares					
West Germany	3.6	5.1[a]	...[e]	...[e]	5.0[h]	3.9[e]	8.9
USA	0.6	1.0	9.0[e]	10.0	1.0[i]	13.3[e]	14.3[e]
France	1.6	...[b]	...	...	2.6[h]	12.9[i]	15.5[i]
Canada	2.2	3.0[b]	1.3	4.3	5.2[h]	...	9.7
Netherlands	3.6	5.2[a]	...	...	5.3[h]	4.4	9.7
Japan	0.6	1.0[b]	...	...	0.6[h]	...	...
UK	1.1	2.4[b]	1.7	4.1	2.7[k]	9.7	12.4
Belgium/Luxemburg	4.0	5.7[d]	...	...	6.4	2.2	8.6
Mexico	3.4	...[d]	...	...	...[k]	...[j]	...
Austria	6.9	9.9[d]	4.0	13.9	7.0[k]	3.4[j]	10.4
Some secondary origin countries							
Switzerland	2.7	4.6[c]	...	...	...	5.5	...
Italy	0.6	1.0[c]	...[e]	...	...	3.8	...
Norway	3.7[f]	5.3[d]	6.0[e]	11.3[e]	...	2.0	...
Ireland	4.3	5.6[c]	2.1	7.7	1.5	4.3	5.8
Australia	1.2	2.9[b]	...	...	2.6	...	...

Note: Definitions of domestic tourism vary considerably and direct comparisons between countries should be made with caution.

a Assumes total fares paid for international tourism are 3.5 times payment to foreign carriers only (the approximate UK ratio).   b Assumes total fares paid for international tourism are 1.75 times payment to foreign carriers only (rather above the US ratio of 1.6).   c Assumes total fares paid for international tourism are 2.5 times payment to foreign carriers only.   d Assumes same fares to expenditure excluding fares ratio as in Netherlands.   e An unusually wide definition of domestic tourism.   f A large element of estimation.   g Assumes an average trip length midway between that of Netherlands and that of UK (15.8 days).   h US average trip lengths: 24 days to Europe and Mediterranean area; 12 days to other overseas areas; 5 days to Canada and Mexico. Canadian trips exclude excursionists; average length 24 days except to USA (7 days).   i Holidays of over four days only.   j In registered tourist accommodation only.   k Assumes same expenditure per week as for Netherlands (derived from expenditure data).

Sources: See Section III for expenditure data; for days spent on tourist trips, see OECD Tourism Policy and International Tourism 1977.

1. In several countries (France, the USA, even the UK) holidays taken away from home already absorb the bulk of annual leave periods (see Table 7). Others might well fall into this category were data available.

2. In some countries (Austria, Norway, and the USA), it is difficult to envisage tourism expenditure, foreign plus domestic, absorbing a very much larger proportion of consumer incomes than they already do. Were data available on domestic tourism expenditure by West Germany, France, the Netherlands, Belgium, Switzerland and Australia, they would almost certainly fall into the same category.

3. Although there are some definitional differences, when compared with data for a few years earlier (see Special Report No. 33, Table 4), a consistent pattern emerges of a rising number of days spent away; generally the rise appears to be rather under half a day extra spent away each year than in the preceding year.

Generally the data in the table underestimate rather than overestimate the amount of travel. Data collection procedures are more likely to omit trips than to double count or exaggerate. Coverage of visits to friends and relatives, and use of second homes, are particularly liable to be omitted unless respondents are specifically probed on these, as they rarely consider them in their own minds to be tourist trips.

The importance of annual leave entitlements

A major implication of the quite high proportions of holiday time and consumer expenditures already absorbed by trips away from home is that international tourism growth will be increasingly determined by:

a.   the growth in annual leave periods;

b.   the extent to which international tourism continues to increase its share of the total tourism market.

If excursionists are excluded, international tourism is essentially an outlet for annual leave periods for the employed population; students apart, their dependants rarely take substantially longer holidays abroad. WTO estimates that paid holidays "account for at least 87 per cent of domestic and international tourist movements throughout the world" (Preliminary Survey on Paid Holidays). Apart from short cross frontier trips, holidays abroad are mainly for periods of one week or more, so there is only limited scope for increased foreign travel stemming from reductions in the working week or increases in the number of public holidays. These extra days are sometimes tagged on to existing holidays abroad, or are used as the basis for, say, a long weekend trip abroad. More often they are taken at home, or used for short domestic trips (to friends and relatives, perhaps), or for stays in second homes. The main existing periods when several public holidays fall closely together, Christmas/New Year and Easter, are widely used as a basis for building holidays of one to two weeks away. The "bridge" concept of making a long weekend around a public holiday falling on, say, a Thursday is increasing in popularity, but, like extra public holidays, creates few new opportunities for trips abroad. Most take them at or near home.

Typical leave periods

Table 7 indicates approximate typical current annual leave periods and the number of public holidays in the more important tourist origin countries. In spite of recent data collection efforts by WTO and some commercial organisations, information on annual leave periods is somewhat inadequate. Note that paid leave periods are normally expressed in terms of days, but for the purposes of assessing the potential for holidays have to be translated into weeks on the basis of the customary working week in each country. Note also that the typical leave periods quoted normally refer to the working population as a whole; middle to upper income groups usually get more (though they may not always take their full entitlement), and it is of course these groups who are particularly prone to take holidays abroad. Ideally information on leave periods should differentiate between socio-economic groups, but, although in principle it would be fairly easy to conduct a survey along these lines in main origin countries, the information does not appear to be available.

Table 7

Annual Leave and Public Holidays

	Normal minimum paid holiday per annum (weeks)	Typical paid holiday period per annum (weeks)	Number of public holidays (days)
Australia	$7\frac{1}{2}$	8	11[b]
Austria	4	$4\frac{1}{2}$	12
Belgium	4	$4\frac{1}{2}$	12[b]
Canada	4	4	11[b]
Denmark	4	$4\frac{1}{2}$	9
France	4	$4\frac{1}{2}$	9[b]
West Germany	4	4	11[b]
Ireland	$3\frac{1}{2}$	$3\frac{1}{2}$	8[b]
Italy	5	5	18[b]
Netherlands	3	$4\frac{1}{2}$	6
Norway	4	$4\frac{1}{2}$	9
Sweden	5	5	10[b]
Switzerland	3	4	8[b]
UK	2[a]	3	8
USA	$1\frac{1}{2}$	$2\frac{1}{2}$	11[c]

a   No legal minimum.   b   Varies by area.   c   Including bridging days.

Main sources: WTO; Income Data Services; The Financial Times.

It will be noted that there is a general tendency for annual leave periods in all countries to move towards four to five weeks; the remarkable figures given for Australia (source WTO) are the main exception. Most West European countries already have typical leave periods in the four to five week range (the UK and Ireland alone among significant origin countries still lag behind). The USA is a more important laggard, but this is partly made up by a fairly widespread provision by which long service employees, with perhaps 15-20 years' service, get extended paid leave (10-15 weeks) as a once and for all bonus or every five years; the concept of the sabbatical is not confined to academic life.

Reductions in the working week instead of longer leave periods –

It is significant that in those countries (most notably France) which established a four week holiday norm many years ago the typical holiday period has only crept slightly upwards over the past ten years or so; professional and management staff may get five or six weeks, but this appears to be a limit. This is probably partly because individuals find it difficult to make effective use of more than about five weeks' holiday a year; indeed professional and management staff often find it impossible to take their full entitlement. It is also because unions, once a four week paid leave entitlement has been achieved, have tended to focus their attentions on securing concessions in other areas. One such area is, of course, a reduction in the working week. Sometimes, as in the UK, this may be no more than a method by which an increased proportion of work is paid for at overtime rates, or of legitimising absenteeism. But pressure is mounting for a real reduction in the working week, already normally five days in many occupations in most industrial countries. Many already informally shrink the week to four and a half days, at least in summer. A formal four and a half day, or even four day, week may not be far off. Indeed it has been suggested that it is the only way by which, in the light of constant productivity improvements, the employed labour force and demand can be kept in balance.

– imply little scope for increased travel abroad

A longer weekend will be used by some to make short trips abroad, mainly to nearby destinations. Urban visits, by for instance the British to Paris or Amsterdam, may be particularly favoured, but apart from shopping trips (already a quite important proportion of travel to the UK), and visits centred on sporting events, these are likely to be mainly by upper income groups. Such trips could have important implications for airlines, and will help improve urban hotel occupancy rates, both seasonally and in weekly patterns (business trips are, of course, concentrated in the mid week period). But even those who engage in such trips during long weekends are unlikely to make more than one or two a year.

Most long weekends will be spent at home, in visits to friends and relatives, and in day motoring trips (including cross border ones for those living close enough). Those who possess second homes, or whose friends and relatives do, will use these more. Indeed a shorter working week may well be a prime reason for acquiring a second home, and the use made of this tends actually to reduce the number of trips staying in hotels; the prosperous minority who used to spend four weeks a year abroad generally spend far less if they obtain a second home. Much the same applies to other new outlets for leisure time, acquired to fill a lengthening weekend. The purchase of a boat with sleeping accommodation (and small boat owners tend to move up to larger ones) often implies an end to holidays abroad – if only to justify the cost. Of course, only a tiny fraction of the population can afford a second home or a fair sized boat, but this is the trendsetting group. And even a more widespread leisure pastime, such as gardening, can reduce the time available for travel abroad. A really keen gardener, who has made this activity a main outlet for his leisure, is often reluctant to leave the garden for any length of time between, say, May and September (in the northern hemisphere).

Table 8. Possible Effective Real Ceilings to Foreign Travel from Major Tourist Origin Countries[a]

	Assumed average leave period available[b] (weeks)				Total nominal weeks available[c] (mn)				Effective real ceilings to foreign travel[d] (mn weeks)				Apparent 1976 penetration level[e]	
	1976	1980	1985	1990	1976	1980	1985	1990	1976	1980	1985	1990	Mn weeks abroad	%
West Germany	4.4	4.7	5.0	5.4	273	292	312	338	102	119	134	153	47.5	47
USA	3.0	3.5	4.0	4.5	645	775	918	1,070	43	56	70	86	32.6	76
France	4.8	5.0	5.2	5.4	254	271	289	308	28	33	37	42	20.1	72
Canada	4.4	4.7	5.0	5.4	101	112	124	140	47	56	62	70	18.4	39
Netherlands	4.7	4.9	5.2	5.4	66	70	77	82	24	28	32	36	11.6	48
UK	3.3	3.8	4.3	4.8	185	216	249	283	27	34	42	50	23.5	87
Belgium/Luxemburg	4.9	5.1	5.3	5.5	49	51	53	55	25	26	27	28	9.9	40
Austria	4.9	5.1	5.3	5.5	39	41	42	44	17	20	21	22	9.3	55

a Japan and Mexico excluded from above table as existing travel levels so far below effective real ceilings that no ceiling constraint likely by 1990. b Assumes that one third of public holidays are available for use on holiday trips. c Assumed average leave period available x projected population. Assumed population growth rates are those projected by the World Bank for the 1976–2000 period (World Development Report, 1978). d Nominal weeks available, reduced by one third (to allow for those unwilling or unable to avail themselves of holiday opportunities), and assuming that the maximum possible shift from domestic to foreign tourism (proportions as in Table 9) is 2 per cent per annum of the domestic tourism share in 1976 in the 1976–80 period, 1.5 per cent per annum of the 1980 share in the 1980–85 period, 1 per cent per annum of the 1985 share in the 1985–90 period, and that there is throughout a foreign share ceiling of 75 per cent. e Figures from Table 9; percentage = per cent of effective real ceiling to foreign travel.

Presumed ceilings to foreign travel

Table 8 suggests effective real ceilings to foreign travel from eight of the ten main origin countries; Japan and Mexico are omitted because travel is at present so far below any possible ceiling levels that any ceiling constraint is unlikely by 1990. The ceilings are based on leave periods available, plus one third of public holidays, multiplied by population and reduced by one third to allow for those unwilling or unable to avail themselves of holiday opportunities. Both the projected leave periods and this proportion are obviously hypotheses. Even greater assumptions are the assumed maximum possible rates of shift between domestic and foreign tourism: 2 per cent per annum of the 1976 domestic tourism share in the 1976-80 period; 1.5 per cent per annum of the 1980 share in the 1980-85 period; 1 per cent per annum of the 1985 share in the 1985-90 period; and, throughout, that there is a foreign share ceiling of 75 per cent of the total. The presumption is, therefore, of a levelling off as ceilings to the foreign shares are approached; these ceilings vary from country to country, reflecting existing shares, which in turn can be taken as largely reflecting the domestic tourism attractions to national tourists of their own countries. Where the domestic tourism share appears relatively small (West Germany, Canada, Belgium and Austria), the effects of varying these assumptions on the foreign travel ceiling are obviously more limited than where domestic tourism is far greater than foreign (the USA, France, and the UK).

Table 8 also shows how 1976 travel abroad from each country seemingly compares with the 1976 effective real ceiling. For most of the countries covered the 1976 penetration levels are around 40-50 per cent, but in the USA, the UK and France they are considerably higher (70-90 per cent). Although figures on existing domestic tourism levels (see Table 6) should be treated with caution, because of definitional differences (partly allowed for in Table 11), there seems little doubt that this difference does exist. It does not, however, imply that the maximum potential growth rates of foreign tourism from the USA, the UK and France are necessarily lower than in other countries. The effective real ceilings to foreign travel grow faster in these three countries. Although leave periods are already comparatively fully absorbed by tourist travel, in all three there is considerable potential for shifting from domestic to foreign tourism, and in the USA and the UK leave periods (currently meagre compared with other countries) are expected to rise quite rapidly.

Potential ceiling limitations are most severe in France, the UK and Austria

Table 9 shows ceiling growth rates derived from the previous table, and the maximum sustainable growth rates possible to move from existing foreign travel levels to the ceilings. The unadjusted figure shows growth (per cent per annum) over the whole period to 1990, assuming that growth does not taper off towards the ceiling growth rate as the ceiling is approached. The tapered off series makes the more realistic assumption that after 0.75 of the ceiling has been reached (at the unadjusted growth rate), progressive tapering off will occur (see footnote for details). These are not of course forecasts. They merely indicate what the highest achievable rates of growth would be given the data presented in this section and on the assumptions stated. The growth rates are in terms of time spent on holidays. Real expenditure per day is, of course, likely to rise, implying faster growth in a travel expenditure series (at constant prices). The table suggests that on this tapered off basis the highest possible growth rates over the whole period to 1990 are in Canada and West Germany; the lowest are in the UK and France.

36

Table 9

Maximum Potential Growth Rate in Foreign Travel in Light of Effective Real Ceilings Imposed by Leave Periods Available (per cent per annum)

	Ceiling growth rate (% per annum)			Travel growth necessary to reach ceiling in 1990 (% per annum)			
					Tapered off[a]		
	1976–80	1980–85	1985–90	Unadjusted	from	Average rate thereafter	Average rate over whole period
West Germany	4.00	2.50	2.75	8.75	1987	6.50	8.00
USA	6.75	4.50	4.25	7.25	1985	5.25	6.50
France	4.25	2.25	2.50	5.50	1980	4.00	4.25
Canada	4.50	2.00	2.50	10.00	1985	6.25	8.50
Netherlands	4.00	2.75	2.50	8.50	1985[b]	5.50[b]	7.25
UK	6.00	4.25	3.50	5.50	1980[b]	4.25	4.50
Belgium/Luxemburg	1.00	0.75	0.75	7.75	1985	5.00	6.50
Austria	4.25	1.00	1.00	6.25	1984	4.00	5.25

a Tapered off: at 0.75 ceiling, difference between growth rate and ceiling growth rate cut by 25 per cent
   " 0.80 " " " " " " " " 45 " "
   " 0.85 " " " " " " " " 60 " "
   " 0.90 " " " " " " " " 75 " "
   " 0.95 " " " " " " " " 90 " "

Assumes growth rate as in unadjusted column until year stated. Tapered off rate given is average from date tapering off starts. b Ceiling effects present in 1976, but because fast ceiling growth rate to 1980 tapering only after then.

Price and Income Elasticities

METHOD USED

In this section calculations are made of the price and income elasticities[1] of foreign tourism from five major origin countries - France, West Germany, Japan, the UK and the USA. It should be emphasised that the method of calculating elasticities used here does not seek to attribute all changes in travel to price and income changes (as do some measures of elasticities). Generally indeed, the results suggest that other elements are, in combination, as important as prices and incomes in determining travel growth.

In assessing the responsiveness of tourism demand to changes in real consumer incomes and to changes in prices, it is necessary to examine trends at the country of origin end. To consider them on a country by country basis at the destination end means that the picture is distorted by changes in fashion for different areas or types of holiday, by changes in the relative prices of holidays in different countries and by possible capacity constraints. Moreover, different national practices in collecting arrivals data, in particular the distinction between frontier arrivals and arrivals at tourist accommodation, mean that any attempt to use arrivals data globally or regionally would be employing a very distorted data base.

Optimally, in the absence of adequate price deflators for tourism expenditure data, and since data for means of travel other than by air are scanty, the tourism figures to be used as a base need to be departure or return figures from origin countries. (To evaluate responses to income and relative price changes, it is necessary for data to be on a volume basis; otherwise inflation distorts apparent relationships.) Unfortunately few countries have collected such data on a consistent basis over a sufficiently long period for analytical purposes. But an increasing number of origin countries do compile figures, primarily for balance of payments data purposes, on tourism expenditure abroad by residents. There are various ways by which these can be adjusted to a constant price basis.

---

1 Price elasticity measures the response of demand for a product, in this case tourism, to a change in prices; it is measured by dividing the percentage change in tourists (numbers, or some other measure of volume) by the percentage change in the price of tourism. Similarly income elasticity measures the response of tourism to an increase in real incomes. Thus if a 2 per cent increase in real incomes is associated with a 3 per cent increase in tourism, the income elasticity is +1.5, while if a 3 per cent increase in the price of tourism (relative to prices generally) is associated with a 6 per cent fall in tourist numbers, the price elasticity is -2.0.

In EIU Special Report No. 33 broadly similar measurements to those described in this section were compiled for the UK, the USA, Scandinavia, and Canada. But data problems made the calculations for Scandinavia and Canada somewhat inconclusive, and there have been significant improvements in several other major origin countries; consequently France, West Germany and Japan have been substituted.

Since the previous report, based essentially on data up to 1974, there have been sharp fluctuations in exchange rates, in comparative rates of inflation, in the growth rates of consumer incomes, and (consequently) in international travel. These fluctuations make it easier to measure price and income elasticities for tourism from major origin countries, and it should be possible to place greater confidence in the results.

In addition to calculating price and income elasticities for total travel, estimates are made of cross price elasticities – that is, how much switching between destinations there is from an individual origin country in response to changes in relative prices in those destinations. Because of data problems these cross elasticities could be calculated only for West Germany, the UK and the USA, and only for certain types of destination, plus some general indications for France.

Travel data

Only a few countries (Canada, Japan, the Netherlands, the UK, the USA, the Scandinavian countries, and, when adjustments are made for changes in definition, France) have compiled estimates of the number of national tourists travelling abroad for a sufficient number of years to be used as a basis for statistical analysis of trends, elasticities, etc. Not all these estimates are compiled in a manner, moreover, that fair confidence can be placed on their reliability. And, total departure or return figures for tourists take no account of changes in length of visit, in geographical pattern of travel, or in real expenditure per day. None-theless where such figures exist, they probably represent the best series for calculating overall price and income elasticities. (It can be argued that changes in expenditure per day and in length of stay are not particularly subject to sharp fluctuations in response to price and income changes, but show only long term trends.)

The only viable alternative data series to these departure or return figures is the figures compiled, for balance of payments reasons, on expenditure on foreign tourism by residents of individual origin countries. These are available for all OECD countries, though not always on a consistent basis over a long period (for instance French data have only relatively recently included inter franc zone travel). Coverage of non-OECD countries is very incomplete, particularly on a long term basis.

It should be emphasised that these expenditure figures generally exclude the major part of the transport cost element of holidays abroad, that is transport paid for in the tourist's home country. For most, but not all, origin countries data do exist on fare payments to foreign carriers, but not on fare payments to domestic carriers (the USA is one of the few countries with information on the latter); since the shares of foreign and domestic air carriers may fluctuate considerably in response to particular types of fare or promotional efforts, it would probably only distort the picture to add in payments to foreign carriers. Moreover, a large part of international transport expenditure, particularly within Europe and North America, is in personally owned motor vehicles. Part of the cost of such travel (fuel purchased abroad) is included in tourism expenditure, but much of it falls under local transport expenditure (e g capital cost of vehicles, insurance, most repairs, etc); yet for countries such as the Netherlands and Belgium travel abroad constitutes a significant share of total mileage by locally owned vehicles.

The exclusion of most transport expenditure is probably less important than it might appear in the context of measuring elasticities. In cross border and other short haul travel (which dominates travel from most major origin countries), the share of transport expenditure in total travel expenditure does not fluctuate much year by year, though it may shift over the long term. The general trend to cheaper air fares relative to prices generally is of rather more significance in relation to countries with substantial proportions of long haul travel.

To be usable for calculation of elasticity, it is necessary to adjust travel expenditure figures to a constant price basis. The approach used has been (unless otherwise stated) to deflate actual data on travel expenditure abroad by the implicit GDP deflation in national accounts data. This, of course, merely eliminates general domestic inflation from the crude data, and shows travel expenditure in terms of national resources devoted to travel. It does not adjust for the actual cost of holidays abroad (a conceptually totally different approach).

Real discretionary incomes data

Discretionary incomes are usually understood to be that part of total personal incomes which individuals are free to spend once tax and other commitments (e g insurance savings schemes, and basic housing costs) have been met and once essentials have been purchased. They are thus a considerably smaller total than disposable personal incomes. They do not, however, normally feature in national accounts statistics. What is and what is not an essential is a matter of opinion, and many people would hold that it varies according to the affluence of the society concerned.

The concept is undoubtedly a useful one, though, as it is out of discretionary incomes that expenditure on holidays and most luxuries and semi-luxuries comes. Since the proportion of discretionary incomes in disposable incomes undoubtedly varies over time, it should be a more appropriate aggregate to compare travel with than, say, disposable incomes.

The term "real discretionary incomes" (the form of incomes considered throughout this section) is used, loosely for convenience, for total disposable incomes at constant prices less expenditure on food, housing, fuel and light. This is, of course, only an approximation to discretionary incomes as commonly understood; no doubt some of the excluded items are far from essentials, while part at least of expenditure on clothing, durables and services does constitute essential expenditure.

Relative prices data

The other major series of data considered in this section as possible influences on travel are relative prices, by which is meant how much faster or slower exchange rate adjusted prices in destination countries rose than did those in the country of origin concerned. This was done by first compiling for 24 major origin or destination countries an exchange rate adjusted consumer price index from 1963 to 1977 (see Appendix 1).

To arrive at a common basis, these indices show consumer prices in each country in terms of a common currency unit, the SDR (effectively the US dollar in earlier years); basic data came from standard UN and IMF sources. By dividing the index for a particular destination country by the index for an origin country, a cross index can be derived, showing whether a particular destination is becoming more or less expensive for the residents of a particular origin country. Referring to the appendix table, it can thus be seen that between 1963 and 1970 exchange rate adjusted prices in Switzerland rose only 9.1 per cent in total more than they did in the UK, while by 1977 the difference had reached 60.5 per cent. For each major origin country an overall index was then compiled through combining the cross indices for the main destinations for travellers from that country. In arriving at these overall indices, the various cross indices were weighted according to the proportion of travel from the origin country concerned going to each. The resulting overall index shows, for example, that in a year when UK prices rose by 5 per cent, and prices in typical destinations rose by 10 per cent (both in terms of a common currency unit), relative prices would rise by just under 5 per cent. Chart D illustrates graphically movements in relative costs from six major origin countries.

It is easy to pick holes in this method of estimating relative prices. The system of weightings might be disputed. The rate of increase in the prices of products which tourists buy may be faster or slower than that of the consumer price index (but see below). Certainly until 1973, and to a degree since then, package tour prices, for instance, tended to follow changes in retail prices with a time lag of almost a year. Most important of all, destination country costs constitute only part of a package tour price, though a much larger part of total holiday cost, particularly in respect of non-package tour holidays. The exclusion of air fares (which do not normally feature in general consumer price indices) might appear particularly serious. But the inclusion of rough indices of air fares in the calculation of cross price elasticities as between destinations of UK and US travel (see relevant subsections on these) does not appear to have made that much difference to the final results.

Unfortunately the data simply do not exist to produce adequate indices of prices of holidays abroad, both package tour and non-package tour, and including personal transport as well as air fares. However, it is worth noting that changes in the main elements on which there are some data, hotel and restaurant prices, have tended generally to keep reasonably close to changes in consumer prices. Chart E illustrates this for five major West European countries . It can be seen that although hotel and restaurant charges have risen consistently faster than consumer prices generally:

HOW RELATIVE COST OF TRAVEL FROM
SIX MAIN ORIGIN COUNTRIES HAS CHANGED

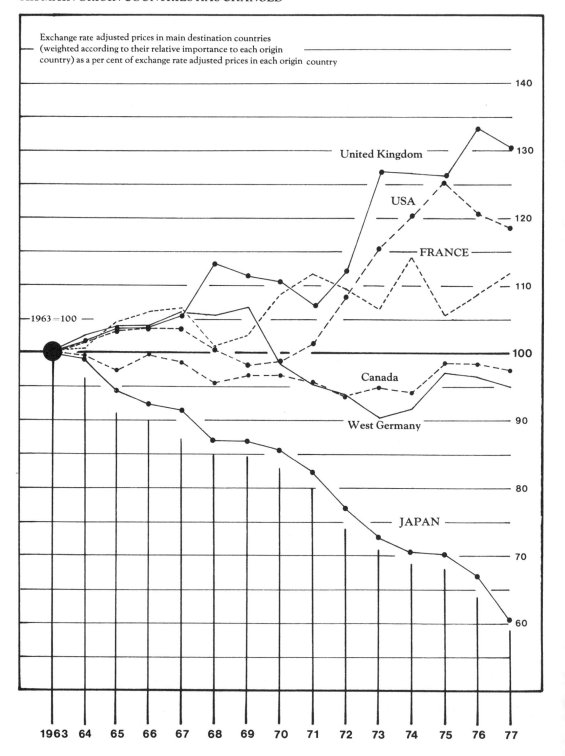

Exchange rate adjusted prices in main destination countries (weighted according to their relative importance to each origin country) as a per cent of exchange rate adjusted prices in each origin country

1963 = 100

United Kingdom
USA
FRANCE
Canada
West Germany
JAPAN

1963 64 65 66 67 68 69 70 71 72 73 74 75 76 77

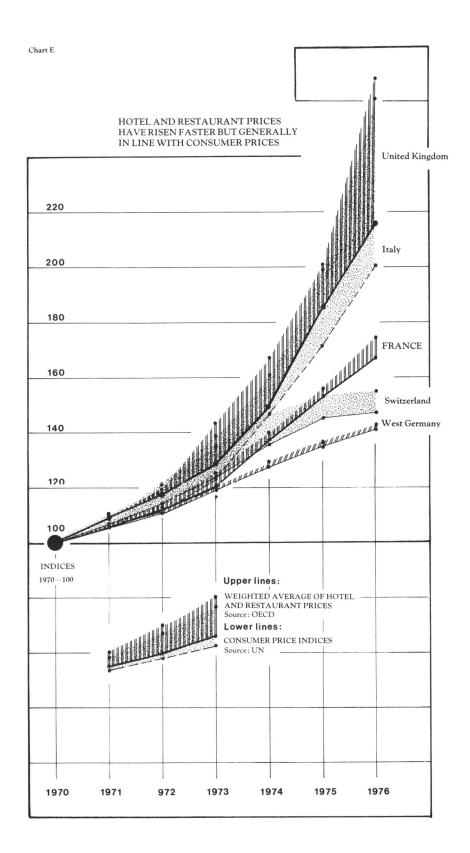

HOTEL AND RESTAURANT PRICES
HAVE RISEN FASTER BUT GENERALLY
IN LINE WITH CONSUMER PRICES

220

200

180

160

140

120

100

INDICES
1970 = 100

United Kingdom

Italy

FRANCE

Switzerland

West Germany

Upper lines:
WEIGHTED AVERAGE OF HOTEL
AND RESTAURANT PRICES
Source: OECD

Lower lines:
CONSUMER PRICE INDICES
Source: UN

1970   1971   972   1973   1974   1975   1976

43

a.   only in Italy (and to a lesser degree the UK) has the increase been much
      faster; probably the hotel prices paid by package tour operators (through
      discounts, etc) have kept still closer in line;

b.   years of rapid increase in consumer prices tend to be years of rapid
      increase in hotel and restaurant prices[1] ;

c   sometimes when hotel and restaurant prices do threaten to get out of
      line (as in Switzerland in 1973 and 1974) increases are held back in
      subsequent years.

As long as the differential between changes in the general consumer price indices
and tourism prices remains reasonably constant over time, use of a special
tourism price index in each country, could one be composed, would make little
difference to the overall picture. If the relative prices are lagged (i e follow
published data some months in arrears) the elasticity calculations can themselves
be made to take this lagging into account. In short, the method used seems the
best possible using readily available data.

Other influences

It must be emphasised that the techniques of regression analysis used do not ignore
all influences on travel other than incomes and price movements. They merely
combine factors such as promotion, changing factors for particular types of holiday,
and exchange control regulations, into a single constant for each origin country.
The implication is that they combine to make travel grow at, say, a steady 5 per
cent a year, while each 1 per cent rise in real discretionary incomes produces,
say, a further 1 per cent rise in travel, and each 1 per cent rise in relative prices
results in, say, a 1 per cent fall in travel. These other influences as a group are
assumed to remain constant over time, though within the group some may increase
or others decline in significance. This is not a very satisfactory presumption, as
in the long run it is obvious that the constant must change (or travel would end
up by absorbing the whole of national income).

In principle, the solution to such problems is to create a model which can reflect
all influences on travel. Unfortunately experience to date with travel models has
not been satisfactory. The problems lie more in the data than in the techniques.
It is difficult enough to define what the influences are; they have to be quantified,
ideally over a run of years, and psychological and sociological influences rarely
can be. An obviously quantifiable element (in principle at least, difficult though it
is to compile the data in practice) is spending on advertising and promotion by the
travel trade; but is the cost effectiveness of such spending constant over time, with
no diminishing returns on the one hand, or effects of improved techniques on the
other?

---

1 Indeed it is possible to estimate coefficients of correlation between percentage
increases in the two series for the six years 1971-76 inclusive. These coefficients
are: 0.81 for the UK; 0.77 each in France, West Germany and Switzerland; but
only 0.54 for Italy.

Use of three year moving averages

Some influences on travel are likely to have only relatively short term effects. To eliminate the complications caused by these is one reason why, when seeking to compile reasonably long term forecasts, it is advisable not to pay overmuch attention to year to year fluctuations in travel or in the main influences on it. Sharp annual fluctuations, as in the past three years, make, moreover, the task of data analysis more difficult. Important though a freak change in travel is for the year to year planning of the travel trade, it may be unnecessary to try to account fully for it in terms of measurable economic and other variables when seeking to establish a basis for relatively long term forecasts; it may also be impossible. Lagged and anticipatory effects of price and income changes on travel are complex; the longer the period over which changes are related to one another, the more this complication can be **bypassed.** It is also perhaps worth observing that, if a past appraisal or a forecast is produced on a year to year basis, there is a great temptation to expect the procedures for long term forecasting to produce valid results for the short term also; this is not the case.

For these reasons the analysis of all series of data has been primarily through the examination of percentage changes per annum in three year moving averages. The use of changes per annum in moving averages, rather than the moving averages themselves, eliminates the influence of the portions of incomes, relative prices and travel which do not change; without this, relationships would appear misleadingly close. The procedure means that data for 13 years (eg 1965-77 inclusive) give ten changes in three year moving averages. A simple grouping into three year periods would enable only three measurements of changes to be carried out for 13 years' data; this is far too few to establish relationships satisfactorily.

Statistical method

For those without some background in statistics a simple **description of the main** procedures involved in this section may be helpful.

The basic **procedure** involved is the standard one of regression analysis. This determines the relationship between a variable or variables (in this report x_1 = change in real discretionary incomes throughout, while x_2 = change in relative prices throughout) and a response in economic behaviour (y = change in travel). In simple regression only one x variable (eg x1) is involved. Multiple regressions can involve two or more x variables. In simple regression where a constant (ie linear) x:y relationship is believed to exist, the procedure is to fit the best straight line to the values of x against y (if the relationship is y = 5 + 2x, y is influenced by a constant of 5 plus twice the value of x at that particular point or period). The best straight line is one where the deviations between the actual values and that line are minimised. **Statistically the method used** here is the most common one – where the sum of the squares of the deviations are minimised (the least squares). Multiple regression is similar, except that one is seeking to minimise the sum of the squares of two or more variables from the line.

While this type of regression gives one the best linear fit between incomes and prices on the one hand and travel on the other, it assumes that each x:y relationship and the constant do not change over time. If it seems they do change, a non-linear function (i e a simple or complex curve) ought to be fitted. Apart from the statistical problems in this, the quantity and quality of data available really mean that the attempt would not be justified; the chances are that the curve linear relationships found would be coincidental rather than causal, and one would be deceiving oneself to try to project them into the future. Though some evidence of changing relationships is found in this section, it is not considered strong enough, or consistent enough, in direction of change to warrant trying to fit non-linear relationships.

It is quite likely that the relationships between income and prices on the one hand and travel on the other do not coincide in time, but travel changes may follow one or more years behind income or price changes; this is a lagged effect. It is possible, moreover, where knowledge of the expected state of an economy is widespread among potential travellers abroad, that travel changes may occur in anticipation of income changes (an anticipatory effect). In attempting to establish best fits, a range of lagged and anticipatory relationships were tested.

It is important to have some measure of how good the fit of a simple or multiple regression equation is. Statistically this can be done through the coefficient of determination, which measures the relationship between the explained (by the equation) and the total variation in the values of y (travel). A coefficient of 0.99 implies that the equation explains almost all the variation, while one of 0.10 indicates that hardly any of it has been explained. Some are more accustomed to the coefficient of correlation as a measure of fit. This shows much the same thing as the coefficient of determination, though its values are invariably higher.

Another measure, appropriate for the analysis of this section and perhaps easier to appreciate the values of, is to assess how large the fluctuations are between the results of applying the equation in the past and actual past travel; this can then be compared with the fluctuations between past travel and a simple straight line fitted to past travel data. (It is clear that any forecasting procedure which would produce past deviations in travel nearly as large as those from a straight line is not very satisfactory as a procedure; it would be better to stick to the far simpler straight line projection). Since the analysis is in terms of per cent changes per annum in three year moving averages so is this measure. Thus one might get mean standard deviation between the results of applying the equation and actual travel of 1.5 per cent per annum (say from 5.5 to 8.5 per cent growth per annum if the average were 7.0 per cent), when the mean standard deviation from trend of actual travel data was 4.5 per cent per annum; one has thus been able to eliminate two thirds of the fluctuations. Mean standard variation is a method of measuring variations which gives proportionately more weight to big variations (which it is important to try to explain) than to small ones (which do not matter so much).

Some cautions

It should be pointed out that a good fit can be achieved when the number of observations is quite small. Obviously this is less likely to be correct than if the same fit were achieved with a far larger number of observations. In this section the number of observations has generally been ten. This is a smaller number than one would wish, and one should be correspondingly cautious in attributing accuracy to the findings. As one goes further back, less data become available and the basis of collection is liable to have changed. It may also be felt that the nature of the travel trade has changed so much that it is not really appropriate to try to fit a linear relationship to data embracing more than perhaps 10-15 years.

Regression analysis only establishes a (past) relationship. It does not establish that the relationship is a causal one – that the x forces did exert a particular influence on y. It is an inference, and it can be a firm and sensible inference, that the relationship is causal. The closer the relationship (the better the fit) and the greater the number of observation points, the more reasonable it is to act on the assumption that the past relationship will continue to hold in the future. But particularly when the relationship is not close, or the number of observation points is small, one should be reluctant to use as a base any equation which seems contrary to general experience or common sense.

THE UK

Overall trends

Chart F illustrates trends in UK travel, measured in two different ways, compared with the development of UK discretionary incomes and the relative cost of travel from the UK. The data used appear in Appendix 2. The following points emerge.

1. The two travel series (visits abroad and expenditure abroad at constant prices) show similar trends in that peaks and troughs coincide and overall trend growth rates are reasonably similar (6 per cent per annum for the number of visits abroad, and 4.4 per cent per annum for real expenditure abroad on a least squares trend basis over 1963-76 – the difference reflecting increasing low cost holiday opportunities over this period). However, the real expenditure series fluctuates considerably more sharply, even on a three year moving average basis, as shown in the chart (the mean standard deviation of the three year moving average of the expenditure series from the trend growth rate is 5.9 per cent, while for the visits abroad series it is only 3.6 per cent). This implies that when economic circumstances are adverse (reflected, for instance, in a slow incomes growth) people do not only reduce the number of trips made abroad but also their expenditure per trip.

2. Periods of rapid discretionary incomes growth coincide with periods of rapid travel growth, as do periods of slow growth in each. There is a possible tendency, though, for the changes in travel to anticipate changes in incomes by one year – suggesting perhaps that people are influenced in their holiday decisions not only by their financial situations at that time, but to a degree also by press reports of how well the economy is likely to perform in coming months.

UK TRAVEL, DISCRETIONARY INCOMES
AND RELATIVE COST OF TRAVEL

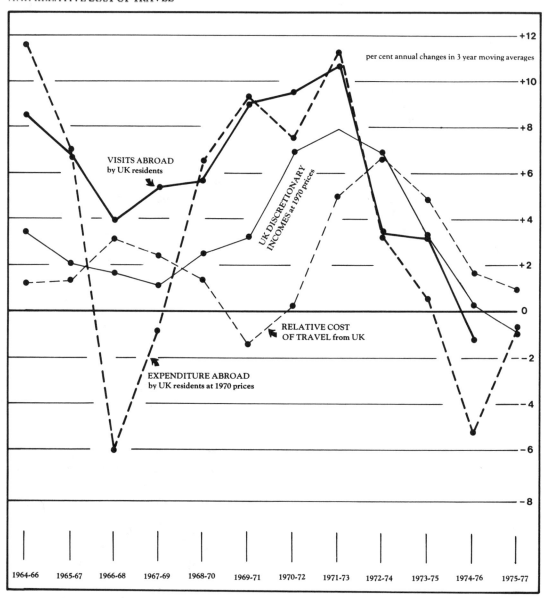

per cent annual changes in 3 year moving averages

VISITS ABROAD
by UK residents

UK DISCRETIONARY
INCOMES at 1970 prices

RELATIVE COST
OF TRAVEL from UK

EXPENDITURE ABROAD
by UK residents at 1970 prices

48

3.   The relative cost of travel from the UK is generally rising, reflecting
        mainly the depreciation of the sterling exchange rate. Periods of rapid
        increase in this relative cost tend to coincide with periods of slow increase
        in travel abroad, whereas when relative prices are growing slowly or
        declining travel tends to expand more rapidly. It seems, though, that the
        effect of price increases on travel is lagged by one year - suggesting,
        perhaps, that in their holiday decisions people are affected partly by their
        own or their friends' experience of how expensive travel abroad had been
        in the previous year, and reflecting also the fact that package holiday
        prices are fixed almost a year in advance of the bulk of holidays being
        taken and that tour operators do not recover the full effect of subsequent
        relative price movements through special surcharges.

Price and income relationships

Table 10 shows six different multiple regression equations derived from the data
which appear on this chart. These explore different time relationships (straight,
anticipatory and lagged) between each of the two travel series and incomes and
relative costs. Three different measures of how well each equation explains
fluctuations in travel are shown. All rank the equations in the same order. The
first two (coefficients of multiple determination and of multiple correlation) are
conventional statistical measures. The third (the percentage reduction in year to
year fluctuations in travel growth rates through application of the equation to actual
past data) may be more comprehensible to those unaccustomed to these statistical
methods. A 50 per cent reduction implies that if, for instance, the average long
term growth rate of travel is 6 per cent per annum, with a fluctuation (mean
standard variation) of 4 per cent per annum either side of this average, the growth
rate in actual travel should normally vary from the growth rate in predicted travel
by only 2 per cent per annum.

The most satisfactory equation relating incomes and relative costs to numbers of
travellers abroad is A3. This implies that travel:

    a.   rises at 4. 05 per cent per annum irrespective of income and price move-
            ments;

    b.   increases by a further 0. 80 per cent per annum for every 1 per cent rise
            in real discretionary incomes one period later (e g the income increases
            in the 1975-77 period stimulate travel rises over 1974-76);

    c.   that each 1 per cent rise in the cost of travel abroad from the UK (relative
            to cost within the UK) reduces travel by 0. 46 per cent.

However, equation A2 is also reasonably satisfactory (this has no anticipatory
income effect), while A1, with no anticipatory or lagged effects, shows fair results.
These imply rather larger price responses, but a more variable income response.

Table 10

Multiple Regression Equations for UK Travel Abroad

Time relationship	Equation	Coefficients of multiple		Use of equation – per cent reduction in mean standard variation in travel
		Determination	Correlation	
A Travel expressed as no. of travellers				
1	$y_1 = 3.86 + 1.09\,x_2 - 0.92\,x_3$	0.625	0.791	38
2	$y_1 = 6.02 + 0.54\,x_2 - 1.01\,x_3$	0.708	0.842	46
3	$y_1 = 4.05 + 0.80\,x_2 - 0.46\,x_3$	0.802	0.895	59
B Travel expressed as real expenditure on travel				
1	$y_1 = 0.26 + 1.80\,x_2 - 1.34\,x_3$	0.703	0.839	46
2	$y_1 = 0.20 + 1.26\,x_2 - 0.76\,x_3$	0.574	0.758	35
3	$y_1 = 4.40 + 1.86\,x_2 + 0.56\,x_3$	0.780	0.883	53

Explanation of equations

y_1A UK travellers abroad to all destinations.

y_1B Expenditure by UK travellers abroad to all destinations.

x_2 "Discretionary" incomes (personal disposable incomes less expenditure on food, housing, fuel and light) at 1970 prices.

x_3 Relative cost of travel abroad from UK (weighted index of exchange rate adjusted consumer prices in major destination countries divided by exchange rate adjusted consumer price index for UK).

Timescales and time relationships

Timescale: A 1965–76
             B 1966–77

Relationships: 1 travel in period x affected by incomes in period x and by prices in period x
                2 travel in period x affected by incomes in period x and by prices in period x – 1
                3 travel in period x affected by incomes in period x + 1 and by prices in period x – 1
                (if 1970–72 is period x, 1969–71 is period x – 1, and 1971–73 period x + 1, etc)

Use of equation – % reduction is mean standard variation in travel
If the mean standard variation in y_1 is 5 per cent and if the application of the equation to actual x_2 and x_3 data results in a mean standard variation of 2.5 per cent between predicted and actually, there would be a 50 per cent reduction.

If incomes and relative costs are related to real expenditure on travel abroad, the statistically most satisfactory relationship - B3 - is a distinctly implausible one, implying as it does that relative price increases result in growing travel, and that the normal situation is for travel to grow quite sharply; however, the more reasonable equation B1 yields only slightly less satisfactory results from the statistical angle. B2, though plausible, is statistically not very satisfactory.

Chart G shows graphically the results that would be achieved over 1965-77 by applying equations A3 and B1 to actual incomes and relative price data, and compares these with actual travel over this period.

Some general conclusions

Taking all six results together (and arbitrarily weighting each by the amount by which its coefficient of multiple determination exceeds 0.500) suggests the following conclusions.

1. The number of travellers abroad from the UK would normally rise by 4.7 per cent per annum, even if there were no income or relative price movements.

2. The volume of expenditure on such travel would, on the same basis, normally fall by 2.3 per cent per annum. (The large difference, which may not of course apply in future years, reflects the increasing availability of cheaper opportunities for travel in the past, even though relative costs of any one type, as used to derive the equations, have risen; a measure of relative prices which was able to take into account the effects on prices of, most notably, the package tour industry should bring the two normal growth rates more into line, but should not affect the elasticity response to changes in movements of relative prices.)

3. The discretionary income elasticity of demand is around 1.2 (thus a 1 per cent increase in discretionary incomes produces a 1.2 per cent increase in travel).

4. The price elasticity of demand is around -0.5 (a 1 per cent increase in the relative cost of travel abroad thus yields a 0.5 per cent fall in travel).

Measuring how relative price movements affect destinations

In addition to the effects on travel of a general change in the relative cost of travel abroad (expressed through a weighted average of relative costs in all destinations), it is interesting to examine the responsiveness of travel to different destinations to movements in relative prices in those destinations. The national holiday surveys conducted in the UK for many years make it possible in addition to measure the extent of switching between holidays taken in the UK to holidays taken abroad in response to movements in their relative prices.

The proportion of all holidays taken
abroad is significantly affected by relative prices

Regression equations analysing the relationship between changes in the cost of
holidays taken abroad and in the proportion of all holidays taken by Britons which
are abroad suggest that, for each 1 per cent increase in the cost of holidays
abroad relative to holidays in the UK, the proportion of all holidays which the
British take abroad falls by 1.8 per cent, counteracting in part a general tendency
for this proportion to increase by 5.7 per cent a year[1].

There is poor evidence on long haul/short haul shifts

The evidence suggests (see data in appendix) that the cost of travel from the UK
to long haul destinations has risen considerably more slowly than to West European
destinations. This applies also, though less markedly, if a rough index of air
fares (derived from total UK airline revenue per passenger-km performed) is
included in the relative cost totals (weighted so as to account for 50 per cent of the
long haul trip cost total, but only 25 per cent of the typical West European trip).
However, the statistical evidence of a relationship between, for instance, periods
when the relative cost of long haul travel declines particularly rapidly and a
sharper growth in the share of long haul travel in the UK total is not very good.
Eight different relationships were tested: taken together, they suggest that for
each 1 per cent shift in relative prices in favour of long haul prices (ie downwards)
its share of the total UK travel market increases by around 0.4 per cent. As this
share was 31.5 per cent (in terms of million days spent) in 1976, the implication
is that the cross price elasticity between long haul and short haul is almost
exactly -1.0. But note that the average coefficient of correlation was only 0.351
and the highest 0.700, and also that the equations suggest that the percentage
share of long haul travel from the UK would have fallen by 0.3 per cent per annum,
but for the favourable price trends.

The UK responds sharply to price changes in West Europe

However, the evidence of price responses in changing patterns of travel from the
UK within West Europe is much clearer. Although the data[2] enable only five
observations for each equation, for six out of the seven main Western European
destinations for British travel plausible price/travel share relationships and

---

1. The equation is $y = 5.71 - 1.77x$, when y is the percentage increase per
annum in the three year moving average of the proportion of all holidays by British
which are taken abroad, and x is the percentage increase per annum one period
earlier (in effect one year) in the three year moving average of the cost of travel
abroad from the UK relative to costs at home. The coefficient of correlation is
0.803. A similar equation without any lagged effect of relative price movements
is $y = 4.80 - 1.34x$ (coefficient of correlation 0.639).

2. There were three year moving averages in: a. changes (per cent points)
during 1969-76 in per cent share of total UK travel to these seven destinations
going to each destination (y); b. per cent changes during 1968-76 in relative prices
in each of these destinations compared with the seven country total (x); in some
cases a lagged relationship (prices in one three year period affecting travel a year
later in the succeeding three year period) was more satisfactory - shown as x_2
on the chart.

UK : PERCENTAGE CHANGES per annum IN 3 YEAR
MOVING AVERAGES OF TRAVEL

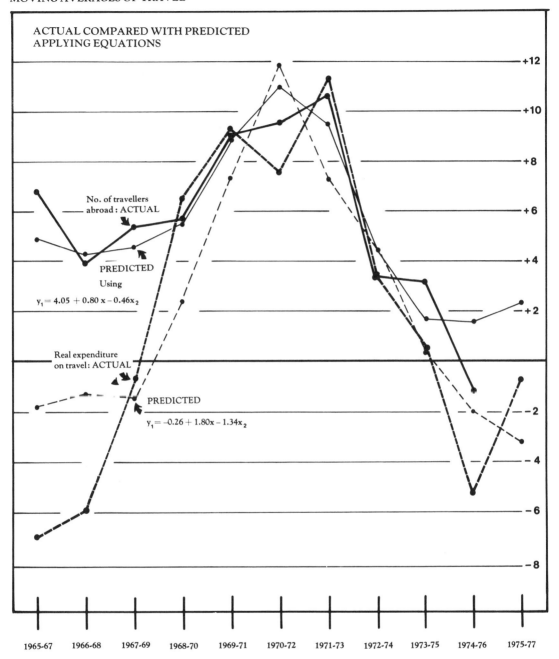

coefficients of correlation (ranging from 0.67 to 0.89) can be derived. The results appear on the accompanying chart. Only for Italy are the results unacceptable (a poor coefficient and a perverse relationship). A possible reason is that the general consumer price index appears in Italy alone to be a poor proxy for tourist prices, the latter rising far faster than prices generally - perhaps because the buoyancy of travel from West Germany, for which Italy is easily the most important Mediterranean holiday area, has made competitive pricing unimportant.

To arrive at constants and price elasticity responses for the data in the chart, it is necessary to express travel changes against a common basis of 100, rather than as changes in percentage shares. This suggests, for the six countries, the following mid period (1973) figures.

Destination	Constant rate of change in travel from the UK, if total travel from UK to seven countries combined remains static (% p a)	Elasticity response: % p a reduction in travel from UK consequent on a 1% increase p a in the cost of travel to that destination compared with seven country average
Spain	5.8	2.3
Irish Republic	-18.8	4.6
France	3.5	1.5
West Germany	5.6	3.2
Austria	1.4	7.0
Switzerland	-1.0	1.4

It can be seen that the constants generally outweigh price responses as determinants of destinations for UK travel. (Constants in this calculation include factors such as changes in the popularity per se of particular types of holiday or destination, responses to marketing and promotional programmes, and in the Irish Republic the repercussions of events in Ulster.) However, price responses are quite marked, most perhaps in the more downmarket destinations (compare Austria and Switzerland). A weighted average cross elasticity for the six destinations is -2.8. This of course implies that, if a country were to reduce its prices to UK travellers by 10 per cent (relative to other countries' prices), it would get over the next three years or so 28 per cent more British travellers than it could otherwise expect, and in the region of 15 per cent more revenue.

THE USA

General trends

Though growth rates in travel (measured in terms of number of travellers abroad, and real expenditure on travel abroad), real discretionary incomes and the relative cost of travel abroad have all fluctuated considerably over the past 15 years, analysis is complicated by two more factors.

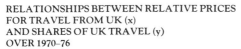

RELATIONSHIPS BETWEEN RELATIVE PRICES
FOR TRAVEL FROM UK (x)
AND SHARES OF UK TRAVEL (y)
OVER 1970–76

No relationship shown for Italy (very poor)

X_2 Indicates that relative prices effect
travel patterns 1 year later in the
3 year moving average

in 3 year moving averages

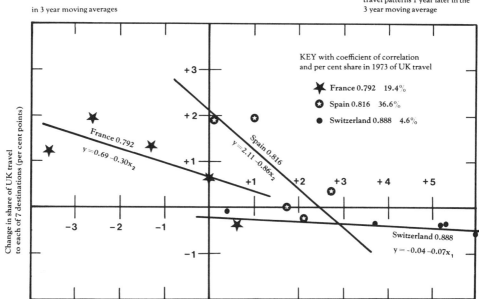

Change in relative prices for each destination
compared with 7 country total (per cent per annum)

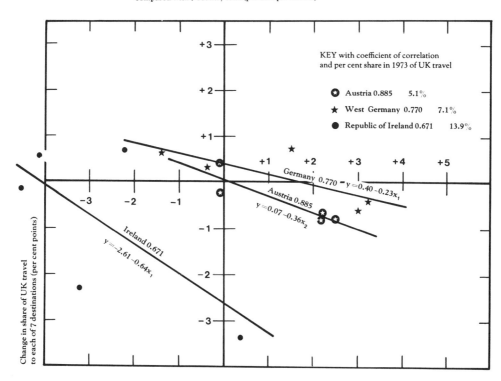

1. A tendency for declines in discretionary incomes growth rates to coincide with falls in the relative cost of travel abroad; not only do these influences thus counteract one another, but it is statistically difficult to disentangle their effects.

2. Analysis of total travel in terms of numbers of travellers is of doubtful value, because it combines large numbers of relatively low spending visitors to Canada and Mexico with smaller numbers of higher spending travellers overseas (67 per cent of US visits abroad in 1976 were to Canada and Mexico, compared with only 45 per cent of travel expenditure).

However, analysis of graphically plotted data suggests:

1. a reasonably good relationship between real discretionary incomes and both travel data series, with a tendency for travel to anticipate income developments (perhaps because press reports on future prosperity affect travel decisions);

2. a clear lagged relationship between the relative cost of travel abroad and travel, however measured (prices tending to affect travel one to two years later).

Discretionary income and price relationships

The table which follows shows six different multiple regression equations relating real discretionary incomes and the relative cost of travel abroad to travel. For all travel abroad only the real travel expenditure series is used, while for overseas and cruise travel (ie excluding trips to Canada and Mexico) the equations explore relationships against both real travel expenditure and numbers of travellers.

Two of the equations for overseas and cruise travel (B1 and C2) yield statistically acceptable results, while the other two (B3 and C1) are reasonable. The equations for all travel abroad are less satisfactory, though not poor. All six equations show positive discretionary income responses and negative relative price responses, as one would expect. The price responses for overseas and cruise travel are, reasonably enough, considerably larger than for total travel abroad. Note, though, that there are big variations in underlying growth rates - a least squares   trend for all travel abroad shows an average growth rate of only 3.3 per cent per annum, against 5.4 per cent per annum for real expenditure on overseas and cruise travel, and 9.2 per cent per annum for numbers going on overseas and cruise trips.

Chart I

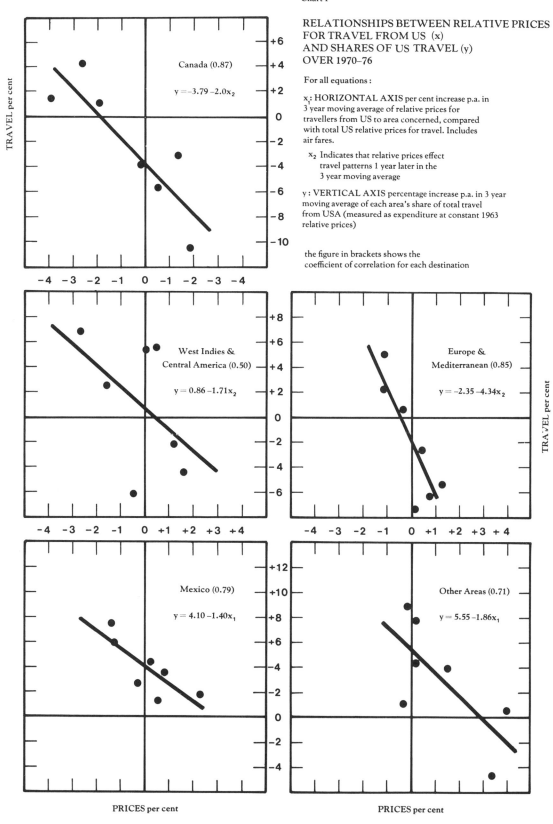

RELATIONSHIPS BETWEEN RELATIVE PRICES
FOR TRAVEL FROM US (x)
AND SHARES OF US TRAVEL (y)
OVER 1970–76

For all equations :

x_1: HORIZONTAL AXIS per cent increase p.a. in
3 year moving average of relative prices for
travellers from US to area concerned, compared
with total US relative prices for travel. Includes
air fares.

x_2 Indicates that relative prices effect
travel patterns 1 year later in the
3 year moving average

y : VERTICAL AXIS percentage increase p.a. in 3 year
moving average of each area's share of total travel
from USA (measured as expenditure at constant 1963
relative prices)

the figure in brackets shows the
coefficient of correlation for each destination

Canada (0.87)

$y = -3.79 - 2.0x_2$

West Indies &
Central America (0.50)

$y = 0.86 - 1.71x_2$

Europe &
Mediterranean (0.85)

$y = -2.35 - 4.34x_2$

Mexico (0.79)

$y = 4.10 - 1.40x_1$

Other Areas (0.71)

$y = 5.55 - 1.86x_1$

PRICES per cent

PRICES per cent

57

Table 11

Multiple Regression Equations for US Travel Abroad Over 1965-76

Time relationship	Equation	Coefficients of multiple		Use of equation – per cent reduction in mean standard variation in travel
		Determination	Correlation	
A All travel abroad – real expenditure				
1	$y_1 = 1.41 + 1.02\ x_2 - 0.14\ x_3$	0.671	0.819	43
2	$y_1 = 2.72 + 0.77\ x_1 - 0.45\ x_3$	0.711	0.843	49
B Overseas & cruise travel – no. of travellers				
1	$y_1 = 8.33 + 1.08\ x_2 - 1.06\ x_1$	0.959	0.979	80
3	$y_1 = 9.42 + 0.87\ x_2 - 1.04\ x_3$	0.851	0.923	61
C Overseas & cruise travel – real expenditure				
1	$y_1 = 6.38 + 0.68\ x_2 - 0.86\ x_3$	0.799	0.894	55
2	$y_1 = 8.71 + 0.17\ x_2 - 1.29\ x_3$	0.962	0.981	81

Explanation of equations

y_{1},A US travellers abroad to all destinations, expenditure at constant prices

y_{1},B US travellers to overseas & cruise destinations only (excludes Canada & Mexico), numbers

y_{1},C US travellers to overseas & cruise destinations only, expenditure at constant prices

x_2 Discretionary incomes (disposable personal incomes less expenditure on food, beverages, housing and household operations) at 1958 prices

x_3 Relative cost of travel abroad from USA (weighted index of exchange rate adjusted consumer prices in major destination countries divided by exchange rate adjusted consumer prices index for USA); for overseas and cruise, index relates to those destinations only

In respect of all the above per cent increases per annum in three year moving averages.

Time relationships

1 Travel in period x affected by incomes in period x and by prices in period x – 1

2 Travel in period x affected by incomes in period x and by prices in period x – 2

3 Travel in period x affected by incomes in period x + 1 and by prices in period x – 1
  (If 1970–72 is period x, 1969–71 is period x – 1, and 1971–73 is period x + 1, etc)

Use of equation – per cent reduction in mean standard variation in travel

If mean standard variation in y_1 is 5 per cent, and if the application of the equation to actual x_2 and x_3 data results in a mean standard variation of 2.5 per cent between predicted and actual y_1, there would be a 50 per cent reduction.

General conclusions on elasticities

Arbitrarily weighting results by the amounts by which the coefficient of multiple determination exceeds 0.500 suggests the following.

1.   Real expenditure on all travel abroad rises by 0.9 per cent for each 1 per cent increase in real discretionary incomes.

2.   Real expenditure on all travel abroad falls by 0.3 per cent for each 1 per cent increase in relative prices.

3.   Overseas and cruise travel (both real expenditure and number of travellers) rises by 0.7 per cent for each 1 per cent increase in real discretionary incomes.

4.   Overseas and cruise travel falls by 1.1 per cent for each 1 per cent increase in its relative price.

Cross elasticities by main area

Statistically acceptable and surprisingly consistent results were obtained by relating movements in relative prices by area visited by US travellers to the shares of total travel going to each area. Naturally, many other factors affect these shares (changes in fashion for particular types of holiday, the impact of promotional programmes, etc). Such elements are reflected in the constants in the equations which follow; thus Mexico, West Indies and Central America, and others areas, are generally increasing in popularity, Canada and Europe are declining. It appears, however, that each 1 per cent by which an area becomes more expensive than other areas reduces travel to it, measured in real expenditure terms, by 2 per cent. (The average value in the equations below, weighted by the respective coefficients of correlation, is - 2.03.) Note that the relative price data used in the equations include a rough index of US international air fares; see the appendix for details. Only the lagged equation for other areas and the unlagged one for Europe and Mediterranean are statistically worthless. Chart I shows graphically the best results for each area.

Table 12

Cross Elasticity Equations for US Travel by Area

	No lagged effects		Lagged by one period	
	Equation	Coefficient of correlation	Equation	Coefficient of correlation
Canada	$y = -4.36 - 2.00x$	0.760	$y = -3.79 - 2.00x$	0.870
Mexico	$y = 4.10 - 1.40x$	0.789	$y = 4.10 - 0.77x$	0.446
West Indies & Cent America	$y = 2.06 - 1.04x$	0.497	$y = 0.86 - 1.71x$	0.497
Europe & Mediterranean	$y = -2.08 - 1.99x$	0.379	$y = -2.35 - 4.34x$	0.845
Other areas	$y = 5.55 - 1.86x$	0.711	$y = 3.06 + 0.08x$	0.029

x = Percentage increase per annum in relative prices for travellers from the USA to area concerned compared with total US relative prices for travel. Air fares included in general indices, assuming that air fares accounted for 15 per cent of total 1971–73 trip cost in Canada and Mexico, 20 per cent in West Indies and Caribbean, 30 per cent in Europe and Mediterranean, and 35 per cent in other areas (all country average, 22.7 per cent).

y = Percentage increase per annum in each area's share of total travel from USA (measured in terms of expenditure at constant 1963 relative prices).

Equations based on three year moving averages over 1967–76 period. Thus seven observations for each area. A lagged effect by one period is, for instance, when relative prices in 1968–70 affect the travel share in 1969–71.

Switching of destinations within Europe in response to price shifts is limited

But while there is reasonable evidence of a marked price response in US travel by
main area, within Europe at least there does not appear to be a great deal of
switching of destinations by US travellers in response to changes in intra-
European relative prices. Thus, while the equations cited above suggest that a
1 per cent increase in the relative price of travel from the USA to Europe (compared
with other destinations) results in a fall of as much as 4 per cent in the number
of travellers, Americans' travel plans within Europe are not very responsive to,
for instance, the increasing cheapness of trips to the UK compared with France.
There are two obvious reasons for this: many visits by Americans to Europe are
multi-country trips in which there is only limited scope for switching periods
spent in different countries; and many Americans are unaware of price differenti-
ations within Europe – tending indeed to regard it as a single entity. Equations
were derived for five main European destinations for US travellers (the UK, West
Germany, Italy, France and Switzerland) and for these five destinations taken
together for the 1967–76 period. Air travel costs were excluded, lagged effects
for one and two periods were considered in addition to straight line relationships.
Thus in total 18 equations were derived.

The equations suggest, though tentatively, that each 1 per cent increase in the
relative cost of travel from the USA to a particular European destination reduces
that country's share of total European travel by 0.6 per cent. (A weighted average
of the combined results for all five countries suggests an elasticity response of
only -0.4 per cent, but when the air fare component, similar for all European
countries, is included the response can be seen to be greater.)

Though the correlations and equations for individual European countries are
generally poor, there is a long term tendency for countries where relative prices
are falling to increase their shares of US travel, and vice versa. Thus the results
for the five countries combined are reasonably similar, though coefficients of
correlation remain poor (around 0.30 for all three calculations).

WEST GERMANY

General trends

Analysis of graphically plotted data for 1963–76 suggests the following.

1. A reasonably good relationship between real discretionary incomes
    growth and tourism growth exists (expressed in terms of total international
    tourism expenditure at 1970 prices – there being historical data on
    numbers of West German travellers abroad for generally only every
    third or fourth year). Tourism growth appears to follow income growth
    with a one to two year time lag – partly reflecting, perhaps, early
    booking on package tours.

2. There is a good relationship between movements in the relative cost of
    travel abroad from West Germany and tourism growth (again expendi-
    ture at 1970 prices); tourism possibly responds to relative price move-
    ments with a one year time lag.

Table 13

Multiple Regression Equations for West German Travel Abroad over 1965–76

Time relationship	Equation	Coefficients of multiple		Use of equation – per cent reduction in mean standard variation in travel
		Determination	Correlation	
1	$y_1 = 5.04 + 0.53\ x_2 - 2.44\ x_3$	0.943	0.971	76
2	$y_1 = 4.27 + 0.68\ x_2 - 2.19\ x_3$	0.951	0.975	78
3	$y_1 = 0.75 + 1.64\ x_2 - 1.05\ x_3$	0.782	0.884	54

Explanation of equations

y_1 = Foreign tourist expenditure by West Germans at 1970 prices (GDP price index used as deflator)

x_2 = Discretionary incomes at 1970 prices (disposable personal incomes less expenditure on food, housing and related items, and adjusted to constant prices)

x_3 = Relative cost of travel abroad from West Germany (weighted index of exchange rate adjusted consumer prices in major destination countries divided by exchange rate adjusted consumer price index for West Germany)

In respect of all the above per cent increases per annum in three year moving averages.

Time relationships

1 Travel in period x affected by incomes in period x and by prices in period x

2 Travel in period x affected by incomes in period x – 1 and by prices in period x

3 Travel in period x affected by incomes in period x – 1 and by prices in period x – 1

Use of equation – per cent reduction in mean standard variation in travel

If mean standard variation in y_1 is 5 per cent and if the application of the equation to actual x_2 and x_3 data results in a mean standard variation of 2.5 per cent between predicted and actual, there would be a 50 per cent reduction.

Examining these data to arrive at multiple regression equations, using percentage changes in three year moving averages of all three data series, yields generally satisfactory results. These are shown in Table 13. Equations 1 and 2 both yield good coefficients of correlation and determination, and broadly similar values for both x_2 (reaction to discretionary income movements) and x_3 (reaction to movements in relative prices). Equation 3 is less satisfactory but still statistically significant. The results are shown graphically in Chart J.

Conclusions on elasticities

Taken together (weighting the results by the amount by which the coefficient of multiple determination exceeds 0.5) the equations give the following results.

1.   Real expenditure by West Germans on travel abroad would normally rise by around 3.7 per cent per annum in the long term if both real discretionary incomes and the relative cost of travel abroad remained unchanged.

2.   Real expenditure on travel abroad rises by 0.9 per cent for each 1 per cent increase in real discretionary incomes.

3.   Real expenditure on travel abroad falls by 2 per cent for each 1 per cent increase in the relative cost of travel abroad.

Were an adequate data series available on the number of West Germans travelling abroad, it seems likely that it would produce rather similar results. A comparison of the data on numbers of travellers for every third or fourth year (when surveys are carried out) with the price adjusted travel expenditure series reveals remarkably similar growth rates; for instance, between 1971 and 1975 the number of visits abroad grew by 31.7 per cent, while real expenditure on travel abroad expanded by 32.8 per cent.

Cross elasticities by country/area of destination

To establish the extent to which travel shifts between areas in response to changes in the relative cost of travel to each a reasonably long series of data is required showing travel by area. Although, for the last few years, a fairly complete break-down of West German travel by country is available, at least within Europe, for only five main West European destinations (all, apart from Italy, countries bordering West Germany) plus the USA and Canada are there data available stretching back to 1970. So cross elasticities have been considered only in relation to these - which exclude such important destinations as Spain and the UK.

In this context, an important characteristic of West German travel expenditure is the high proportion of the total spent in Western European bordering countries - 55 per cent in 1976 (22.6 per cent in Austria, the most important single destination for West German tourists, 9.8 per cent in Switzerland, 8.7 per cent in France, 7.3 per cent in the Netherlands, 2.5 per cent in Denmark, and 1.8 per cent in Belgium). Much of the rest was spent in countries near to West Germany, though not actually sharing a border (18 per cent of total expenditure was in Italy, 2.9 per cent in the UK, and 1.5 per cent in Yugoslavia). West Germany's central location in Europe has, of course, much to do with this, many visits to Austria, the Netherlands and Denmark in particular being no more than day trips - and as such not likely to be particularly price sensitive.

Chart J

COMPARISON OF ACTUAL GROWTH IN
WEST GERMAN TRAVEL WITH PREDICTED TRAVEL
using three different regression equations

SEE TEXT FOR DETAILS AND EXPLANATION

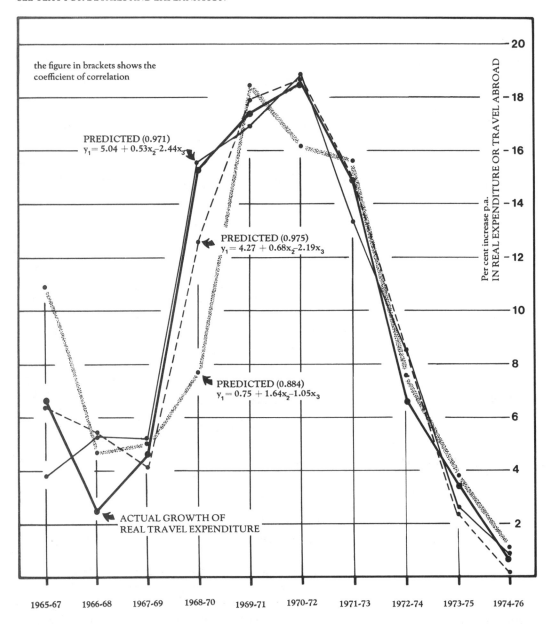

the figure in brackets shows the
coefficient of correlation

PREDICTED (0.971)
$y_1 = 5.04 + 0.53x_2 - 2.44x_3$

PREDICTED (0.975)
$y_1 = 4.27 + 0.68x_2 - 2.19x_3$

PREDICTED (0.884)
$y_1 = 0.75 + 1.64x_2 - 1.05x_3$

ACTUAL GROWTH OF
REAL TRAVEL EXPENDITURE

Per cent increase p.a.
IN REAL EXPENDITURE OR TRAVEL ABROAD

1965-67   1966-68   1967-69   1968-70   1969-71   1970-72   1971-73   1972-74   1973-75   1974-76

The predominance of travel to nearby countries and of non-package tour travel means that the exclusion, from indices of relative prices, of air fares and of discount prices obtained by tour operators is of less significance than for other origin countries.

A comparison was made of percentage shares of West German travel expenditure (constant 1963 relative prices) from 1970 to 1976 for five main West European destinations (Austria, Italy, Switzerland, France and the Netherlands), and separately for the USA plus Canada against all West European destinations, against changes in the relative prices of travel from West Germany to each of these destinations (fluctuations above or below the combined total relative price movements for each group). Among individual countries only for Switzerland (an elasticity response of -1.2) and for the USA plus Canada (-2.7) were there statistically worthwhile and consistently plausible results; a problem is that, using the technique of changes in three year moving averages in each series, only four observations were possible for each country, well below what is necessary to be able to hope to arrive at statistically worthwhile results.

However, taking the five West European countries together (shifts in the pattern of travel to these in response to changes in the relative prices of travel to each), and thus obtaining 20 observations, it seemed that there was a clear tendency for those where prices were falling relative to the five country total (Italy and France) to increase their travel shares at the expense of Switzerland, Austria and the Netherlands. No doubt other reasons than price were partly responsible, but two different equations, one based on a lagged response of travel to price shifts, showed similar results, and implied that, for each 1 per cent increase in prices in a particular country relative to the five country total,that country's share of West German travel expenditure in real terms fell by fractionally over 1 per cent. The two equations were:

$$y = -0.12 - 1.13x \quad \text{(coefficient of correlation 0.671)}$$
$$y = -0.02 - 1.21x \quad \text{(coefficient of correlation 0.653)}$$

where y is the percentage increase per annum in the share of real travel expenditure and x is the percentage increase per annum in relative prices for West German travel (compared with the five country total). The second equation presumes a lagged response of one period, and both equations were based on percentage changes per annum in three year moving averages.

A not dissimilar cross elasticity (-1.1) appeared to be implied by taking a weighted average (weighted by coefficient of correlation) of the x values for six different equations exploring the relationship of travel shifts between OECD Europe as a whole and the USA plus Canada to changes in the relative costs of travel to these areas.

FRANCE

General trends

Two data series exist indicating the growth over the past ten years or so of travel abroad from France; the number of foreign holiday trips made in the summer period and total tourism expenditure abroad at current prices – which can be adjusted to a constant price basis by using the GDP price index as a deflator. Unusually, given the impact of cheaper air fares in real terms, the expenditure series on a constant price basis rises significantly faster (4.3 per cent per annum on average over the 1965–76 period) than does the number of trips series (2.5 per cent per annum over the same period), although the French currency (and hence relative prices) has only depreciated modestly against the currencies of main destination countries. One reason is an increasing proportion of trips made outside the summer holiday peak, and perhaps an increasing proportion of business trips; comprehensive data on both these is largely lacking – though destination country figures give some clues. Another reason is that the typical trip made is becoming more expensive in real terms; the French traveller is moving up market in the type of holidays taken and is travelling further afield.

Both series are growing more slowly than for most other major origin countries. Holiday opportunities within France and the innate conservatism of most French holidaymakers are reasons. Perhaps as important, though, is the fact that the great majority of French workers have had four weeks' annual leave for many years, and that progress towards five and six week norms is slow; in many other countries typical leave periods have, until recently, been only two or three weeks. The implication is of an approaching ceiling to French travel at least in terms of number of trips.

Analysis of the responsiveness of travel abroad from France to fluctuations in personal incomes and in the relative cost of travel abroad is not facilitated by this possible change in pattern because of an approaching physical ceiling to travel. And there are other difficulties.

1. The growth in discretionary incomes at constant prices (and indeed of most other macroeconomic aggregates) has been much more regular and uninterrupted in France, even since 1973, than in other major Western economies; this makes analysis of relationships statistically more difficult, and could be expected to smooth the travel trend.

2. Nor have there been sharp fluctuations since 1973, as in many other countries, in the relative cost of travel abroad.

3. Original data on the number of summer holiday trips taken should not be regarded as statistically precise measures (as is reflected by their publication rounded to the nearest 100,000).

Graphical analysis of data series

Largely because of these factors, both graphical and statistical analyses indicate rather weak relationships between French travel abroad, whether measured in terms of the number of summer holiday trips made, or in terms of real travel expenditure, and real disposable incomes on the one hand or relative cost of travel abroad on the other. Graphical analysis does, however, suggest the following conclusions.

1. On a year to year basis there is a strong relationship between relative prices for travel abroad and the number of trips taken abroad (remember point 2 above, though), and a rather less good one, possibly with the effects lagged by one year, between relative prices and real expenditure on travel abroad.

2. Over a longer term, using three year moving averages for all series, the relationship between relative prices and travel is less clear; but, as already noted, there has been an absence of sharp price movements which alone could be expected to produce real changes in travel. There is also some evidence that the relative price/travel relationship may be rather different in the 1970s than in previous years.

3. Relationships between the steadily growing discretionary incomes series, even on a year to year basis, and travel are difficult to identify, and seem slight; this may be because the French put a high priority in their personal budgets on traditional annual holidays, and are unlikely to be deflected from these by comparatively small fluctuations in the economy. Signs of relationships are, however, evident, possibly with a one year lagged response.

Simple regression equations

In view of the general absence of strong relationships between discretionary incomes, relative prices and travel, it seemed worth testing simple regressions before undertaking multiple regression analysis. Altogether, four different equations were arrived at, seeking – through direct and through lagged relationships – to link the real discretionary incomes series to the two different travel series.[1] None produced adequate coefficients of correlation, but taking the results[1] together suggests that in the medium to long term a 1 per cent increase in real discretionary incomes produces an increase of around 1.4 per cent in travel abroad, and that this effect tends to be a lagged one, by one period (e g discretionary incomes in 1965-67 affect travel in 1966-68).

---

1 The two best for the ten periods 1965–67 to 1974–76 were:

$y = -4.74 + 1.20 \ x_1$ (coefficient of correlation 0.428)
$y = -8.94 + 1.80 \ x_2$ (coefficient of correlation 0.498)

when y = per cent increase per annum in the three year moving average of the number of summer holiday trips taken abroad

   x = per cent increase per annum in the three year moving average of discretionary incomes in constant 1970 prices

   x_1 indicates a direct time relationship between the two series x_2 is when discretionary incomes in one period (e g 1965–67) affect travel in the subsequent overlapping period (e g 1966–68).

None of the six equations tested relating changes in three year moving averages over 1965-67 to 1974-76 in the relative cost of travel abroad from France and in travel (two travel series for each of which a straight, a one period lagged response and a two period lagged response were tried) yielded worthwhile coefficients of correlation and a plausible negative response (i e an increase in relative prices producing a fall in travel). So, the possibility that this might be partly because the relationship had changed was explored. The period was split into two, 1965-67 to 1969-71 and 1970-72 to 1975-77. The results of the twelve equations were slightly more encouraging, though the strongest of the negative coefficients of correlation was still only 0.608 (an equation which suggested that in the more recent period a 1 per cent increase in relative prices produced, without any lagged effect, a 0.6 per cent fall in foreign tourist expenditure at constant prices). Taken together, they suggest that in the 1965-67 period a 1 per cent increase in relative prices produced a lagged 0.3 per cent fall in travel abroad, while in the 1970-72 period it resulted, without any time lag, in a 0.6 per cent fall.

For the more recent period, from 1970 to 1976, regressions were also tested between changes in relative prices and changes in travel on a year to year (rather than three year moving average) basis. When travel was measured on the number of summer holiday trips basis, a strong response and a good unlagged relationship appeared; the equation was $y_1 = 3.96 - 1.89x$ and the coefficient of correlation was 0.942, when y_1 is the per cent increase per annum in the number of summer holiday trips taken, and x is the per cent increase per annum in the relative cost of travel abroad from France. (But remember that this travel series may be an unreliable one, and that the relationship is based on six observations only.) The relationship with percentage increases per annum in real travel expenditure (as y_2) was weaker, and relative prices appear to affect travel one year later; the equation was $y_2 = 8.47 - 0.47x$, and the coefficient 0.664.

Multiple regression analysis

Five different regression equations were derived for the 1965-67 to 1974-76 period in percentage changes per annum in three year moving averages between:

x_2 = discretionary incomes at constant 1970 prices

x_3 = relative cost of travel abroad from France

$y_1 a$ = summer holiday trips abroad made by French residents.

The equations reflected five different time relationships[1] between the data series. A similar series of five regression equations was derived for the same period and for the same x values but with $y_1 b$ = expenditure on travel abroad by France at constant 1970 prices. The time relationships[1] were the same as for the first series.

---

1 These were (taking 1974-76 travel as an illustration):

A 1974-76 travel affected by 1974-76 discretionary incomes and by 1974-76 relative prices. B 1974-76 travel affected by 1974-76 discretionary incomes and by 1973-75 relative prices. C 1974-76 travel affected by 1974-76 discretionary incomes and by 1972-74 relative prices. D 1974-76 travel affected by 1973-75 discretionary incomes and by 1974-76 relative prices. E 1974-76 travel affected by 1973-75 discretionary incomes and by 1972-74 relative prices.

Only three of the ten equations yielded both positive x_2 values and negative x_3 values, as one would expect (ie an increase in incomes brings an increase in travel, while an increase in relative prices brings a fall in travel). None of these had reasonable coefficients of correlation, indeed only one exceeded 0.5. In the remaining seven equations three yielded positive x_2 values, while only one had the expected negative x_3 value, and all of these had coefficients of correlation of under 0.5.

It is obvious that only slight value can consequently be placed on the results. It is nonetheless worth noting that the two most satisfactory equations were:

$y_1a = -11.36 + 2.25 \ x_2 \ - 0.59 \ x_3$ (coefficient of correlation 0.544)

$y_1a = -5.85 + 1.41 \ x_2 \ - 0.32 \ x_3$ 'coefficient of correlation 0.445)

The second is an unlagged relationship (A in the footnote), while the first involves lagging both price and income effects (E).

It is also worth noting that of the six positive x_2 values, five had coefficients of correlation in excess of 0.4 (though only one in excess of 0.5). These five x_2 values were 2.25, 1.93, 1.41, 1.20, and 0.43, suggesting that a 1 per cent increase in real discretionary incomes produces an increase of around 1.5 per cent in travel.

The x_3 values, both positive and negative, are generally small; two of the four negative values were under 0.1, and the others only 0.3 and 0.6. Relative prices appear therefore to have had little effect on French travel in the longer term.

General conclusions on elasticities

No reasonably firm conclusions can be drawn on the responsiveness of French travel abroad to movements in discretionary incomes or in relative prices. However, the evidence does suggest the following conclusions.

1. Over the period 1965–76 each 1 per cent increase in real discretionary incomes yielded an extra 1.4 to 1.5 per cent increase in travel abroad (however measured).

2. Year to year increases in relative prices produce a similar scale response (a fall of around 1.5 per cent) in travel abroad; this response is possibly lagged by one year.

3. The effects of changes in relative prices are predominantly short term; in the medium to long term effects appear slight. However, they have become somewhat more noticeable in the 1970s than was the case in the 1960s; a 1 per cent increase in relative prices now yields a 0.5 per cent fall in travel, roughly double the previous response.

4. But for the steady increase in real discretionary incomes, travel measured in terms of summer holiday trips would actually have fallen by around 6 per cent a year over this period; travel would also have fallen, though only by around 3 per cent per annum, if measured in terms of real travel expenditure. Relative price movements have not made much difference, mainly because these have been far smaller (a net 4 per cent increase over the whole eleven year period, as against a net increase in real discretionary incomes of 88 per cent), and partly because the elasticity response appears to be smaller.

Some evidence on cross elasticities

Apart from destination country data, unreliable as a guide to long term travel
trends particularly on a comparative basis, there are no data on numbers of
French travellers going to different destinations,covering a reasonable run of
years. And only for French travel to the USA and Canada is expenditure data
available over a long period. The character of such travel is so different from
the bulk of French travel that it is not surprising that no usable results can be
obtained by comparing for the 1964-76 period trends in the relative cost of travel
to the USA from France (compared to costs in other destinations) with changes in
the share of total travel expenditure made in North America. It is evident too
that the boom in French travel to the USA from 1966 to 1970, succeeded by a
decline in 1973 and then by a modest recovery, have only to a minor extent been
caused by changes in relative prices.

However, it is useful to compare the relative price of travel from France to three
major destinations for which travel expenditure data exist for the years concerned
(West Germany, the UK and North America) with their shares of the three country
total of French travel expenditure in the years immediately before the world
economic upheaval from end 1973 and in the most recent years available (1975-76).
The number of observations is, of course, far too small to make valid comparisons,
but the series corresponds almost precisely to a straight line; the equation fitting
this implies that for each 1 per cent by which the cost of travel from France to
any one of these destinations rises faster than does the average cost of travel
from France, travel to that destination falls by 2.5 per cent. Though the coefficient of correlation is high, little reliance should be placed on so limited a
number of observations, and it must be admitted the cross elasticity response
does seem rather high.

JAPAN

General trends

For more than ten years up to 1973 the number of Japanese abroad had risen
steadily at an annual average rate of 37 per cent, culminating in a 64 per cent
increase in that year. The increase in international tourist expenditure at constant
prices has been only slightly less dramatic – around 26 per cent a year on average.
This rapid growth in travel coincided with a steady increase in real discretionary
incomes, averaging 11.5 per cent a year, and with a comparatively slow but nonetheless steady decline in the relative cost of travel abroad from Japan.

From 1974 onwards the growth rate of Japanese travel abroad has slowed to only
about 7.5 per cent a year on average in terms of numbers of travellers, while in
real expenditure terms travel actually fell in 1974 and 1975, since recovering
to only a little above its former levels. Simultaneously the growth in real
discretionary incomes has slowed to around 3 per cent a year, though the real
cost of travel abroad has continued to decline at around its former pace.

Although one would therefore expect to be able to arrive at fairly good statistical relationships between the growth of discretionary incomes, movements in relative prices, and travel abroad by Japanese, it would be misleading to attribute the trends in travel described above solely to extreme responses to fluctuations in discretionary incomes and in the cost of travel abroad. The elasticity responses arrived at later in this subsection are indeed implausibly high. At least as important was the low absolute level of Japanese travel abroad in 1963 (under 100,000 Japanese out of a population of 96 mn), a low base from which rapid growth was always likely once the fashion for travel abroad - a product perhaps of more outward looking attitudes - spread among Japanese. The progressive elimination of currency and other restrictions on travel abroad also played a major role.

Elasticity responses -

Graphical analysis of movements in real discretionary incomes and in the relative cost of travel abroad from Japan against the number of Japanese travelling abroad and against real expenditure on travel abroad suggests a reasonably good fit between discretionary incomes and both travel series; conceivably, though, the elasticity response of the number of Japanese travelling abroad to incomes changes is lagged by one year, while that of the real expenditure series anticipates income changes by one year (plausible reasons can be advanced for either hypothesis, but hardly for the combination). A fair fit can also be obtained between both travel series and changes in relative prices of travel abroad, though it must be admitted that it seems inherently unlikely that a change from a rate of decline in relative prices of around 2.5 per cent a year in the 1960s to around 5 per cent a year in the early 1970s would have had a really dramatic effect on travel growth rates; the relative price series (which, as in most other countries, excludes changes in the air fare element - a rather more serious deficiency in the case of Japan, in view of its location, than in Western Europe) is probably too stable to base sound analysis on. There appears no graphical evidence of any lagged, or anticipatory, response of travel to changes in relative prices.

Table 14 shows the results of four multiple regression equations exploring the statistical relationships between discretionary incomes, relative prices and travel. Two of the equations relate the independent variables to the number of Japanese travelling abroad, and two to real expenditure on travel abroad; in the first a lagged income response is investigated (e g incomes in 1972-74 affect number of travellers in 1973-75), in the second an anticipatory income response.

All the equations are statistically significant, though the second is barely so. But none has a particularly high coefficient of correlation. They show remarkably similar results.

1.   A normal tendency (without any income or price induced changes) for travel to decline quite rapidly - by between 12 and 17 per cent a year.

2.   A high responsiveness of travel to changes in the growth rate of real discretionary incomes - an elasticity of between 2.8 and 3.6.

3.   Three of the equations suggest that a fall in relative prices of 1 per cent sparks off an increase in travel of around 2 per cent; the fourth suggests a higher elasticity, of -4.2.

Table 14

Multiple Regression Equations for Japanese Travel Abroad over 1965-76

Time relationship	Equation	Coefficients of multiple		Use of equation – per cent reduction in mean standard variation in travel
		Determination	Correlation	
1	$y_1A = -11.72 + 3.60\ x_2 - 1.99\ x_3$	0.709	0.842	46
2	$y_1A = -13.31 + 3.50\ x_2 - 2.17\ x_3$	0.308	0.555	17
1	$y_1B = -14.14 + 3.07\ x_2 - 1.81\ x_3$	0.502	0.708	29
3	$y_1B = 17.34 + 2.84\ x_2 - 4.23\ x_3$	0.613	0.783	38

Explanation of equation

y_1A = Number of Japanese residents travelling abroad

y_1B = Foreign tourist expenditure by Japan at 1970 prices (GDP price index used as deflator)

x_2 = Discretionary incomes at 1970 prices (disposable personal incomes less expenditure on food, housing and related items, and adjusted to constant prices)

x_3 = Relative cost of travel abroad from Japan (weighted index of exchange rate adjusted consumer prices in major destination countries divided by exchange rate adjusted consumer price index for Japan)

In respect of all the above, per cent increases per annum in three year moving averages.

Time relationships

1 Travel in period x affected by incomes in period x and by prices in period x

2 Travel in period x affected by incomes in period x – 1 and by prices in period x

3 Travel in period x affected by incomes in period x + 1 and by prices in period x

Use of equation – per cent reduction in mean standard variation in travel

If mean standard variation in y_1 is 5 per cent and if the application of the equation to actual x_2 and x_3 data results in a mean standard variation of 2.5 per cent between predicted and actual, there would be a 50 per cent reduction.

In spite of these statistical findings, it seems distinctly improbable that Japanese travel abroad would have actually fallen over the 1965–76 period had real discretionary incomes and relative prices remained constant. Nor does it seem likely that long term elasticities could really be around 3 or more, or that the price elasticity could be around –4. A more plausible scenario is for a normal tendency for travel (in terms of numbers of travellers) to rise by 8 per cent a year, for an income elasticity of 1.8 and a price elasticity of –1.5; this can be fitted to the travel trend, though with a lower coefficient of correlation than the first equation in the table. Applying the same elasticities to the series on real travel expenditure (the third equation on the table) implies a normal growth rate of travel of 0.4 per cent a year.

GENERAL CONCLUSIONS

Elasticities for total travel

The relatively sharp fluctuations in incomes, consumer prices and exchange rates, and in travel since 1973 enable rather firmer conclusions on elasticities to be drawn than was possible at the time that Special No. 33 was being compiled. The results imply a fractionally lower typical income elasticity than then seemed indicated (+ 1.0 to + 1.8), and a rather lower typical price elasticity than was then suggested (– 1.0 to – 1.6). It is perhaps not surprising, though, that the travel response to the relatively small price movements which had been typical up to 1974 should appear to be proportionately larger than for big price movements; in both periods quite a number of travellers, particularly those on business or visiting friends and relatives, are unlikely to alter their plans because of changes in the cost of travel abroad.

The results of the more recent calculations are summarised in Table 15. For explanations and qualifications see the general introductory part of this section and the pages dealing with the individual countries. The results on the UK, the USA and especially West Germany are, it should be noted, considerably more solidly based statistically than those on France and Japan.

1. Typically a 1 per cent increase in real discretionary incomes appears to result in an increase of between 1.0 and 1.5 per cent in travel abroad (whether measured in terms of numbers of travellers or real expenditure); the best statistical fits for Japan suggest a substantially greater response than this, but such results seem inherently somewhat implausible. Conceivably, income elasticity declines as income per head rises (among highly advanced countries at least, a levelling off as a ceiling to foreign travel approaches; the reverse would probably apply to countries at an early stage in the industrialisation process).

2. Price elasticity seems, except in West Germany, to be generally lower than income elasticity. Typically a 1 per cent increase in the relative cost of travel abroad from a particular origin country results in a fall of under 1 per cent in travel abroad. But price elasticity seems to vary more between countries than does income elasticity, from –0.3 in the USA to a statistically indicated – 2.7 in Japan. Even where the elasticity response appears high, movements in relative

Table 15

Summary of Findings on Long Term Elasticities of Tourism Demand from Main Origin Countries

| | Constant | | Income elasticity | Price elasticity | How adequate a statistical relationship |
	No. of travellers basis	Real expenditure basis			
UK	+4.7	-2.3	+1.2	-0.5	reasonable
USA: all travel	...	+2.1	+0.9	-0.3	reasonable
overseas & cruise travel only	+8.8	+7.8	+0.7	-1.1	good
West Germany	...	+3.7	+0.9	-2.0	good
France	-6.0[b]	-3.0[b]	+1.5[b]	-0.5[a]	poor[b]
Japan	+8.0[b]	+0.4[b]	+1.8	-1.5[b]	poor[b]

a In the 1960s price elasticity appears to have been smaller; and, on a year to year basis, there seems to be a price elasticity of around − 1.5. b Best fit equations consistently produce large negative constant growth rates (around − 14 per cent per annum) and high elasticity responses (around +3.2 for income elasticity and around − 2.7 for price elasticity); statistical relationships for these equations are only fair, and it seems likely that the big income elasticity response, particularly, reflects to a large degree a coincidental rather than a causal relationship.

prices have affected travel considerably less than have income changes; this is because on a long term basis annual average growth rates in discretionary incomes have generally been higher than have been rates of increase or decline in relative prices.

2. It does seem that there is a tendency for price effects to be lagged by one period - that is, for the average change in real cost of travel in, say, 1974-76 to affect the average rate of growth in travel in 1975-77. Indeed, in the USA there were slightly better fits for price effects lagged by two periods than by one. On the other hand, there was no real evidence of lagged effects for either West Germany or Japan. There is slight evidence of lagged income effects for West Germany and France, but in the UK and possibly also Japan the evidence pointed to an anticipatory effect (e g the average growth of real discretionary incomes in 1974-76 affecting the average rate of growth in travel in 1973-75).

4. The constant (reflecting what the growth of travel would be in the absence of any discretionary income or relative price movements -in other words the combined effect of all other influences on travel) varies considerably from country to country. It is normally (France being the exception) higher when travel is measured in terms of numbers of travellers than when real expenditure on travel abroad is the basis. This is probably because the method of deflating expenditure at current prices to a constant price basis is unable to take into account in any specific manner the impact on travel of the package tour industry and of cheaper air fares (in relative terms). It is not suggested that it implies a trend to cheaper types of holiday in real terms or a reduction in the average length of stay. The negative constants indicated for France and (in the original best fit statistical calculations) for Japan seem inherently improbable, but note that the statistical reliability of the findings on these two countries is well below those for West Germany, the USA and the UK.

Cross price elasticities

In addition to the reaction of total foreign travel from a country to changes in the cost of travel abroad[1], there is generally fair evidence that travellers switch their pattern of travel between destinations in response to changes in the cost of travel to one destination as against another. It is not, of course, suggested that this is the sole, or even the main, reason for such switching. Fashion and promotional efforts are at least as important (in statistical terms the constant affecting the share of total travel from a particular origin country going to a particular destination country is usually considerably larger than are the effects of a price response).

---

1. Note also that there is evidence for the UK that the share of foreign travel in total travel (foreign and domestic) is quite responsive to shifts in the relative cost of each. The tendency is for the proportion of foreign travel to rise steadily (by 5.7 per cent annually of its share), and for each 1 per cent rise in the cost of foreign travel compared with domestic to reduce this share by 1.8 per cent a year.

The findings on cross price elasticities as between foreign destinations can be summarised as follows.

UK. There is some, though not very strong, evidence that the proportion of long haul travel in total travel rises by 1 per cent for each 1 per cent fall in the cost of long haul travel (including fares) relative to short haul. There is rather better evidence of a switching between European destinations in response to changes in relative prices in each. Indicated elasticities range from –1.4 up to –7.0, or around –2.8 on average. This implies that a 10 per cent reduction in prices in one destination relative to others could be expected in the long term to result in 28 per cent more British travellers and 15 per cent more tourist revenue.

USA. A not dissimilar (–2.0) average total cross price elasticity for travel by main area (Canada, Mexico, West Indies and Central America, Europe and Mediterranean, and other destinations) can be derived for US travel. The price response appears particularly high for travel to the European and Mediterranean area (–4.3). But there is little evidence of switching between European destinations in response to changes in relative prices in each; the indicated typical elasticity response, based on rather poor statistical relationships, is –0.6. This seems plausible as many trips to Europe by Americans are multi-country, and there is only limited scope for switching periods spent in each; it is also arguable whether Americans are very aware of changing relative prices within Europe.

West Germany. Statistical evidence is not strong, but does suggest that, while there is quite a marked switching of travel to North America vis-à-vis Western Europe in response to changes in relative prices (a cross price elasticity of –2.7), between major West European destinations the response is less marked (–1.2); this could well be because most countries seem quite cheap to the affluent West Germans.

France. Tentative conclusions based on only a handful of observations (nevertheless producing an excellent statistical relationship) suggest that for travel to West Germany, the UK, and North America a 1 per cent increase in the cost of travel to a particular destination is reflected in a 2.5 per cent reduction in the relative amount of travel to that destination.

Japan. No data on which to base estimates.

Forecasts
by Country of Origin

In this section forecasts of total travel are compounded by country of origin. The final forecasts themselves are presented in tabular form in Section I – to avoid repetition. Section VII then splits the forecasts for main origin countries into bordering country travel, other short haul travel and long haul travel. The data base for the forecasts was derived and explained in Section III, the measurement of price and income elasticities was discussed in Section V, and the possible sloping ceilings to travel (related essentially to annual leave periods) were outlined in Section IV. Forecasts are first made without ceiling effects, and these, inevitably arbitrary, are than introduced. The forecasts concentrate on the ten main origin countries (72.3 per cent of 1976 world tourism expenditure), and then rather cruder calculations for minor origin countries and areas are made.

Reliability of forecasting

Long term forecasting of any kind can be expected to produce only approximations to the future situation. Perhaps because tourism growth reflects a human behavioural response to, for instance, higher incomes, changed prices, etc, tourist forecasts are subject to particularly wide potential margins of error. Could sound statistical confidence limits be attached to upper and lower ends of a forecast range (e g 90 per cent confidence that travel will fall between, say, 125 and 150), the limits would be likely to be so wide that the forecast was of little practical use, except by in effect ignoring the limits and employing the mid point of the range as a management tool. And, in fact, it is not possible to attach formal statistical limits to tourism forecasts; the past statistical data are inadequate to permit the necessary calculations. A common alternative in long term forecasting is to present forecasts in the form of high, central and low, or simply as a range (high and low only). This could imply an equally large high/low differential. (If, for instance, one took it that the constant for a particular country is most unlikely to be below 3 per cent per annum or above 5 per cent per annum, the income elasticity most unlikely to be below 1 or above 1.5, the price elasticity below –1 or above –1.5, the forecast income growth below 3 per cent per annum or above 4 per cent per annum, and relative prices for travel abroad are likely to fall by at least 1 per cent per annum and at most 2 per cent per annum, then growth rates could be anything between 7 per cent and 14 per cent per annum – not really very helpful.) In practice, it is reasonable to presume that neither will all forces making for low growth coincide, nor will all forces making for high growth. Indeed, if the number of variables were large, it would be possible to allow for this statistically; with only five, as here, it is not. The forecaster usually first frames a central forecast and then indicates the degree of uncertainty by putting in a + or – 5 per cent spread, if he is fairly confident, 10 per cent if less so, and so on. This is the procedure adopted in this report. It is, obviously, arbitrary.

MACROECONOMIC FRAMEWORK

Assumptions on incomes growth and relative price movements –

The analysis of price and income elasticities in Section V confirms the widespread view that the growth of consumer incomes and changes in the cost of travel abroad are the major quantifiable determinants of expenditure on travel abroad at constant prices, though in general the constant (reflecting all other types of influence combined) is as, or more, important. It is therefore necessary prior to making the actual travel forecasts to assume some reasonably likely rates of income growth and to assume the trend of exchange rate adjusted prices (ie whether movements in exchange rates between individual tourist origin and corresponding destination countries overcompensate, compensate precisely, or undercompensate for changes in relative prices). Neither of these can, of course, be forecast precisely. Nor does this report claim to be based on any original work in these areas. The projected growth rates and trend of exchange rate adjusted prices employed are essentially assumptions, though it is hoped realistic assumptions. They are based on a whole range of medium to long term forecasting exercises undertaken by other organisations, both official and private. The assumptions derived from this work are the author's own.

– and some general assumptions

Underlying all these, are some still broader assumptions on the general world economic environment.

1. There will be no direct military confrontation between major powers, and hostilities between lesser powers will have limited economic impact in a global context; they will not require major increases in military spending.

2. There will be no major breakdown in the world economic system, leading, for instance, to generalised global depression or to a more rigid division into economic blocs; on the contrary, international economic cooperation will tend to increase in scope.

3. There will be no dramatic long term shifts in the pricing of resources (as occurred with oil in the mid 1970s) and hence in the shares of world income accruing to different country groups.

Forecasts of discretionary incomes growth

Table 16 shows the actual growth of GDP and discretionary incomes over 1966–76, and the projected growth in these over the period to 1990. For the 1976–80 period GDP projections are based on actual developments in 1977 and 1978 and on national short to medium term projections for 1979 and 1980 – more often provided by private than by public organisations. Thereafter the projections are derived entirely from the work in this field of other organisations, many of them of a confidential nature. The work done by the World Bank underlying its assessment of the framework for developing country growth might be mentioned in particular (see, for instance, its World Development Report, 1978).

Table 16

GDP and Discretionary Income Growth for Main Tourist Origin Countries. Past and Projected Growth Rates
(per cent per annum)

| | Actual 1966–76 | | Projected | | | | | |
| | GDP at constant prices[a] | Discretionary incomes at constant prices[b] | GDP at constant prices | | | Discretionary incomes at constant prices[b] | | |
			1976–80	1980–85	1985–90	1976–80	1980–85	1985–90
West Germany	3.5	3.9	3.25	4.25	4.25	4.00	5.25	5.25
USA	3.2	2.6	3.50	3.75	3.75	4.25	4.75	4.75
France	4.8	5.9	3.75	4.00	4.00	4.75	5.00	5.00
Canada	4.3	6.8	3.50	4.00	4.00	4.25	5.00	5.00
Netherlands	4.7	4.7	2.75	4.25	4.25	3.50	5.25	5.25
Japan	8.1	9.7	5.25	5.50	5.50	6.50	6.75	6.75
UK	2.0	3.3	2.25	2.75	2.75	2.75	2.75	2.75
Belgium/Luxemburg	3.9	6.4[c]	2.50	4.00	4.00	3.25	5.00	5.00
Mexico	6.1	5.3[c]	4.75	5.50	5.50	6.00	6.75	6.75
Austria	4.3	6.0	2.75	4.00	4.00	3.50	5.00	5.00

a Source: OECD, except Mexico (UN). b Defined as personal disposable incomes, less expenditure on food, housing, fuel and light at constant prices; some slight variations in definition between countries. Original data from OECD, except Mexico (UN). c Private consumption.

79

It will be noted that in the 1966-76 period for most countries the growth of discretionary incomes outstripped that in GDP by, typically, a ratio of 1.20-1.40 to 1. In the USA, however, for reasons which are not very clear, the reverse occurred, and in the Netherlands there was no differential (there is no figure for Mexico). Normally one would expect household disposable incomes to rise at much the same pace in the long term as GDP (perhaps a little slower, because of an increased government share of national disposable incomes), but that discretionary incomes as defined for the purpose of this exercise would rise appreciably faster, as people spend a smaller proportion of their incomes on the basics of food and housing. It will be noted that the assumed discretionary growth rates (rounded to the nearest 0.25 per cent) are throughout for all countries except the UK 1.25 times the projected GDP growth rates. For the UK, it is assumed there would be no differential post 1980 with an increased, and urgently needed, shift to a higher proportion of GDP going on investment spending.

Probably the best basis for GDP growth forecasts for secondary tourist origin countries are the World Bank projections to 1985, as shown in Table 17. Figures in brackets in the last column are the implied discretionary income growth rates, on a 1.15:1 ratio to GDP growth (1.25:1 for Western industrial countries), rounded to 0.25 per cent.

Table 17

Percentage Growth Per Annum in GDP

	1960-70	1970-75	1975-85
Low income Asian countries	2.4	3.9	5.1 (5.75)
Low income African countries	4.3	2.8	4.1 (4.75)
Middle income countries	6.3	6.4	5.9 (6.75)
All developing countries	5.5	5.9	5.7 (6.50)
Western industrial countries	4.9	2.8	4.2 (5.25)
Centrally planned economies	6.8	6.4	5.1 (5.75)

Source: World Bank, World Development Report 1978 (except last column).

Trends in relative price movements

The events of the 1970s have demonstrated all too clearly that any attempt at forecasting inflation rates and still more exchange rate movements for any period in excess of a year or so is likely to be almost immediately overtaken by some unforeseen event. Fortunately, in the context of this exercise, the two do tend to cancel each other out: an above average rate of inflation is usually reflected in exchange rate depreciation, bringing the rate of increase in exchange rate adjusted consumer prices nearer the all country average. (Of course the interaction is not directly with consumer prices but, predominantly, with the prices of goods entering into international trade; however, the trend of the two is likely to be similar.)

Nonetheless, there have, of course, been some fairly substantial adjustments in relative exchange rate adjusted prices in recent years. Rates of change per annum appear in the last three columns of Table 18. They show the following trends.

1. Since 1966, West Germany, the Netherlands, Belgium, Austria, and most markedly of all Japan have become relatively cheaper countries to travel from and relatively more expensive to travel to.

2. The USA, Canada, and the UK have become relatively more expensive to travel from and relatively cheaper to travel to (though the reverse has applied to the UK since 1976).

3. France has roughly held its ground, while Mexico, after becoming relatively cheaper to travel from up to 1976, has become markedly more expensive since then.

The distinction between the last (twelfth) column and the tenth is that the tenth compares exchange rate adjusted prices with an OECD average, while the last column is weighted to take into account the destinations visited by a particular origin country. This is more accurate but is difficult to project from. The two series show similar results, apart from Canada and Mexico, because most of their travel is to one country – the USA.

It will be noted that exchange rate adjusted relative price movements have been much sharper in terms of annual rates of change since 1976 than in the preceding ten years. This is, of course, partly because up to 1970 inflation was fairly modest in most important countries and exchange rate adjustments were few and small; indeed the really rapid process of adjustment has been since 1973. It is also partly because it is only in a longer term context that the smoothing effect of sharp exchange rate movements compensating for differential rates of inflation becomes operative.

Medium term prospects for exchange rate adjusted prices

Undeniably the world exchange rates structure in 1971 did not reflect the real values of the currencies concerned. The question is whether the shakeout since then, notably during the years of generally floating exchange rates, has brought the world closer to true equilibrium, that is, to a position where, if rates of domestic inflation were to be similar, exchange rates would bear broadly the same relationship to one another as at present (ie differential inflation rates would be roughly matched by exchange rate changes, so relative exchange rate adjusted prices would remain unchanged). As far as West European currencies are concerned there are signs that this is the case, and the planned creation of the Ecu should enable EEC currencies other than the £ to keep generally in line. (Although outside the Ecu system, the Austrian schilling is so bound up with the DM that much the same applies). It is hoped that the £ will be kept in touch with the Ecu, and there are reasonable prospects that for the next year or so divergences will be little more than accounted for by a higher than average rate of inflation. In the latter part of 1978, the weakness of the US dollar, and linked to it the Canadian dollar, and the continued strength of the yen suggest that these currencies have still to reach an equilibrium level. Yet, following the reaction to Opec oil price increases announced in December 1978, it is difficult to envisage the US dollar sinking much further over the next two years except insofar as is made necessary by comparatively rapid inflation.

Table 18

Exchange Rate Adjusted Price Trends in Main Tourist Origin Countries

	1966	1976				1978				Percentage change pa in exchange rate adjusted consumer price index above or below all OECD		Percentage change pa in relative cost of travel from abroad[c]
	Units of currency per $	Units of currency per SDR	Exchange rate index (1966=100)	Consumer price index (1966=100)	Exchange rate adjusted consumer price index (1966=100)	Units of currency per SDR	Exchange rate index (1966=100)	Consumer price index (1966=100)	Exchange rate adjusted consumer price index (1966=100)	1966-76	1976-78[b]	1966-76
West Germany	4.00	2.91	72.8	155.1	213.0	2.42	60.5	165.3	273.2	0.9	3.1	0.7
USA	1.000	1.155	115.5	175.2	151.7	1.301	130.1	204.7	157.3	-2.0	-6.0	-1.5
France	4.94	5.52	111.7	200.6	179.6	5.54	112.1	245.1	218.6	-0.8	0.6	-0.2
Canada	1.084	1.140	105.2	177.4	168.6	1.542	142.3	211.6	148.7	-1.3	-11.4	0.7
Netherlands	3.62	3.05	84.3	196.6	233.2	2.71	74.9	221.0	295.1	1.8	2.4	1.7
Japan	360	343	95.3	233.6	245.1	251.2	69.8	266.3	381.5	2.3	12.6	2.5
UK	0.357	0.640	179.3	258.5	144.2	0.649	181.8	329.5	181.2	-2.3	2.1	-2.5
Belgium/Luxemburg	50.0	44.6	89.2	186.0	208.5	38.2	76.4	209.7	274.5	0.7	4.3	0.6
Mexico	12.50	17.82	142.6	232.9	232.9	29.60	236.8	350.5	148.0	1.8	-19.3	0.5
Austria	26.00	20.72	79.7[a]	175.6	220.3	17.71	68.1[a]	192.9	283.3	1.2	3.2	1.5
All OECD	x	x	100.0	195.2	195.2	x	100.0[a]	234.3	234.3	-	-	-

Notes: Rates are period average, except in 1978 for which latest available data are used (December 18 exchange rates, after announcement of oil price increases September consumer prices except Mexico, August).

A low exchange rate index implies currency appreciation and a lower than average exchange rate adjusted consumer price index implies that exchange rate depreciation has more than compensated for a higher than average rate of domestic inflation (eg UK 1966-76) or has added to a lower than average rate of domestic inflation (eg USA 1966-76). A higher than average exchange rate adjusted consumer price index implies that exchange rate appreciation has more than offset a low rate of domestic inflation (eg West Germany 1966-76), or is insufficient to offset a high rate of domestic inflation (eg Japan 1966-76). Above average exchange rate adjusted consumer price indices indicate countries which are becoming relatively cheaper to travel from or relatively more expensive to travel to (reflected in positive figures in the last two columns). In contrast, countries with below average exchange rate adjusted consumer price indices (negative figures in the last two columns) are becoming relatively more expensive to travel from, and relatively cheaper to travel to.

a Taken as identical to a SDR. b 2.25 years (1978 is September, not period average data). c Relative exchange rate adjusted consumer price indices between origin country concerned and main destination countries (weighted by importance). See Section V for methodology.

Assumptions on relative prices

Looking beyond 1980 it is presumed that an equilibrium level is being approached and that, therefore, the relative cost of travel from main tourist origin countries will change at only half the average annual rates for 1966-76 and 1976-78 (ie the latter period is therefore weighted more heavily than the former. The assumptions on relative prices are therefore as in Table 19. The picture is of generally small adjustments except for Japan (a continued significant decrease in the real cost of travel abroad) and Mexico (an increase).

Table 19

Assumed Relative Prices for Travel Abroad From Main Origin Countries
(per cent changes per annum)

	Relative to all OECD countries			Adjusted for destination pattern of travel[c]	
	1976-78[a] actual	1978-80[b] assumed	1976-80 total	1976-80	After 1980
West Germany[d]	-3.1	-0.5	-2.0	-1.7	-0.6
USA	6.0	1.0	3.8	0.9	0.6
France[d]	-0.6	-	-0.3	1.0	0.3
Canada	11.4	-	6.4	3.3	0.6
Netherlands[d]	-2.4	-	-1.4	-0.6	-0.6
Japan	-12.6	-2.0	-8.0	-9.0	-2.9
UK[e]	-2.1	1.5	-1.8	-1.6	0.2
Belgium/ Luxemburg	-4.3	-	-2.4	-1.7	0.6
Mexico	19.3	-	10.9	7.4	1.7
Austria[e]	-3.2	-	-1.8	-1.5	-0.8

Note: The change of signs (from + to -) from previous table is because this table shows relative cost of travel abroad, not relative internal prices.

a 2.25 years. b 1.75 years. c Pattern of travel weighted as in Section V; relative prices vis-à-vis countries not listed above, as for OECD average. d Ecu member. e Exchange rate movements likely to be reasonably close to Ecu.

For minor origin countries it is assumed that relative prices for travel abroad will remain unchanged throughout the forecast period. In aggregate, this assumption is probably fair enough, although it is obvious that some groups of countries (oil rich Middle Eastern ones, perhaps) are likely to benefit from a falling relative cost of travel, while others (in Africa perhaps) will find the cost rising. Generally, and not surprisingly, countries where real GDP has been rising at an above average rate have tended in the past to benefit from a falling relative cost of travel; and vice versa. This tendency - which perhaps is less marked than one might expect - is likely to continue.

PRESUMED ELASTICITIES

Table 20 shows for the ten main origin countries:

1. Actual rates of travel growth (real expenditure basis) between 1966 and 1976, with adjustment to constant prices by two different methods:

    A.   deflated by US GDP price index and by decline of dollar against other currencies (as in the main data base table in Section 3);

    B.   adjusted by national GDP price indices at constant exchange rates – showing the proportion of origin country resources devoted to tourism (as used for calculation of price and income elasticities of tourist demand in Section V).

Not surprisingly, in view of the rather slow rate of US domestic inflation and the fairly modest depreciation of the US dollar up to 1976, the second method in all cases shows a slower rate of growth than the first method. Differentials range from around 2 per cent per annum (the USA itself, the UK and France) up to around 6 per cent per annum (West Germany, Japan and Mexico). The average differential (weighted by GDP) is 3.2 per cent per annum.

2. Discretionary incomes growth and changes in the relative cost of travel abroad over 1966-76. These have been calculated as explained in Section V.

3. The equations (constant, income elasticity and price elasticity) used in conjunction with the forecast income growth and price changes presented earlier in this section to produce travel forecasts without any ceiling constraints. These equations and past changes in incomes and relative costs (as in 2 above) roughly fit real travel growth over 1966-76 (adjustment to constant prices as in method B). The fit against growth between 1966 and 1976 alone would be unlikely to be a precise one, as it is improbable that all the data sets for these two years would both fall on to fitted trend lines.

Framing the constants and elasticity responses

The constants and elasticities in Table 20 for West Germany, the USA, France, Japan and the UK have, of course, been derived essentially from Section V, but with some adjustments to bring them more in line with one another, particularly for those countries for which the statistical relationships established were poor. The constants and elasticities for the remaining countries are drawn by analogy with these five countries, taking into account, of course, actual travel growth and actual discretionary incomes and relative price movements over 1966-76.

Table 20

Travel, Discretionary Income and Relative Cost Changes over 1966-76 and Constant, Income and Price Elasticities used for Forecasting (Ter. Main Origin Countries)

	International tourism expenditures ($ mn)				% growth p a (1966-76)		Discretionary incomes % growth p a at constant prices (1966-76)	Relative cost of travel abroad % change p a (1966-76)	Equations used for central forecasts		
	1966	1976 Current prices	Constant 1966 prices A	B	A	B			Constant (% pa)	Income elasticity	Price elasticity
West Germany	1,573	8,954	6,240	3,466	14.75	8.25	3.9	-0.7	3.7	0.9	-1.50
USA	2,657	6,856	4,778	3,978	6.00	4.00	2.6	1.5	2.5	0.9	-0.75
France	1,304	3,434	2,393	2,019	6.25	4.50	5.9	0.2	-	0.9	-0.75
Canada	836	2,589	1,804	1,322	8.00	4.75	6.8	-0.7	-	0.7	-0.75
Netherlands	374	1,886	1,314	934	13.50	9.50	4.7	-1.7	2.5	1.0	-1.25
Japan	118	1,663	1,159	770	25.75	20.50	9.7	-2.5	2.0	1.5	-1.50
UK	832	1,799	1,254	1,037	4.25	2.25	3.3	2.5	-	1.2	-0.75
Belgium/ Luxemburg	320	1,609	1,121	880	13.25	10.75	6.4[a]	-0.6	2.5	1.1	-1.25
Mexico	479	1,575	1,098	604	8.75	2.25	5.3[a]	-0.5	-	0.5	-0.50
Austria	171	1,518	1,058	851	20.00	17.50	6.0	-1.5	6.0	1.5	-1.25

Note: Constant price adjustment methods: A Adjusted by US GDP price index and for decline of $ against other currencies as measured by SDR value. B Adjusted by national GDP price index and at 1966 exchange rates (ie reflects origin country resources spent on tourism).

a Private consumption expenditure.

Sources: International tourism expenditures, see Section III; discretionary incomes and relative prices, see Section V.

It may be remembered that the best fit equations for France and the UK (real
expenditure travel series only) indicated negative constants (i e that in the absence
of favourable income or relative price movements travel abroad would normally
fall year by year). But the statistical relationships were not good. Among the
countries not covered, the most plausible price and income elasticities also
yielded a small negative constant for Canada and a large one for Mexico. It seems
inherently unlikely that constants could be negative (except conceivably for
Mexico). So elasticities have been adjusted to bring these constants to zero while
retaining overall equations which nonetheless explain most travel growth in the
light of past discretionary income growth and relative price movements. It might
be pointed out that although a negative constant plus, say, a fairly high income
elasticity may yield the statistically best fit, it may be possible to achieve only a
slightly poorer statistical fit by eliminating the negative constant and lowering
the income elasticity. And, of course, provided the growth rate of incomes is
not too dissimilar to that in the past, the two methods would produce broadly
similar forecasts. It might be thought, though, that the elimination of the negative
constant for Mexico yields implausibly low income and price elasticities (incomes
rose rapidly over the 1966-76 period and the relative cost of travel abroad fell).

THE FORECASTS

The framework and system described in the foregoing subsections have been used
to derive the central growth rates without ceiling restrictions presented in
Tables 21 and 22 for, respectively, main origin countries and other areas.

Table 21

Main Origin Countries' Projected Central Growth Rates in Real
International Tourism Expenditure 1976-90 without Ceiling Restrictions
(per cent per annum)

Main origin countries	Actual[a]	Projected		
	1966-76	1976-80	1980-85	1985-90
West Germany	8.25	9.8	9.3	9.3
USA	4.00	5.7	6.3	6.3
France	4.50	3.5	4.3	4.3
Canada	4.75	0.5	3.1	3.1
Netherlands	9.50	6.7	8.5	8.5
Japan	20.50	16.1	16.4	16.4
UK	2.25	4.5	3.2	3.2
Belgium/Luxemburg	10.75	8.2	7.2	7.2
Mexico	2.25	-0.7	2.5	2.5
Austria	17.50	13.1	14.5	14.5

a Deflators: exchange rate adjusted national GDP price indices.

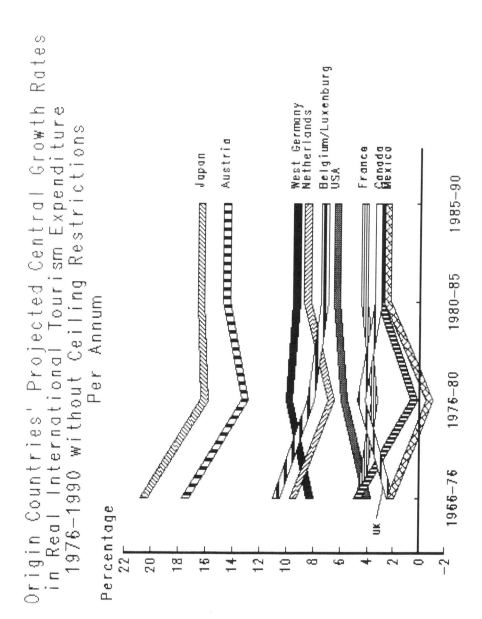

Origin Countries' Projected Central Growth Rates
in Real International Tourism Expenditure
1976-1990 without Ceiling Restrictions
Per Annum

Figure 2

87

In all cases the deflator used has been the national GDP price index (or nearest equivalent in, for instance, Eastern Europe) adjusted to SDR terms to compensate for exchange rate changes – as was done in the elasticity calculations of Section V. Usual international sources (UN, IMF and OECD) are the original data sources to derive these deflators. Where a group of countries is involved (as, for instance, in other Asia), national GDP price indices adjusted for exchange rate changes were weighted according to 1976 travel expenditures to arrive at a group deflator. But for non-listed minor countries in Western Europe and Oceania the deflator used is the same as the average for the larger groups within which these countries fall (secondary Western European destinations and Australasia).

Separate estimates are shown in Table 22 for all secondary origin countries with 1976 travel expenditures estimated in excess of $200 mn, except for East Germany, Poland, Iran, Turkey, Hong Kong and Puerto Rico. The inadequacy of the data on travel expenditures by these countries is the main reason.

Problems with deflators for the Middle East

Generally the system used to derive the forecasts appears to work fairly well. But for Middle Eastern countries the general system of tourism expenditure deflator used to arrive at constant price estimates of travel expenditures between 1966 and 1976 implies that real tourism expenditure actually fell by 3.75 per cent per annum between 1966 and 1976 – distinctly improbable, although it must be remembered that the big rise in Middle Eastern travel abroad had barely started in 1976. In view of the rapid real GDP growth (estimated at around 9.5 per cent per annum for the whole Middle East over 1966-76) this implies an implausibly big negative constant. The reason is that internal prices rose so dramatically between 1966 and 1976 (by 25 per cent to 30 per cent per annum for many important countries) and, because of the impact of higher oil revenues, there was little change in exchange rates; indeed Saudi Arabia coupled an increase in internal prices of approaching 1,700 per cent with a strengthening currency. So in resource terms, relative to domestic prices, foreign travel became cheaper at so dramatic a pace (19 per cent per annum for the whole Middle Eastern area over 1966-76) that it outstripped a 12.5 per cent per annum increase in normal travel expenditures in current dollar terms.

In fact there is no really adequate way of assessing how fast in real terms travel from Middle Eastern countries did grow between 1966 and 1976. Indeed, the data base itself for expenditures in current price terms is poor (see Section III), largely because of incomplete documentation of travel between Arab countries (which constitutes a large part of their travel expenditures); and big differences in arrivals growth rates and expenditures per day as between Arab and other destinations make it, as usual, impossible to place much reliance on arrivals data. A simple alternative method of deflating the travel expenditure estimates is, as in Section III, to adjust simply for the US purchasing power of the dollar and for the depreciation of the dollar. This produces an implied real travel growth rate for Middle Eastern countries of 8.5 per cent per annum – and no doubt a much faster growth since then. But even this is below real GDP growth (9.5 per cent per annum), suggesting a negative constant. And the relevance of US internal prices as a component of the deflator would be difficult to justify. A more rational alternative is to use an index of import prices, adjusting also for the decline in the purchasing power of the dollar. An important price index

Table 22

Secondary and Minor Origin Countries – Projected Central
Growth Rates in Real International Tourism Expenditure without Ceiling Restrictions
(per cent per annum)

W Europe	1966–76 actual Real tourism expenditure[a]	GDP (volume)	1966–76 implied constant tourism growth rate[b]	Projected GDP growth 1976–80	Projected GDP growth 1980–90	Projected real tourism expenditure[b] 1976–80	Projected real tourism expenditure[b] 1980–90
Secondary:							
Switzerland	5.00	2.3	2.2	1.75	2.50	4.4	5.3
Sweden	6.25	3.2	2.3	1.50	3.00	4.2	6.1
Denmark	6.75	3.3	2.6	2.25	3.25	5.4	6.7
Italy	10.50	4.1	5.4	2.75	3.75	8.8	10.1
Norway	13.50	4.5	7.9	3.50	4.50	12.3	13.5
Spain	9.00	5.6	2.0	4.00	5.50	7.0	8.9
Finland	8.25	5.1	1.9	2.50	4.50	5.0	7.5
Ireland	5.75	3.9	0.9	3.50	4.00	5.3	5.9
Total	7.00						
Others	−1.00	5.6	_[c]	5.00	5.50	6.3	6.9
All other W Europe	6.25						
E Europe (inc USSR)							
Total	8.75	4.8	3.2	4.75	5.00	8.7	9.0
Australasia & Oceania							
Secondary:							
Australia	8.00	4.4	2.5	3.00	4.25	6.3	7.8
New Zealand	9.75	2.3	6.9	2.00	2.50	9.4	10.0
Total	8.50	5.1	_[c]	5.00	5.00	5.8	5.8
Others	–						
All Australasia, etc	8.25						
Middle East							
Total	4.25[d]	9.5	4.0[d] or –	7.50	7.00	12.5	8.0

(continued)

Other Asia (exc Japan)							
Total	5.50	5.9	−1.3	5.50	6.00	5.0	5.6
Latin America & Caribbean							
Secondary:							
Brazil	23.00	9.5	12.1	6.50	6.00	19.6	19.0
Others (exc Mexico)	4.50	4.3	−0.4	4.25	4.50	4.5	4.8
Total	8.00						
Africa							
Total	1.75	5.0	−4.0	4.50	5.00	1.2	1.8

a Deflators: exchange rate adjusted national GDP price indices (or nearest equivalent). b Assumed elasticity responses of real tourism expenditure to real GDP of 1.25 for Western industrial countries, and of 1.15 for other countries; this is equivalent to elasticity responses of around 1 against real discretionary incomes; relative price effects are taken as being the same in the forecast period as in the past. c Presumed (negative implied by data taken as resulting from underestimated real tourism growth). d See text.

for all developing countries (source IMF) used in this way suggests a real travel growth for all Middle Eastern countries of only 2.25 per cent per annum between 1966 and 1976, again implying a negative constant; this would be even more marked were an import price index for Middle Eastern countries only to be compiled and used!

Yet another approach is not to consider real growth from Middle Eastern countries in resource terms at all, but against costs in destination countries. Data problems bedevil this approach, but if exchange rate (against the SDR) adjusted prices in some known main destination countries for Middle Eastern travellers are taken as representative, an average annual cost increase of 4.7 per cent over 1966-76 can be applied to the 53 per cent of Middle Eastern travel expenditure believed to be long haul (France 6 per cent, UK 3.7 per cent, and USA 4.3 per cent). Similarly 11.4 per cent per annum may be typical for the 47 per cent of intra Middle Eastern travel (Egypt 4.2 per cent, Iran 24.3 per cent, Iraq 12.3 per cent, Lebanon 5.8 per cent and Syria 10.4 per cent). The weighted average increase is 7.8 per cent per annum, which implies a 1966-76 real travel growth of around 4.25 per cent per annum. This figure appears in Table 25. It still suggests a negative constant at any but a very low income elasticity. If the constant is taken as nil, the income elasticity to arrive at the past 4.25 per cent per annum growth would be 0.45. At the likely GDP growth rates this implies that real future travel will grow at only 3.4 per cent per annum in 1976-80 (a figure almost certainly already overtaken by events) and 3.2 per cent per annum after 1980.

Assumptions on Middle East

Given this situation there appears no alternative to ignoring apparent past trends in looking to future Middle Eastern travel, and to assuming a typical 1.15 elasticity response to real GDP, a high constant of 4 per cent per annum in 1976-80, and a nil constant thereafter. This suggests growth rates of around 12.5 per cent per annum up to 1980, and 8 per cent per annum thereafter. These are purely arbitrary assumptions employed to give global coverage in the forecasts. (If the 1976-80 rate still seems low in the context of recent trends in travel to Europe, it must be remembered that travel within the Middle East has been less dynamic and that much of the European growth has been at the expense of intra Middle Eastern travel - especially to the Lebanon.)

Effects of varying the coefficients

Table 23 shows the effects of varying elasticity responses (adjusting the constants to compensate for these), income growth rates and relative cost movements for two major origin countries - West Germany and the UK. The first is an example of a country with rapidly growing incomes and travel and with favourable relative price trends. The second is illustrative of a country where travel and incomes are growing slowly, and where relative price movements have been adverse. While the various higher and lower assumptions taken do not perhaps extend plausibility to its limits, an assumption that, for instance, long term discretionary income growth in the UK will only be 2.25 per cent per annum is distinctly pessimistic (it was 3.3 per cent per annum over 1966-76), while a similar 5.75 per cent per annum assumption for West Germany (compared with a surprisingly low actual past 3.9 per cent) appears distinctly optimistic.

Table 23

Some Alternative Forecasts for West Germany and the UK

	Constant[a]	Income elasticity	Price elasticity	Projected % growth pa in real tourist expenditure 1976-80	1980-90
Different elasticity responses					
West Germany – basic	3.7	0.9	-1.50	9.8	9.3
– high income elasticity	2.5	1.2	-1.50	9.8	9.7
– low income elasticity	4.4	0.7	-1.50	9.7	9.0
– high price elasticity	3.3	0.9	-2.00	10.3	9.3
– low price elasticity	4.0	0.9	-1.00	9.3	9.3
UK – basic	0.0	1.2	-0.75	4.5	3.2
– high income elasticity	-1.0	1.5	-0.75	4.3	3.0
– low income elasticity	1.0	0.9	-0.75	4.7	3.3
– high price elasticity	1.3	1.2	-1.25	6.6	4.3
– low price elasticity	-0.6	1.2	-0.50	3.5	2.6
Different income growth rates	1976-80	1980-90		1976-80	1980-90
West Germany – basic	4.00	5.25		9.8	9.3
– higher	4.50	5.75		10.3	9.8
– lower	3.50	4.75		9.4	8.9
UK – basic	2.75	2.75		4.5	3.2
– higher	3.25	3.25		5.1	3.1
– lower	2.25	2.25		3.9	2.6
Different relative cost movements					
West Germany – basic	-1.7	-0.6		9.8	9.3
– higher	-1.0	0.5		8.8	7.7
– lower	-2.4	-1.5		10.9	10.7
UK – basic	-1.6	0.2		4.5	3.2
– higher	-0.9	1.3		4.0	2.3
– lower	-2.3	-0.7		5.0	3.8

a Different constants necessary to fit past data associated with different elasticity responses.

It can be seen that for both countries the variations introduced make a significant difference to forecast growth rates. But they do not make a really big difference. In the 1980-90 period the spread of annual growth rates for West Germany is 7.7 per cent per annum to 10.7 per cent per annum, compared with the basic forecast of 9.3 per cent per annum. But of the nine different forecasts only two (both the result of big variations in relative price movements) vary by more than 0.5 per cent per annum from the basic 9.3 per cent rate. Similarly for the UK the spread of growth rates for 1980-90 is 2.3 per cent per annum to 4.3 per cent per annum, against the basic forecast of 3.2 per cent per annum. Only two of the nine forecasts vary by more than 0.6 per cent from the basic 3.2 per cent rate (one is for the higher relative cost assumption and the other for the higher price elasticity assumption).

Possible range of variations for high and low forecasts

Of course a combination of, say, the high income and high price elasticities, high income growth and low relative costs for travel abroad would bring a bigger differential, as could a combination of all factors, making for slow growth. But such combinations are not perhaps very likely. For both countries it seems reasonable to set the likely upper growth rate at around 1 per cent above the basic rate (ie at 10.3 per cent per annum for West Germany and 4.2 per cent per annum for the UK). The likely lower growth rate could be set at 1 per cent below the basic rate (ie 8.3 per cent per annum for West Germany and 2.2 per cent per annum for the UK). Thus the forecast low growth rate for West Germany would still be almost double the forecast high growth rate for the UK (against almost triple for the basic forecast). Much the same results - relatively small differentials between forecasts - would be likely for other origin countries.

Adjustment for ceiling effects

A comparison of the central growth rates with the sloping ceilings to foreign travel (stemming essentially from annual leave periods) suggested in Section IV implies that foreign travel from the following six major origin countries is likely to be affected by ceilings before 1990:

West Germany
France
Netherlands
Belgium/Luxemburg
Austria
USA

Table 24

Ceiling Adjustments for Major Origin Countries Affected

	W Germany	France	Netherlands	Belgium/ Luxemburg	Austria	USA
Central travel growth without ceiling (% pa)						
1976–80	9.8	3.5	6.7	8.2	13.1	5.7
1980–85	9.3	4.3	8.5	7.2	14.5	6.3
1985–90	9.3	4.3	8.5	7.2	14.5	6.3[a]
Per cent of ceiling reached in 1976	47	72	39	40	55	76[a]
Ceiling effects starting from (year)	1985	1984	1990	1986	1980	1983[a]
Central travel growth with ceiling (% pa)						
1976–80	9.8	3.5	6.7	8.2	13.1	5.7[a]
1980–85	9.0	4.2	8.5	7.2	6.1	6.1
1985–90	6.0	3.7	8.4	4.9	1.5	5.6
final year (1990)	4.4	3.5	8.2	3.3	1.0	5.4
Per cent of ceiling reached in 1990	93	82	76	88	100	84

a Ceiling grows faster than central travel forecasts up to 1980.

Other major origin countries seem unlikely to be affected. Although the UK is already close to the ceiling, a rapid ceiling growth rate is likely to outstrip that in travel abroad. Among secondary origin countries, travel from the Scandinavian countries and Switzerland could be affected by ceiling limitations, though data do not permit estimates to be made.

Table 24 shows the effects of applying ceiling effects gradually as the ceiling is approached (by the same method as in the final table in Section IV) for the four main origin countries affected. It can be seen that the effect is only marginal for the Netherlands. It is sharper (starting in the mid 1980s) for West Germany, Belgium/Luxemburg, France and the USA. For the first two the 1985-90 travel growth rate is reduced by around a third, and the final year growth rate more than halved. For France and the USA the effects are rather less marked. But the rapid travel growth without ceiling effects for Austria and the slow growth of the ceiling there mean that the ceiling effects are severe for this country and are likely to make themselves felt from 1980. The Austrian travel growth rate would be only 6.1 per cent per annum in 1980-85 (against 14.5 per cent without ceiling restrictions), and only 1.5 per cent in 1985-90, with the actual ceiling itself being reached in 1987.

Possible ceiling effects in secondary origin countries

Among secondary origin countries which could be affected by the ceiling some very broad assumptions can be made.

1 Switzerland was at the West German/Austrian average for ceiling penetration in 1976 (51 per cent) and ceiling growth rates would be at around the average for these countries (4.5 per cent per annum in 1976-80 and 1.75 per cent per annum thereafter).

2. Sweden, Denmark and Norway were at the West German/Netherlands/Belgium/UK average for ceiling penetration in 1976 (55 per cent) and had ceiling growth rates of around the average for these countries (3.75 per cent per annum in 1976-80, and 2.5 per cent per annum thereafter).

Putting these assumptions against projected real tourism expenditure growth rates suggests that Switzerland would not in fact be affected by the ceiling. Sweden and Denmark would be affected, but not severely. Norway would, however, be severely affected, almost as severely as Austria, with the high without ceiling central growth rates being pushed down sharply from the early 1980s. Implied growth rates (per cent per annum) are as shown below.

	No ceiling restrictions			With ceiling restrictions		
	1976-80	1980-84	1985-90	1976-80	1980-84	1985-90
Sweden	4.2	6.1	6.1	4.2	6.1	5.9
Denmark	5.4	6.7	6.7	5.4	6.7	5.9
Norway	12.3	13.5	13.5	12.3	7.3	3.6

Some kind of adjustment is also needed for Brazil, where real travel expenditure grew by some 23 per cent a year between 1966 and 1976, and where projected central growth rates are 19-20 per cent per annum. Growth at this rate would mean that by 1990 only West Germany, the USA, Japan, France and the Netherlands spent more on foreign travel, distinctly implausible even for so large a population and such a rapidly growing economy. Much of the growth in Brazilian travel has been because the benefits of development have accrued predominantly to a small, wealthy segment of the population. Both in terms of socioeconomic groups and regionally, Brazil is in effect two nations. There is a limit to the amount of travel which the wealthy group can undertake. This has been reflected by an arbitrary tapering off of the constant from 12.1 per cent per annum in 1966-76 to 8 per cent per annum in 1976-80, to 5 per cent per annum in 1980-85 and to 3 per cent per annum in 1985-90.

High and low growth rates adopted

Analysis of the effects on the central forecasts of varying underlying assumptions for West Germany and the UK suggested that it is reasonable to put high and low growth rate limits 1 per cent per annum respectively above and below the central growth rates. True statistical limits, could these be compiled with high confidence rates attached, would undoubtedly be much wider, but consequently not very helpful. These somewhat arbitrary + or - 1 per cent per annum limits have been attached to all countries, although the confidence which can be given to these limits for major origin countries, and particularly those on which elasticity calculations were carried out in Section V, is certainly greater than for secondary and minor origin countries. The forecasts for developing countries, most notably Middle Eastern ones, are especially tentative. It might be argued that, for those countries where the central growth rate is affected by ceiling limitations, the high growth rate should be little if any higher. This view would be reasonable had it been possible to calculate the ceiling and its growth with greater accuracy. It might also be said that a 0.5 per cent low growth rate for Austria in 1985-90 (when the central growth rate is severely restricted by the ceiling to 1.5 per cent per annum) is unrealistically low; but as this is the only country so drastically affected the 0.5 per cent low rate has been retained for the sake of consistency.

Forecasts
by Length of Haul

In this section, the total travel forecasts derived in the previous section are
divided between:

   a.   expenditure on trips to bordering countries (including those divided by
        a narrow strip of water, such as the English Channel);

   b.   expenditure on other short haul travel (generally travel within the
        same continent or subcontinent, except where the distance makes a
        trip necessarily over about 1,750 nautical miles);

   c.   expenditure on long haul travel.

The work concentrates on the ten major origin countries, and concludes with some
crude estimates for other countries, essentially for purposes of aggregation to
global totals only. The base for the forecasts is the division of travel expenditures
between these three elements in the data base (see Section III). It may be
remembered that in some cases the division of travel expenditures by haul length
involved a fair element of estimation (notably for Mexico and Belgium and to a
rather lesser extent France and Japan among main origin countries). These
figures also exclude international fare payments, obviously therefore exaggerating
the apparent share of cross border travel (though this is nonetheless of great
importance), and reducing the apparent long haul share. Use of a more accurate
and complete 1976 breakdown - could this be compiled - would not, however, in
itself yield significantly different growth rates in each type of travel; it would
only affect the forecast shares of travel by type. But for planning purposes it is
probably growth rates, particularly relative growth rates, which are of more
importance than the forecast absolute amounts.

Estimates of the past development of travel shares by haul length -

Table 25 presents estimates of the development between 1969 and 1976 of the
percentage shares by haul length of each major origin country's expenditure on
international travel (excluding fare payments). The 1976 breakdown (the base)
is at 1976 prices, while breakdowns for preceding years in general reflect
volume changes in each travel type fitted to this 1976 breakdown (i e they could
be regarded as being at 1976 rather than current prices). The methods by which
these changes in shares have been assumed do vary somewhat from country to
country, depending on the data available; so they are not strictly comparable.
The methods are referred to briefly in footnotes to the table (a full description
would be extremely lengthy). The most common method has been to aggregate
recorded arrivals data compiled by main destination countries for each type of
travel (either weighting the data where expenditure shares are known, or, for
instance, dividing hotel arrival figures by a constant to bring them better into

Table 25

Percentage Shares of Travel by Haul Length

	1969	1970	1971	1972	1973	1974	1975	1976	Coefficient of correlation	Trend line projections 1980	1985	1990
UK[a]												
Cross border	24.1	22.5	21.5	19.0	21.4	20.6	20.6	20.5	0.67	18.2	16.6	14.0
Other short haul	53.1	54.2	55.4	58.0	57.7	53.9	52.8	50.9	0.33	52.1	50.4	48.8
Long haul	22.8	23.3	23.2	23.1	20.9	25.5	26.5	28.6	0.73	29.7	33.4	37.0
USA[b]												
Cross border	44.8	44.1	46.0	44.4	46.4	49.2	48.7	50.9	0.90	53.7	58.3	62.9
Other short haul	12.3	10.5	10.1	10.9	12.3	12.4	12.9	11.5	0.42	12.9	13.8	14.7
Long haul	43.0	45.3	43.9	44.8	41.3	38.4	38.4	37.6	0.87	33.3	27.9	22.4
West Germany[c]												
Cross border	44.8	46.2	44.7	44.0	45.3	46.7	43.7	44.7	0.17	44.5	44.1	43.8
Other short haul	48.1	47.2	48.6	48.3	46.1	44.1	46.8	46.2	0.61	44.1	42.3	40.5
Long haul	7.1	6.6	6.7	7.7	8.6	9.2	9.5	9.1	0.91	11.4	13.6	15.7
France[d]												
Cross border	73.6	71.7	70.1	66.7	64.2	63.4	61.8	58.1	0.99	50.1	39.3	28.6
Other short haul	2.8	2.9	3.3	3.0	3.1	3.1	3.2	3.2	0.66	3.4	3.7	3.9
Long haul	23.6	25.4	26.6	30.3	32.7	33.5	35.0	38.7	0.99	46.5	57.0	67.5
Netherlands[d]												
Cross border	37.5	36.0	35.7	35.4	32.8	33.7	35.0	35.8	0.51	33.0	31.4	29.9
Other short haul	55.4	56.1	56.2	54.7	56.4	55.5	54.6	52.7	0.65	52.8	51.2	49.6
Long haul	7.1	7.9	8.1	9.9	10.8	10.8	10.4	11.5	0.94	14.2	17.4	20.5
Belgium/Luxemburg[d]												
Cross border	65.2	64.0	61.6	57.1	55.9	53.5	51.8	50.9	0.99	40.8	29.7	18.6
Other short haul	30.2	30.5	32.3	36.3	37.4	39.4	41.4	40.4	0.97	49.2	58.1	66.9
Long haul	4.6	5.5	6.1	6.6	6.7	7.1	6.8	8.7	0.93	10.0	12.2	14.5
Austria[d]												
Cross border	87.9	86.5	86.1	85.1	84.2	83.6	82.8	81.7	0.99	78.5	74.3	70.1
Other short haul	6.4	7.0	7.2	7.5	7.8	7.9	8.5	8.9	0.99	10.1	11.7	13.4
Long haul	5.7	6.5	6.7	7.4	8.0	8.5	8.7	9.4	0.99	11.4	14.0	16.5
Canada[e]												
Cross border	71.4	67.2	65.5	64.5	65.3	62.8	61.5	67.0	0.64	59.7	55.7	51.8
Other short haul	-	-	-	-	-	-	-	-	-	-	-	-
Long haul	28.6	32.8	34.5	35.5	34.7	37.2	38.5	33.0	0.64	40.3	44.3	48.2
Japan[f]												
Cross border	-	-	-	-	-				-	-	-	-
Other short haul	12.2	12.6	13.0	13.4	13.8	13.4	13.8	15.0	0.93	15.8	17.4	19.1
Long haul	87.8	87.4	87.0	86.6	86.2	86.6	86.2	85.0	0.93	84.2	82.6	80.9
Mexico[g]												
Cross border	88.8	88.1	89.2	90.5	91.4	92.5	92.8	92.1	0.93	51.8	99.2	102.6
Other short haul	0.3	0.3	0.3	0.3	0.3	0.3	0.3	0.3	1.00	0.3	0.3	0.3
Long haul	10.9	11.6	10.5	9.2	8.3	7.2	6.9	7.6	0.93	3.9	0.5	-2.9

Note: Percentages may not always add up to 100 because of rounding.

a Basis: mn days spent abroad (source: BTA). Irish Republic, France and Belgium counted as bordering countries; all travel outside Europe counted as long haul. b Basis: total expenditure by area adjusted for relative price movements (source: OECD Tourism Annual). Caribbean and Central America counted as short haul. c Basis: total expenditure by area adjusted for relative price movements (source: OECD Tourism Annual) with European OECD split between cross border and other short haul according to relative growth rates in destination countries arrivals data; USA and Canada plus other countries used as basis for long haul share. 1976 data base used as basis for shares. d Basis: derived from growth rates in many destination countries' arrivals data (main source: OECD Tourism Annual), weighted to represent comparative importance and using 1976 data base as basis for shares. e Basis: tourism expenditures (source: OECD Tourism Annual) adjusted for relative price movements. f Very approximate estimates for pre-1976 shares: Hong Kong, South Korea and Philippines only considered short haul. g Very approximate. Long haul estimates based on Canada, Spain, Italy and UK arrivals data. Trend line projections obviously represent an impossible situation.

line with frontier arrivals figures). The changing pattern thus revealed is then expressed in changes in percentage shares taking the 1976 expenditure breakdown as base. Gaps in data and changes in methods of recording mean that the procedure is in practice less straightforward than it might appear. The estimates for Mexico and Japan are particularly rough.

– are projected on a trend line basis into the future

The table also shows the results of simply projecting these past travel shares into the future, by fitting a trend to them. This is a crude indication of what would happen if apparent past trends were continued to 1990, and discounts any changes in the underlying factors which affected these shares. The simple least squares method used to fit the trend line treats the percentages as absolutes, not as percentages. So it is possible for a rapidly growing percentage eventually to be over 100 or a declining one to be negative – a logical impossibility. (This in fact happens with Mexico.) The method also yields some quite high coefficients of correlation (most notably for Austria), which alternative methods might not.

Changes in travel patterns –

Table 25 does, however, suggest some interesting differences in the changes in travel patterns.

1. Travel to bordering countries as a percentage of the total is falling in most countries, very slowly from West Germany, slowly from the Netherlands, quite rapidly from Austria, Canada and the UK, and very rapidly from Belgium and France (so rapidly indeed that a continuation of this trend at the same rate as in the past is distinctly implausible beyond the mid 1980s).

2. Travel to bordering countries as a percentage of the total is rising slowly from Mexico (though the data do not allow one to be definite about this); it is rising quite rapidly from the USA.

3. Other short haul travel as a percentage of the total is generally tending to rise, slowly from France, Japan (though data are poor) and the USA, quite rapidly from Austria and Belgium.

4. It is tending to fall, slowly, from West Germany, the Netherlands and the UK.

5. Long haul travel as a percentage of the total is generally rising either quite rapidly (Austria, Belgium, Canada, West Germany, the Netherlands and the UK), or very rapidly (France – perhaps so rapidly that the trend could not continue long).

6. From Japan (where the vast majority of travel has been long haul) it is declining slowly. It is declining more rapidly from the USA and Mexico (where its share is already small – so the trend could not continue).

98

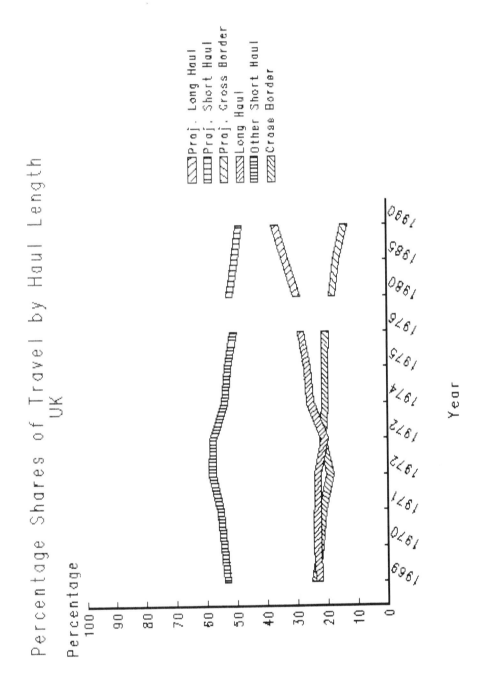

Figure 3

99

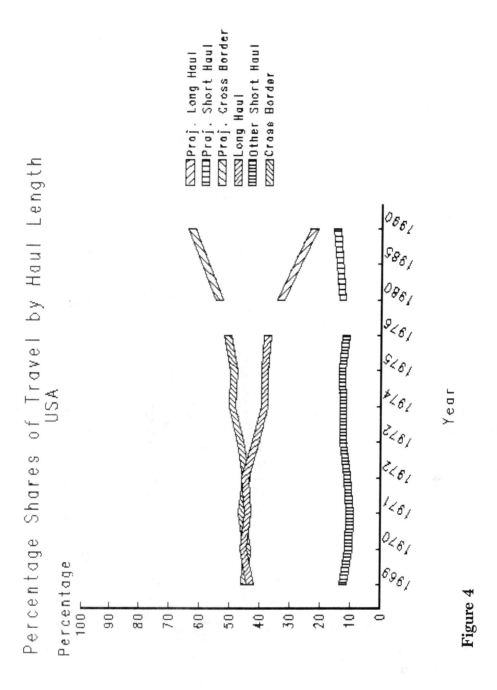

Percentage Shares of Travel by Haul Length
USA

Figure 4

100

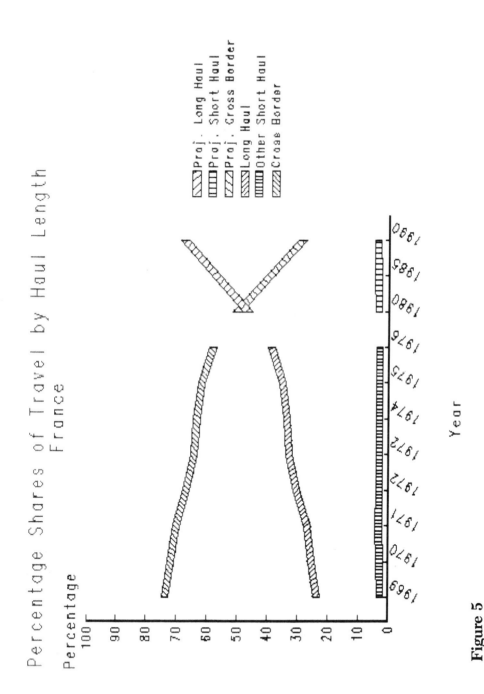

Figure 5

101

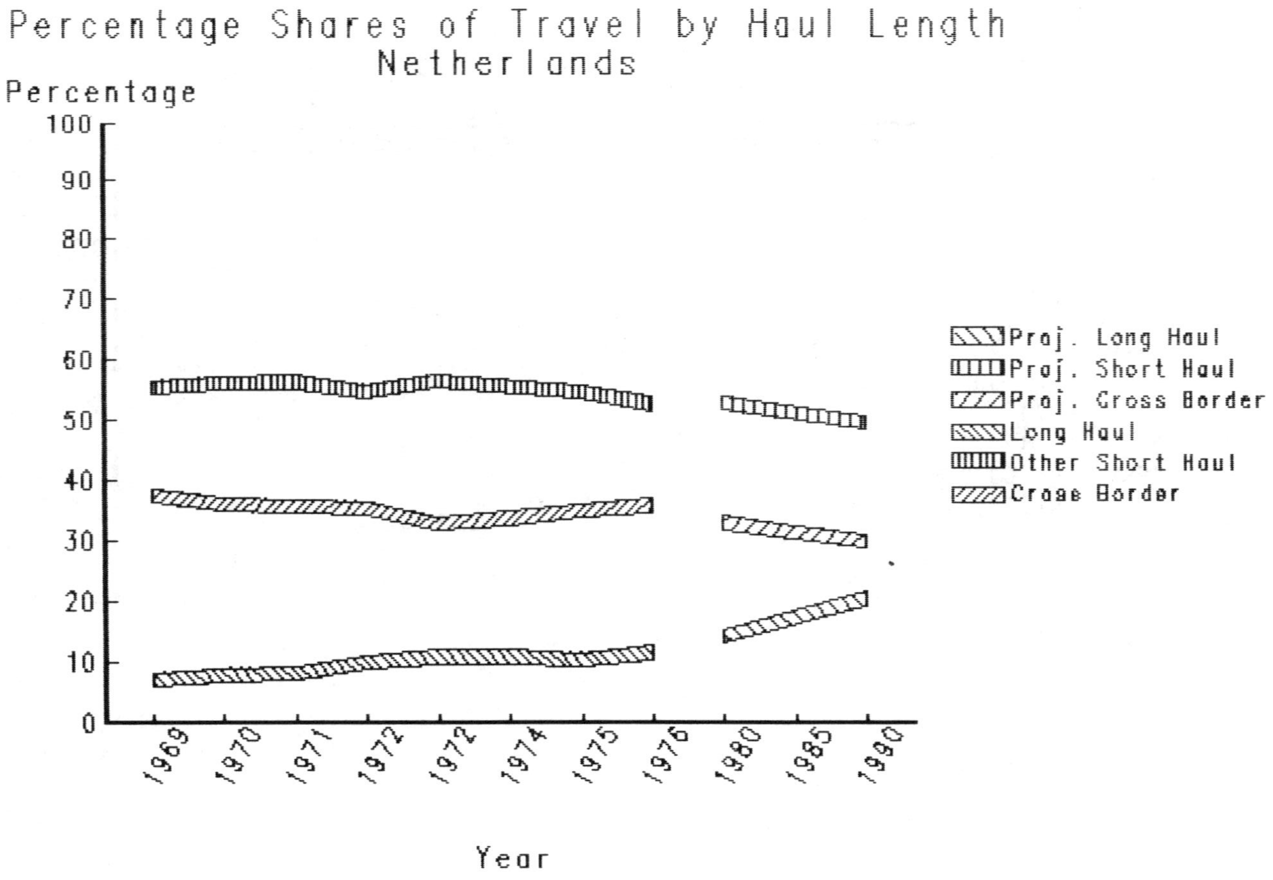
Percentage Shares of Travel by Haul Length
Netherlands
Percentage
100
90
80
70
60
50
40
30
20
10
0
1969
1970
1971
1972
1972
1974
1975
1976
1980
1985
1990
Year
Proj. Long Haul
Proj. Short Haul
Proj. Cross Border
Long Haul
Other Short Haul
Crose Border

Figure 6

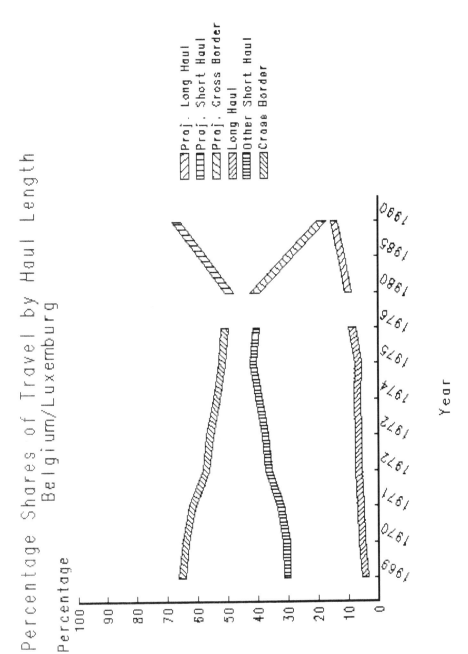

Figure 7

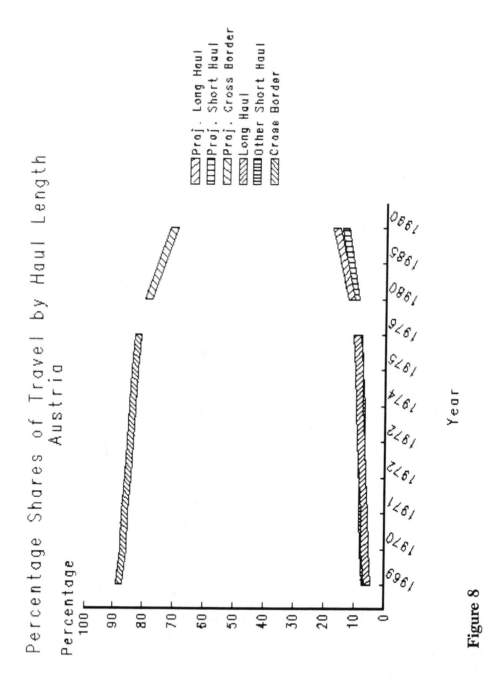

Figure 8

104

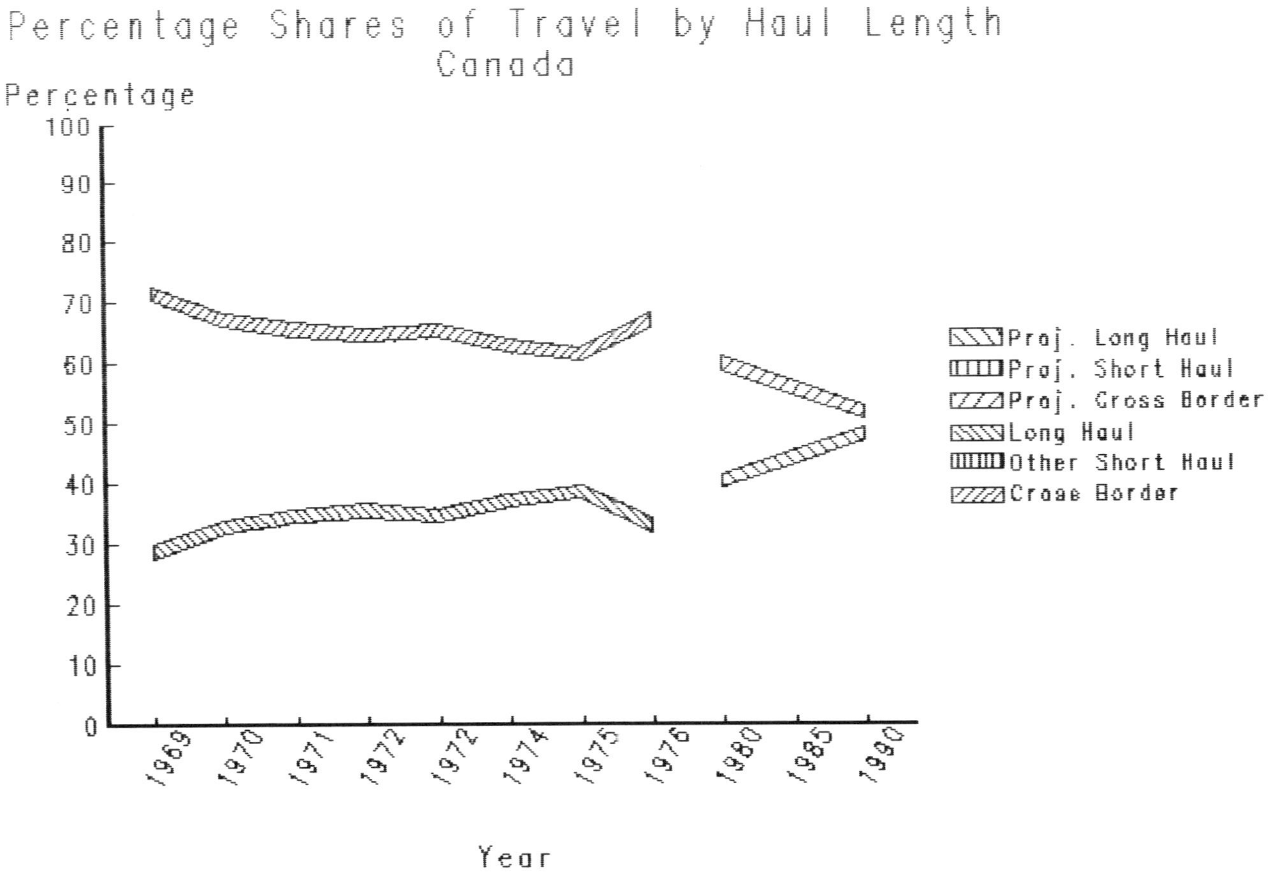

Percentage Shares of Travel by Haul Length
Canada

Percentage

Proj. Long Haul
Proj. Short Haul
Proj. Cross Border
Long Haul
Other Short Haul
Cross Border

Year

Figure 9

105

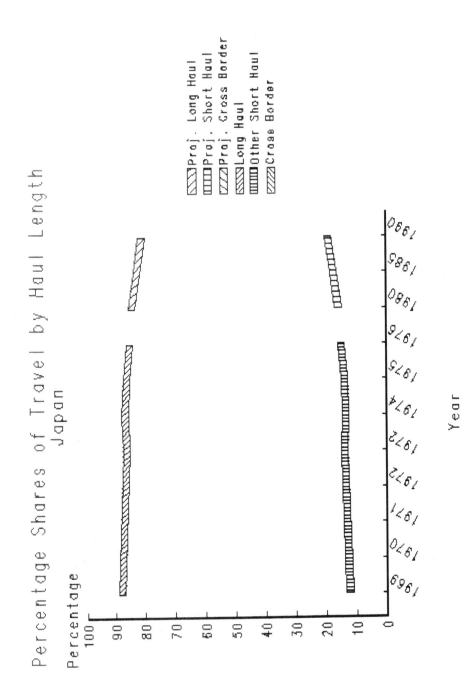

Figure 10

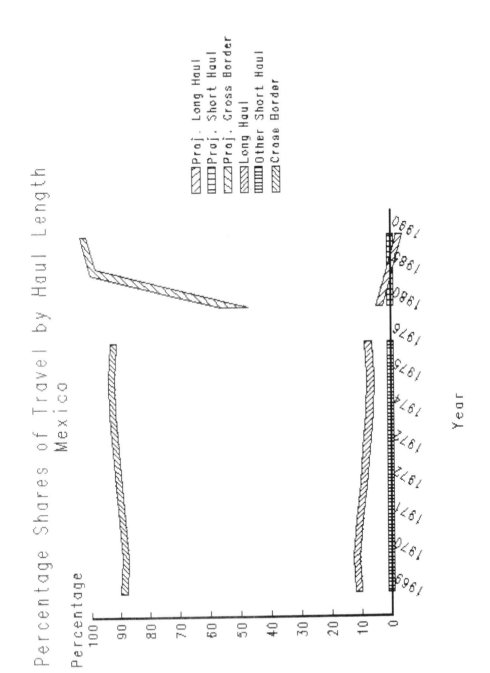

Figure 11

Table 26

Percentage Shares of Travel by Haul Length at 1976 Relative Prices

	1969-76 total change in relative prices for haul length above or below total relative price movements (%)	1969-76 change p a in travel share resulting from relative price movements (percentage points)	Percentage shares								Coefficient of correlation	Trend line projections (% shares)		
			1969	1970	1971	1972	1973	1974	1975	1976		1980	1985	1990
UK														
Cross border	-11.2	0.37	26.7	24.7	23.3	20.5	22.5	21.3	21.0	20.5	0.86	16.7	12.8	8.8
Other short haul	6.7	-1.06	45.7	47.9	50.1	53.7	54.5	51.8	51.8	50.9	0.62	56.3	60.0	63.7
Long haul	-18.6	0.69	27.6	27.4	26.6	25.8	23.0	26.9	27.2	28.6	0.07	27.0	27.2	27.5
USA														
Cross border	-5.5	0.48	48.1	47.0	48.4	46.3	47.8	50.2	49.2	50.9	0.70	51.8	54.1	56.3
Other short haul	11.1	-0.26	10.5	9.0	8.8	9.8	11.5	11.9	12.6	11.5	0.75	13.9	16.0	18.2
Long haul	-2.1	-0.22	41.4	44.0	42.8	43.9	40.9	37.9	38.2	37.6	0.80	34.3	29.9	25.5
West Germany														
Cross border	10.3	-1.00	37.8	40.2	39.7	40.0	42.3	44.7	42.7	44.7	0.91	48.5	53.1	57.8
Other short haul	-10.3	0.84	54.0	52.2	52.8	51.7	48.6	45.8	47.7	46.2	0.93	40.8	34.8	28.8
Long haul	-12.6	0.16	8.2	7.6	7.5	8.3	9.1	9.5	9.6	9.1	0.82	10.7	12.1	13.4
France														
Cross border	5.5	-0.67	68.9	67.7	66.8	64.0	62.2	62.1	61.1	58.1	0.98	52.7	45.3	37.9
Other short haul	6.5	-0.03	2.6	2.7	3.1	2.9	3.0	3.0	3.2	3.2	0.86	3.5	3.9	4.3
Long haul	-13.0	0.70	28.5	29.6	30.1	33.1	34.8	34.9	35.7	38.7	0.98	43.8	50.8	57.8
Netherlands														
Cross border	7.1	-0.43	34.5	33.4	33.5	33.7	31.5	32.8	34.6	35.8	0.24	34.7	35.3	36.0
Other short haul	-1.0	0.24	57.1	57.6	57.4	55.7	57.1	56.0	54.8	52.7	0.84	51.8	49.0	46.1
Long haul	-11.1	0.19	8.4	9.0	9.1	10.6	11.4	11.2	10.6	11.5	0.88	13.5	15.7	17.9
Belgium/Luxemburg														
Cross border	-3.0	0.20	66.6	65.2	62.6	57.9	56.5	53.9	52.0	50.9	0.99	40.0	27.9	15.9
Other short haul	2.0	-0.23	28.6	29.1	31.1	35.4	36.7	38.9	41.2	40.4	0.97	50.2	60.2	70.1
Long haul	-4.1	0.03	4.8	5.7	6.3	6.7	6.8	7.2	6.8	8.7	0.92	9.8	11.9	14.0
Austria														
Cross border	0.7	-0.03	87.7	86.3	85.9	85.0	84.1	83.5	82.8	81.7	0.99	78.6	74.6	70.6
Other short haul	4.3	-0.04	6.1	6.8	7.0	7.3	7.7	7.8	8.4	8.9	0.99	10.2	12.0	13.8
Long haul	-5.0	0.07	6.2	6.9	7.1	7.7	8.2	8.7	8.8	9.4	0.99	11.2	13.4	15.6
Canada														
Cross border	-5.2	0.76	76.7	71.8	69.3	67.5	67.6	64.3	62.3	67.0	0.85	56.7	48.9	41.2
Other short haul	-	-	-	-	-	-	-	-	-	-		-	-	-
Long haul	14.7	-0.76	23.3	28.2	30.7	32.5	32.4	35.7	37.7	33.0	0.85	43.3	51.1	58.8
Japan														
Cross border	-	-	-	-	-	-	-	-	-	-		-	-	-
Other short haul	9.7	-0.27	10.3	11.0	11.6	12.3	13.0	12.9	13.5	15.0	0.98	16.9	19.9	22.9
Long haul	-3.9	0.27	89.7	89.0	88.4	87.7	87.0	87.1	86.5	85.0	0.98	83.1	80.1	77.1
Mexico														
Cross border	-2.2	0.68	93.6	92.2	92.6	93.2	93.4	93.9	93.5	92.1	0.01	93.1	93.1	93.1
Other short haul[a]	-	-	0.3	0.3	0.3	0.3	0.3	0.3	0.3	0.3	1.00	0.3	0.3	0.3
Long haul	17.9	-0.68	6.1	7.5	7.1	6.5	6.3	5.8	6.2	7.6	0.10	6.6	6.6	6.6

a Assumed no changes in this minor element.

Note: See text and footnotes to preceding table for method of compiling this table and qualifications attached to it.

An obvious, important reason for these changes in patterns is that while for some countries the relative cost of travel to bordering countries has been falling and that to more distant destinations rising (e g the USA), for other countries the reverse is true (e g the Netherlands). Table 26 shows the possible effects on travel patterns of past movements in relative prices. The method of estimating relative prices is as used in Section V (Price and Income Elasticities). It may be remembered that air fare components were excluded. Inclusion of these (were it possible) would generally make the cost of long haul travel somewhat cheaper relative to short haul than the figures used imply. Consequently, rather more of the general increase in the long haul share is probably attributable to relative price changes than the table implies. For all countries and all haul lengths a cross price elasticity of -1.5 was used (i e the change in travel pattern resulting from a change in the relative cost of, for example, long haul travel as against short haul). This is rather different from some of the average cross price elasticities calculated in Section V (-2.0 for US travel, for instance), but in view of the tentative nature of these estimates it seemed sensible to standardise on a typical figure.

It is important to note that the table is based on 1976. For earlier years it shows what relative shares of travel would have been had relative prices been as in 1976. This is clearly a purely hypothetical concept, and of use only for making trend line projections of what travel shares would be in the future in the absence of any relative price movements. In other words it reflects simply the constants in travel shares (e g the growing comparative popularity of particular holiday types), and seeks to exclude price effects. Trend line projections are shown in the table, again simply as a crude indication of what would happen if past trends were continued in 1990. The simple least squares method of trend line fitting to percentages has again been used; as already noted, it has disadvantages. The incidence of price effects has been spread equally over the whole period. Although use of moving averages with perhaps lagged price effects would be preferable in principle, it makes little difference in practice to the projections and, in view of the approximate nature of the whole exercise, appears an unnecessary refinement.

- and are less sharp if price effects are excluded

Generally the effect of eliminating price responses, as reflected in this table by comparison with the preceding one, is to reduce the speed at which changes in travel patterns take place. The movements in most countries for most types of travel are in the same direction. Exceptions are West Germany and Netherlands travel to bordering countries (which when price effects are excluded appear to be rising gently from the Netherlands, quite rapidly from West Germany, rather than falling gently); other short haul travel from the UK (rising quite rapidly when price effects are excluded instead of falling gently); while for Mexico, price effects appear to account for all changes in travel patterns (so all three types of travel appear stable). This could be interpreted as implying that the actual price responses are larger than the -1.5 cross price elasticity used, particularly for long haul travel, where it was not possible to take into account the impact of air fares (but note that the Section V estimates suggested that inclusion of air fares in the calculations for the UK and the USA did not make much difference to the elasticity response itself). However, in the absence of stronger evidence on cross elasticities, the use of a comparatively high elasticity response is difficult to justify.   109

Moreover, there are a few instances where, in contrast to the general tendency, the exclusion of price effects actually accelerates changes in the pattern of travel as shown in the previous table; in other words constants affected travel patterns appear larger than previously implied, the price effects tending to soften natural trends.

Future travel shares by length of haul for main origin countries

Table 27 which follows presents forecast shares of travel expenditure to 1990 by length of haul for the ten main origin countries. From these, growth rates per annum for each type of travel are derived. These are presented (to avoid repetition) in Section I. It should be re-emphasised that, because of the approximate nature of the breakdowns of travel expenditure by haul length, it is these growth rates which should be regarded as being significant, not the absolute dollar amounts (in constant prices), or the percentage shares.

The percentage share forecasts are largely based on the preceding analysis. Generally, each forecast share is roughly midway between the two trend line projections (the unadjusted one and the one eliminating the effect of responses to changes in relative prices). The implication of a straight averaging of the two would be that future changes in relative prices for different haul lengths will, on a per annum basis, be only half as sharp in the 1976-90 period as during the 1969-76 period. Generally this may not be an unreasonable assumption, in that the period of radical adjustment to compensate for the past failure of exchange rates (during the years when they were more or less fixed with only occasional adjustments) to reflect differential rates of inflation may be virtually over; from 1976 onwards, changes in exchange rates may fit fairly closely to differences in the pace of inflation in different countries. It should be remembered, too, that the forecasts of total travel do take into account total relative price movements for each origin country. So an averaging procedure would assume that the rate at which (for instance) long haul travel becomes relatively cheaper compared with cross border travel from the Netherlands is halved, within the framework of the relative cost of total foreign travel from the Netherlands falling slightly (by 0.6 per cent per annum) over the whole forecast period.

Adjustments made to produce percentage share forecasts

A simple averaging procedure has, however, been used only as a basis for the percentage share forecasts. It has been adjusted in four main respects.

1. To allow for apparent actual changes in travel shares since 1976, most notably the surge in long haul travel following cheaper fares on the North Atlantic. North Atlantic travel from the UK rose by around a third in 1978 alone, and by around a quarter from other West European countries.

2. To compensate for the statistical deficiencies in the simple method of trend line fitting used, which for instance tends to exaggerate proportional changes in falling travel shares in the later years, particularly for a travel type whose share is small.

3. To take account of the probability that air fares having fallen more (in real terms) for long haul travel than for short haul in recent years (particularly in the

first two forecast years 1977 and 1978 - and reflected in the changes noted in 1 above) will from around 1980 fall more rapidly for short haul travel. This applies mainly to travel from and within Western Europe. The estimate of British Airways that its short haul passenger fare yield will drop by 42 per cent in real terms by 1986 against a drop of only 28 per cent for long haul travel could probably be applied generally to air travel from and within Western Europe. In contrast the tendency will probably be for long haul fares for North American travellers to continue to decline relative to short haul - already of course much cheaper on a per mile basis than in the rest of the world. So these air fare trends (relative to those in 1969-76 which were reflected in the constants underlying the rates of change in Table 26) could be expected to boost long haul shares for all major origin countries, apart from Japan, up to 1980, but thereafter to boost the short haul share in respect of travel from Western Europe.

4. Where appropriate, adjustments have also been made for special factors. For instance, one of the reasons for the past fall in the share of cross border travel from the UK has been the Northern Ireland situation which has affected travel to the Irish Republic. This factor is unlikely to produce a continuing decline in such travel (indeed there are signs that it has already begun to recover). The effects of socio-political tensions in the Caribbean on US travel is another special factor. Finally, the extremely sharp fall in Mexican long haul travel on a simple trend line basis appears unrealistic to be used on a 50/50 basis in an averaging procedure, particularly in view of the likely impact of soaring oil revenues on the economy in the 1980s. This new general economic situation is likely to be reflected in an increase in the proportions of long haul and other short haul travel, and the forecasts reflect this.

Special ceiling type adjustments for France, Belgium and Canada

The procedures used do, however, produce some rather improbable 1985 and 1990 travel shares for France and Belgium. The long haul share of French travel expenditure was by 1976, at 39 per cent, well above that for other West European countries and has been rising rapidly. Even if there were no changes in relative prices to boost this share (as happened in the past), the 1990 long haul share would be, on a projection of past trends, 58 per cent, and the bordering countries' share (58 per cent in 1976) would be down to 38 per cent. In the context of a forecast of rather slow total travel growth from France, this seems distinctly unlikely. Some ceiling to the long haul share must soon begin to operate and the shares have been quite sharply adjusted to allow for such effects. The bordering country share of travel expenditure from Belgium has been falling rapidly and the other short haul rising rapidly in recent years. This, too, if continued, would by the mid 1980s reveal what would perhaps be an unlikely situation (bordering 30 per cent of the 1985 total on a simple trend line projection against 51 per cent in 1976, and other short haul 58 per cent against 40 per cent in 1976), although the forecast growth rate of Belgian travel is much faster than that of French. Some similar ceiling type adjustments have been made. The rapid shift in Canadian travel from cross border to long haul would, if continued in the 1976-80 period when total travel is forecast to grow only slowly, result in a sharp fall in cross border travel; though some decline may be realistic, particularly with the cheaper transatlantic fares, a sharp fall does not seem likely. Similarly it seemed appropriate to introduce some ceiling type effects, limiting the shift from cross border to long haul post 1980.

Table 27

<u>Forecast Shares of Travel by Haul Length</u>
(per cent of total)

	1976	1980	1985	1990
UK				
Cross border	20.5	18.7	16.5	14.8
Other short haul	50.9	50.8	52.5	52.8
Long haul	28.6	30.5	31.0	32.7
USA				
Cross border	50.9	50.9	54.3	56.9
Other short haul	11.5	12.4	13.4	14.9
Long haul	37.6	36.7	32.3	28.2
West Germany				
Cross border	44.7	45.9	48.1	49.5
Other short haul	46.2	41.8	38.3	34.5
Long haul	9.1	12.3	13.6	16.0
France				
Cross border	58.1	52.8	47.9	46.1
Other short haul	3.2	3.6	4.2	4.4
Long haul	38.7	43.6	47.9	49.5
Netherlands				
Cross border	35.8	33.3	33.1	32.6
Other short haul	52.7	51.4	49.8	47.6
Long haul	11.5	15.3	17.1	19.8
Belgium/Luxemburg				
Cross border	50.9	44.8	40.3	36.4
Other short haul	40.4	44.2	47.7	50.0
Long haul	8.7	11.0	12.0	13.6
Austria				
Cross border	81.7	78.0	73.9	68.4
Other short haul	8.9	10.0	12.0	14.1
Long haul	9.4	12.0	14.1	17.5
Canada				
Cross border	67.0	61.8	57.7	54.1
Other short haul	-	-	-	-
Long haul	33.0	38.2	42.3	45.9
Japan				
Cross border	-	-	-	-
Other short haul	5.0	16.4	19.1	22.1
Long haul	95.0	83.6	80.9	77.9
Mexico				
Cross border	92.1	92.4	91.0	89.4
Other short haul	0.3	0.3	0.5	0.6
Long haul	7.6	7.3	8.5	10.0

Forecast shares for major origin countries –

The resulting forecast shares of travel by haul length from the ten main origin countries are shown in Table 27. The actual constant price dollar amounts and growth rates appear in Section I.

1. The long haul share is expected to rise rapidly from most countries, although from the USA and Japan it is forecast to decline somewhat.

2. The bordering traffic share is expected to fall from most countries, quite rapidly from many. But from West Germany and the USA it should rise slightly.

3. The other short haul share is expected to rise generally, but not from West Germany or the Netherlands.

– and for minor

Purely as a basis for compounding global aggregates, future market shares for lesser origin countries have been projected, taking the 1976 data base situation as in Section III as a starting point. For Western European countries, other than the six major origin countries, the presumption is for these countries taken together that the rates of shift of percentage shares from cross border and other short haul traffic to long haul travel would be identical in each forecast period (1976–80, 1980–85 and 1985–90) to the combined total for the six major countries. Thus between 1976 and 1980 the cross border share of travel from the six main West European origin countries is forecast to fall by 2.1 per cent of the 1976 share (from 47.5 per cent of the total to 46.5 per cent – in terms of percentage points the change is, of course, less); the other short haul share by 4.7 per cent; while the long haul share is forecast to rise by 16.8 per cent. Applying these changes to the 1976 other West European travel shares by haul length and adjusting the result to make the total equal 100 produces forecast 1980 shares of 34.1, 36.7 and 29.2 respectively (against 35.6, 39.0, and 25.4 in 1976). The same process was adopted for 1985 and 1990.

Around 43.5 per cent of 1976 travel expenditure by countries other than the main ten origin countries is accounted for by other Western Europe. The travel patterns of the remaining 56.5 per cent tend to be heavily biased towards particular haul lengths, so moderate changes in shares do not make a great deal of difference. Thus Australian and New Zealand travel is all long haul, as is most Middle Eastern, other Asia, and African travel. For all these countries it is presumed that the rate of shift of percentage shares from cross border and other short haul travel will be identical in each forecast period to the combined total for the major origin countries plus other Western Europe. This is of course a somewhat sweeping assumption, but the data for a more calculated approach do not exist. Nor indeed, if, for example, the haul length distribution of African travel were to change in a radically different way to the rest of the world would this make much difference to the global total.

Part Two:
The Economic
and Social Impact of
International Tourism on
Developing Countries

Introduction

Aim of this Special Report

This Special Report has as its purpose the identification and examination of the many types of economic and social impact created by international tourism, an assessment of these impacts on developing countries and the suggestion of measures which will help to reduce problems associated with international tourism, thereby increasing the benefits accruing to developing countries.

It has not been the intention of this Special Report to resolve the dilemma as whether tourism is a "blessing or a blight", the opposing camps' views being well summed up by the World Tourism Organization (WTO).

"For many observers.... the benefits, both economic and social, conferred by tourism are so obvious as to be hardly worthy of deeper examination. They point to.... the Spanish example where tourism could be held to be the stimulus behind a whole economy's expansion and has seemingly enabled the largely farming communities of Spain's Mediterranean seaboard to move, relatively painlessly, from a life lived at near-subsistence level to one enjoying a relatively high prosperity in less than two decades. It is assumed that tourism is capable of similar successes in developing countries all over the world, whatever the nature of their economies or their social structure. At the other extreme are those who doubt.... whether tourism confers any economic benefits at all, and who are convinced that it is socially very damaging. This attitude is specially prevalent in the Caribbean where it has been claimed that tourism has exacerbated social tensions, where a relatively low proportion of tourist expenditures have been retained in the island economies, and where it has had, apparently, a detrimental effect on the local wage structures, most notably in the agricultural sector.... Such adverse comment regularly includes accusations of neo-colonialisation - the perpetuation of the subservience of poor peoples to affluent visitors, and the creation of further wealth for foreign investors through the labour of the underprivileged. " (56e)

The author's view is that the truth lies somewhere between these two extremes. Planned, controlled and coordinated, tourism can be a useful tool to assist economic development; but, if allowed to develop in a haphazard fashion, tourism's negative features swiftly assume supremacy, resulting in minimal economic benefits and great social costs.

The following objectives were established at the outset.

1. To review the past and current economic and social impact of international tourism on developing countries.

2. To identify examples of, and reasons for, problems in developing countries arising from international tourism.

3. To suggest two categories of measures to alleviate these problems:

    i. a basic framework for all developing countries to follow in their tourism planning, measurement and control;

    ii. areas for collaboration on a regional and/or international basis.

The method employed in the preparation of this report was to draw together several of the past programmes of research undertaken in specific countries in order to complete an assessment of the various types and degrees of impact of international tourism. Using the problems arising from these examples, the "state of the art" in dealing with them is appraised. The presentation is deliberately simple (other than the occasional resort to some elementary algebra, no mathematics are used in the text, instead being subordinated to a technical appendix). This approach has been adopted in order that the report may fulfil the principal intention of acting as a basic primer on the subject for those relatively new to it. We believe that most benefit will be obtained by those who:

    i. are embarking on, or are in the early years of, a career in tourism in, or dealing with, developing countries;

    ii. require a general overview on the subject to guide future policy and strategy decisions.

As such, it should be particularly useful as an aid in training the staff of national tourism administrations and transnational corporations dealing with developing countries.

Section II contains an introduction to the international tourism market (its size, characteristics, structure and methods of operation) with particular emphasis on developing countries' involvement. Section III identifies a wide range of areas where international tourism can have an impact. The contrasting effects which can be brought about are exampled from the research undertaken. Examination is made of the effects of, and reasons behind, a number of problem areas. Particular attention is paid to earnings (i e whether the net income from international tourism is sufficient to warrant government support over other sectors). In Section IV, procedures, methodologies and policies are described which are aimed at reducing the problems identified in the preceding section.

Developing or less developed countries. The definition used throughout this Special Report is that adopted by the UN in its statistical series (a full analysis is given in Appendix 7). Though this pays less than full attention to the level of economic development of the countries concerned, it is considered to be the only practicable definition from the point of view of enabling a statistical analysis (albeit limited) to be made.

No two developing countries are identical. The report therefore treats them in broad categories or types. The criteria for grouping developing countries have been:

    i.   distance from major tourist generating markets;

    ii.   level of economic development;

    iii. type and extent of tourism resources;

    iv.   extent of development of, and dependence on, tourism sector.

TOURISM STATISTIC RECORDING AND COMPILATION

The different ways tourism is measured

The UN Conference on International Travel and Tourism in Rome in 1963 adopted certain definitions of the terms "visitor", "tourist" and "excursionist". These are reproduced in Appendix 8. A further meeting of the UN Statistical Commission in 1965 stressed that the compilation of statistics according to the 1963 definition would be almost impossible for the Scandinavian countries where there are no frontier formalities. With the reduction of such formalities through the spread of regional agreements like the EEC this type of problem is increasing rather than diminishing.

It is further exacerbated by the fact that the UN conference did not lay down procedures to record tourism flows. Consequently, countries have adopted differing methods and not all figures are comparable. Sir George Young (57) comments: "The rather unsatisfactory situation that exists at the moment is that... some countries collect statistics of arrivals at the frontier and many of these distinguish between tourists – those who stay more than 24 hours – and day excursionists. Other countries collect statistics of arrivals at registered accommodation but there is no international agreement as to what accommodation should be registered; and even if there was it would exclude visits to friends and it would lead to multiple recording of mobile tourists."

Inspection of the returns submitted to WTP by 106 countries for their tourism sectors in 1976 indicates the extent of the problem.

    Countries recording all visitors   75

    Countries recording tourists   68

    Countries recording arrivals at
       registered tourist accommodation   52

Figures of tourist receipts present problems of equal magnitude. There is little consistency as to whether earnings from excursionists (i e cross border visitors or cruise passengers) should be included or not; some countries include the earnings of the national flagcarrier; and there are many instances where the Central Bank's data for tourism receipts vary widely from data issued by the tourism authorities. To take just one case in point - Iran. WTO statistics based on returns from the Ministry of Information and Tourism run at around one third the level of data presented in the UN Statistical Yearbook based on IMF data obtained from official balance of payments returns.

Tourism Receipts in Iran
($ mn)

	1974	1975	1976
WTO	65.6	123.4	142.4
UN	201.0	362.0	431.0

Standardising tourism data will be a long, slow process

Clearly, then, inter-country comparisons have to be conducted with great caution until all countries (at least the major tourist receiving ones) compile standardised, comprehensive data using internationally accepted definitions, or until regular programmes of sample surveys are established by the appropriate tourism authorities to produce such data.

In the last three years a number of tourism statistic guidelines have been issued by bodies such as OECD and the UN (see Appendix 11) and the WTO has published handbooks on sampling methods and forecasting techniques. The trend is, therefore, in the right direction, but the signs are that the process of developing a standardised system of tourist flow measurement will be a long and slow one, owing to the reduction in frontier formalities noted above and a major shortfall in trained manpower in NTAs (see below).

The position is such that, as stated by BarOn (3) in his paper to Esomar in October 1977, the published data do not enable reliable answers to many vital questions facing tourism authorities, such as:

-   How many people tour abroad each year?

-   The frequency of travel, especially - how many holiday abroad every year?

-   How long are trips abroad and how many countries are visited?

-   The average (and distribution of) stay of different types of tourists in specific countries and resorts.

-   The proportion of international tourist nights spent in accommodation establishments and its relationship to domestic tourism demand (by season, resort, type of accommodation).

-   Changing patterns of tourism and their causes.

- The effectiveness of promotion campaigns - of Government Tourist Offices, publicity, special attractions, subsidies, etc.

These shortcomings are all connected with first generation tourism statistics, i e the recording of movements. It is little wonder, then, that information is so sparse on the economic and social impact of tourism which requires the compilation of second generation tourism statistics, e g employment, import content of tourism receipts.

IGNORANCE OF TOURISM'S ADMINISTRATORS

Tourism's impact has not been properly studied -

As a result (though some would argue it is the cause) of these deficiencies in tourism statistics and their gathering, the government officials charged with the administration of the tourism sector are ignorant of its effects. Writing in 1972, Sir George Young noted that many key questions are not so much unanswered as unasked and that implicit assumptions which may have been valid in the 1950s are not being challenged. ''Does tourist expenditure really filter through to, and benefit, the local economy; or has the emergence of international airlines, international hotel companies, international travel agents and international banks meant that the benefits of tourist expenditure are now being siphoned away and reverting to the tourist's country of origin rather than his destination? Is it the case that the taxpayer or the ratepayer of the tourist destination is in fact subsidising the tourist... by paying through taxes and rates for expensive tourist infrastructure and capital gains for hotels, without receiving adequate benefit? Is the traditional machinery of local government geared to the priorities and requirements of local residents, able to control or plan for an ever-increasing influx of visitors from abroad? To what extent is the sustained and costly effort made by tourist authorities on behalf of many historic cities to attract and accommodate more tourists undermining their very appeal as tourist destinations? If there are saturation levels beyond which further growth in tourist arrivals brings more problems than rewards, what is being done to calculate those levels and see that they are not exceeded? On a national level, is it really in the best interests of LDCs to graduate from an agricultural economy to a service economy based on tourism without the intermediate stage of a manufacturing economy? Might the effort of diverting a country's labour force into the tourist industry - where productivity gains are difficult to achieve - impede growth rather than accelerate it?'' (57)

- particularly by the industry's administrators

Nor do matters appear to have changed a great deal in the six years since these information gaps were identified. It is true that the oil price rises and subsequent global recession forced governments to reconsider their priorities and some of them paid close attention to tourism. However, much of the initiative for the tourism impact studies undertaken has come from academic circles and there remains much ignorance among tourism administrators. Furthermore, those studies which have been undertaken have been of a once-off nature and few LDCs have set in process the machinery to gather the necessary data to enable ongoing assessment of tourism's impacts.

In his review of tourism in 1977 in The Big Picture, Somerset R Waters identifies "one of the greatest problems now concerning the worldwide travel industry" as being the fact that "government leaders and academic economists who influence government policy do not know how little they know about the enormous economic impact of tourism."(53) There has been little attempt to measure the economic impact of the rapid increase in transportation (aircraft fleets, private car owner-ship, international hire car networks) and accommodation facilities. With the development of computer systems like the UK Post Office's Prestel and the arrival of the microprocessor, which are facilitating communication and coordination of travel and tourism, the urgency of the need to measure this impact will become ever more pressing.

The Tourism Industry

As a backcloth to the assessment of international tourism's impact on LDCs, this section contains an analysis of the characteristics, size, growth and structure of the industry.

CHARACTERISTICS OF TOURISM

An invisible export with differences

The UN/WTO definition of tourism (reproduced in Appendix 3) recognises three elements:

   i.   purpose (includes all purposes except permanent migration);

   ii.   time (excludes stays under 24 hours - excursionists - or over one year -- migrants);

   iii. particular situations (excludes sea cruise passengers and transit traffic).

The term "visitor" is used to include the categories noted above which are excluded from the 'tourist" grouping.

As in trade, in tourism a distinction is drawn between domestic (or internal) and foreign (or international) tourism. This report concentrates on international tourism because it is this sector that has the widest range of economic (e g balance of payments) and social (e g different languages, cultures) impacts. The implications of international tourism for domestic tourism are, however, included in the evaluation of the costs (e g overcrowding of tourist facilities thereby preventing their use by domestic tourists) and benefits (e g reduced price of facilities to local residents brought about by foreign tourists taking up the spare capacity). In this connection, it is important to note that domestic tourism (involving stays of at least one night away from home) outstrips international tourism by 4:1 (according to a WTO survey) in terms of movements.

In economic terms, international tourism is an invisible export which differs from other forms of international trade in several ways.

1. The consumer "collects" the product from the exporting country, thereby eliminating any freight costs for the exporter, except in cases where the airlines used are those of the tourist receiving country.

2. Demand for the pleasure segment of international tourism is highly sensitive to non-economic factors such as local disturbances, political troubles and changes in the fashionability of resorts/countries created largely by media coverage. At the same time, international tourism is in general both price and income elastic. Changes in either of these two variables normally result in a more than proportional change in pleasure travel[1].

3. By means of specific fiscal measures, the exporting (tourist receiving) country can manipulate exchange rates so that those for tourists are higher or lower (normally the latter in order to attract a greater number of tourists) than those at which other foreign trade takes place. At the same time, tourists are permitted to buy in the domestic market at the prices prevailing for the local resident (exceptions being the duty free tourist shops operated in many Caribbean islands and elsewhere).

4. Tourism is a multifaceted product which directly affects several sectors in the economy (e g hotels and other forms of accommodation, shops, restaurants, local transport firms, entertainment establishments, handicraft producers) and indirectly affects many others (e g equipment manufacturers, utilities).

5. Tourism brings many more non-pecuniary benefits and costs (i e social and cultural) than other export industries.

SIZE AND GROWTH OF INTERNATIONAL TOURISM

Trends over the last 15 years

The WTO reports that, in 1978, there were between 260 and 265 mn international tourist arrivals in the world, an increase of between 8 and 10 per cent on 1977. The corresponding rise in international tourist receipts was 11 per cent - to a 1978 level in excess of $60 bn. Over the 15 years between 1963 and 1978, international tourist arrivals rose at an annual average rate of 7.7 per cent, whilst receipts from international tourism recorded an average growth of over 13.6 per cent per annum in current terms.

The average levels of growth in tourist arrivals were achieved in spite of the impact of the Opec decision to boost oil prices (to the extent that the price of aviation fuel quadrupled between March 1973 and March 1974). This had the effect of causing a decline in tourist arrivals in 1974 (the first for over two decades), followed by a year of slow recovery in 1975. By 1976, however, the recovery was complete and new record levels of tourism were being established.

---

1 The evidence on price and income elasticity is somewhat conflicting. Bond and Ladman (4) found that US tourism to Latin America was price inelastic (0.71) due to the fact that, at the time of their research, travel to alternative destinations was relatively much more expensive. They found that income elasticity was around unity (0.99). Edwards, however, found that "income elasticities of demand appear to lie between 1.0 and 1.8" and "relative price elasticities...between 1.0 and 1.6".

An apparently different picture emerges when international tourist receipts figures are examined. Growth has been consistent throughout the last 15 years and the rate of growth only slightly impeded by the oil price increases. However, the data in Table 1 relate to receipts in current terms, not at constant prices, and the high rates of growth are principally due to inflation, particularly in 1975 when a 2 per cent increase in tourist arrivals produced a 17 per cent rise in tourist receipts and in 1976 when a 2.8 per cent volume growth was accompanied by a 28 per cent value increase.

Table 1

International Tourist Arrivals and Receipts, 1963-1978

	Tourist arrivals		Tourist receipts [a]	
Year	No. (mn)	Annual increase (%)	Amount ($ mn)	Annual increase (%)
1963	93	14.2	8,300	6.4
1964	108	16.1	9,600	15.7
1965	116	6.9	11,000	14.6
1966	131	13.2	12,500	13.6
1967	140	6.6	13,400	7.2
1968	140	0.1	13,800	3.0
1969	154	10.3	15,400	11.6
1970	168	9.3	17,900	16.2
1971	182	7.8	20,900	16.8
1972	198	9.1	24,200	15.8
1973	215	8.6	27,600	14.0
1974	209	-2.8	29,000	5.1
1975	213	2.0	34,000	17.2
1976	219	2.8	43,500	27.9
1977	240	9.6	54,000	24.1
1978 [b]	260 to 265	8.3 to 10.4	60,000 to 62,500	11.1 to 15.7

Average annual rate of growth (%)	Tourist arrivals	Tourist receipts
1963-1970	8.9	11.6
1970-1978	5.6 to 5.9	16.4
1963-1978	7.1 to 7.2	14.1 to 14.4

a Current prices. b Preliminary estimates.

Source: WTO.

LDCs' share of international tourism

How are LDCs faring in attracting international tourists and reaping the foreign exchange benefit? The official data give only a superficial answer and cannot be fully relied upon because, as pointed out in Section 3 (Areas of Economic and Social Impact, page 142) the numbers of countries filing returns to the WTO are incomplete (and vary from year to year) and their methods of compiling statistics differ from each other and are frequently changed.

The most comprehensive attempt at analysing LDCs' performance in international tourism is presented in the 1975 study prepared by the then International Union of Official Travel Organisations (now WTO) for the UN Economic and Social Council (Ecosoc). Using the UN Council for Trade and Development (Unctad) definition of

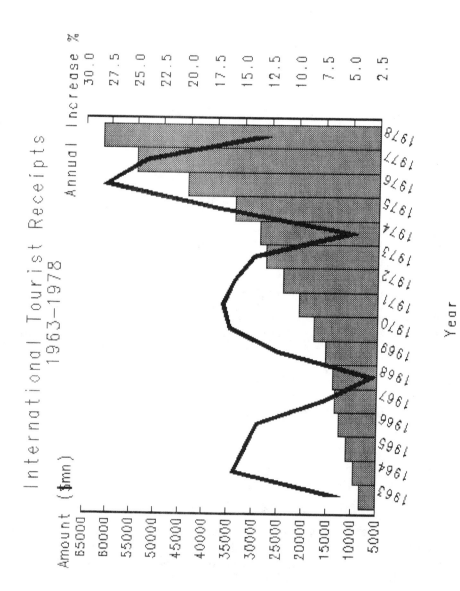

Figure 1a

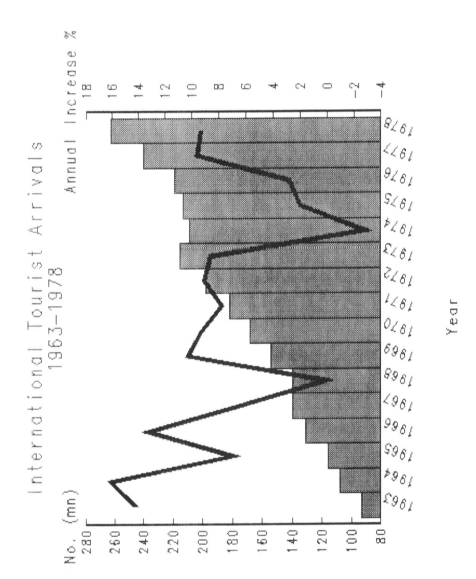

Figure 1b

127

LDCs, this study found that around one fifth of tourism expenditure accrued to LDCs over the period 1962 to 1973. Some growth had occurred in LDCs' share over the period but this increase had been small. The IUOTO report (49) pointed out, however, that LDCs' share of world tourism receipts had become slightly larger than their share of international trade. Over the 1962-73 period their relative share of tourism receipts rose from 18.8 per cent to 20.8 per cent, while their share of world trade fell from 20.5 per cent in 1962 to stabilise at around 18 per cent.

Despite the optimistic tone of the comments in the IUOTO report, the trends of the data in Table 2 are perturbing. LDCs achieved a fairly rapid (16 per cent per annum) growth in tourist arrivals between 1962 and 1973, nearly doubling their market share. In terms of receipts, however, their progress was nowhere near so marked - a 13 per cent average annual increase but an improvement in market share of only 2 percentage points. LDCs, therefore, lost out to developed countries in terms of earnings per tourist over the period. This concern is heightened by the fact that the erosion of LDCs' gross tourism receipts (not reflected in the IUOTO/WTO figures) is greater than that of their developed country counterparts. This is due, in part, to the locus of control of distribution and, in some cases, to the ownership of LDCs' tourist products being with corporations or individuals based outside the LDC (see Structure of the Tourism Industry, page 136). Another factor contributing to the high rate of leakage of LDCs' tourism receipts is their need to import many items (e g construction materials, food and beverages) in which developed countries are much nearer self-sufficiency.

Table 2

LDCs' Share in World Trade and Tourism, 1962-73

| Year | Tourist arrivals | | Tourist receipts | | Trade |
	No. (mn)	% of world total	Amount ($ mn)	% of world total	% of world total
1962	6.0	7.3	1,468	18.8	20.5
1968	10.3	7.4	2,348	17.0	18.5
1969	13.4	8.7	2,539	16.5	18.1
1970	16.2	9.6	3,389	18.9	17.8
1971	20.1	11.1	3,865	18.5	18.0
1972	26.7	13.5	4,909	20.3	18.0
1973	29.4	13.7	5,737	20.8	18.1

Source: IUOTO report for UN Ecosoc.

The data deficiencies referred to earlier make it impossible to update the figures in Table 2 on a directly comparable basis. To produce estimates of LDCs' performance over the last five years it has been necessary to use a basket of 30 countries (see footnote to Table 3 for the countries and the criteria for their selection). Between them the 30 countries account for around two thirds of international tourism activity in LDCs.

The trends noted during the previous decade appear to have continued over the last five years. LDCs' share of tourist arrivals has continued to increase - from 13.7 per cent in 1973 to around the 15 per cent mark in 1977, when international tourist

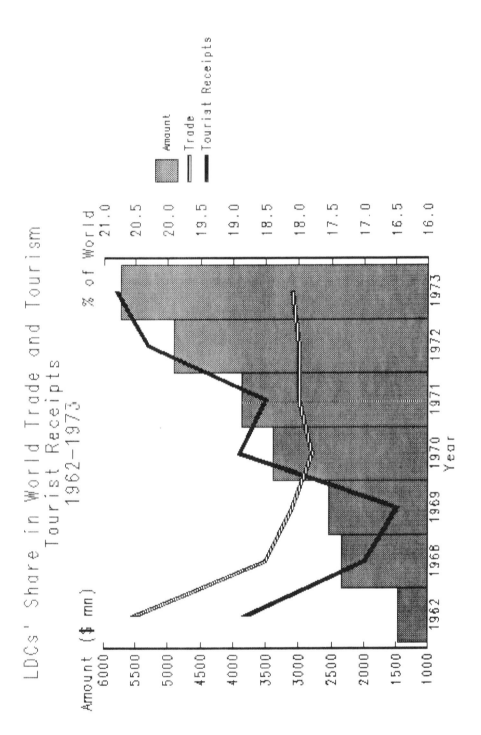

Figure 2a

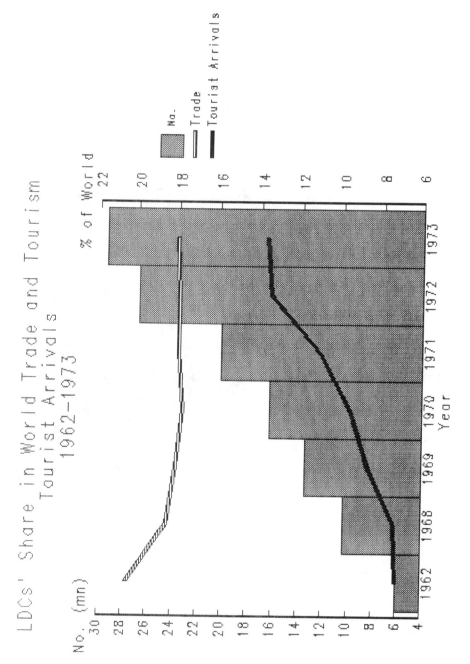

LDCs' Share in World Trade and Tourism
Tourist Arrivals
1962-1973

Figure 2b

130

arrivals in LDCs are estimated at between 34 and 38 mn. However, no growth has been recorded in LDCs' share of international tourists' expenditure. Indeed, a decline appears to have taken place, a 20.8 per cent share in 1973 dropping to around 18 per cent in 1977, when LDCs' tourism receipts were between an estimated $9.5 bn and $10 bn. One implication of these trends is that tourists are spending less (relative to visits to developed countries) per trip to LDCs. Examination of the sample countries suggests one major cause - with the notable exception of Egypt (which has benefited by attracting high spending tourists from fellow Arab states), the average receipts per tourist arrival trend in those countries which are beginning to establish themselves as important tourism centres (e g Brazil, Venezuela) is noticeably downward as a result of lower budget tourists being attracted by cheaper group package tours. Certainly LDCs' rate of increase in tourism earnings has fallen far below their increase in debt - to $190 bn in 1976 and may be as high as $300 bn currently - brought about by the Opec oil price increases. LDCs' tourism receipts were equivalent to over 6 per cent of LDCs' export earnings in the early 1970s, a contribution which fell to below 3 per cent in 1974 in the wake of the oil producing states' vastly increased income from oil exports, but has since recovered to 3.4 per cent in 1977. Excluding Opec states, LDC export earnings doubled between 1973 and 1977, while tourism receipts rose by around 70 per cent over the same period (assuming that the tourism performance of Opec and non-Opec LDCs does not vary significantly).

Table 3

Growth in LDCs' Trade and Tourism, 1973-77

	% change over previous year		Exports		% of world trade	
Year	Tourist arrivals	Tourist receipts	Inc Opec	Exc Opec	Inc Opec	Exc Opec
1974	0.2	9.8	104.3	46.9	26.9	11.9
1975	6.4	9.4	-6.9	-3.4	24.2	11.3
1976	5.6	20.4	21.1	21.2	25.7	11.9
1977	8.0	18.2	12.8	18.7	25.6	12.5[a]

1977
No. tourists (mn):	34 to 38
% of world total:	14.2 to 15.8
Tourist receipts ($ bn):	9.5 to 10
% of world total:	17.6 to 18.5

a Estimates based on partial data only.

Source: Based on WTO and UN data for basket of 30 LDCs.

The LDCs were: Africa: Benin, Egypt, Ghana (replaced by Nigeria in receipts calculations), Kenya, Morocco, Tunisia, Tanzania, Upper Volta (replaced by Sierra Leone in receipts calculations), Zaire; Americas: Bermuda, Bahamas, Barbados, Brazil, Costa Rica, Haiti, Jamaica, Mexico (excluding border tourism), Puerto Rico, Venezuela; Asia: Bangladesh, Cyprus, Hong Kong, India, South Korea, Philippines, Singapore, Sri Lanka, Thailand, Turkey; Oceania: French Polynesia. The countries were selected to be as representative a cross-section as possible taking account of geographic spread, extent of economic development, range of tourism resources, state of development of tourism sector and the various political and social systems. The primary criteria for inclusion in the sample obviously had to be the preparation of usable tourism data series covering the last five years. The data used were extracted either from WTO or UN sources; only one source was used for each country in the sample.

TRENDS IN TOURISM

The post-1960 boom in tourism (domestic, as well as international) has been brought about by a combination of increased wealth and awareness among consumers and technological advances which have served to reduce the real costs of travel. The 13 per cent average annual increase in the current terms value of world trade over the last two decades has served to maintain growth in business tourism. The positive determinants of increased leisure tourism can be considered in two broad classifications: demand and supply.

Factors affecting demand for tourism

Personal disposable income. Despite the hiccoughs created by the 1973/74 oil price rises and subsequent worldwide recession, there has been a steady rise during the last two decades in the purchasing power and discretionary incomes of the populace of almost all countries. This has enabled middle and, increasingly, lower income groups to spend part of their income on non-essentials such as leisure travel.

Paid holidays. Paid leave entitlements (excluding public holidays) have nearly doubled during the last 20 years to a current average of just under four weeks. Furthermore, as noted by Edwards (21f), further increases of 1 to 1.5 weeks may be expected over the next decade.

Urban build-up. People living in urban areas are subject to greater social tensions and pressure than their rural counterparts. The increasing urbanisation of the post-war period has highlighted the need for leisure activities and rest in a different environment.

Awareness and attitudes. Greater awareness of, and interest in, foreign countries has been generated by higher education and the mass media. This in turn has led to new attitudes towards leisure travel. Once considered a luxury, an annual holiday is now widely viewed as a necessity and part of the consumption pattern of all but the most underprivileged social groups. Evidence of this is provided by a WTO survey which sought to ascertain the proportion of the population who would be prepared to forgo or cut down on various products/services.

Item	% of sample willing to forgo/cut down
Holidays	6
Comfort	9
Food	14
Other recreational activities	16
Car travel	27
Clothing	28

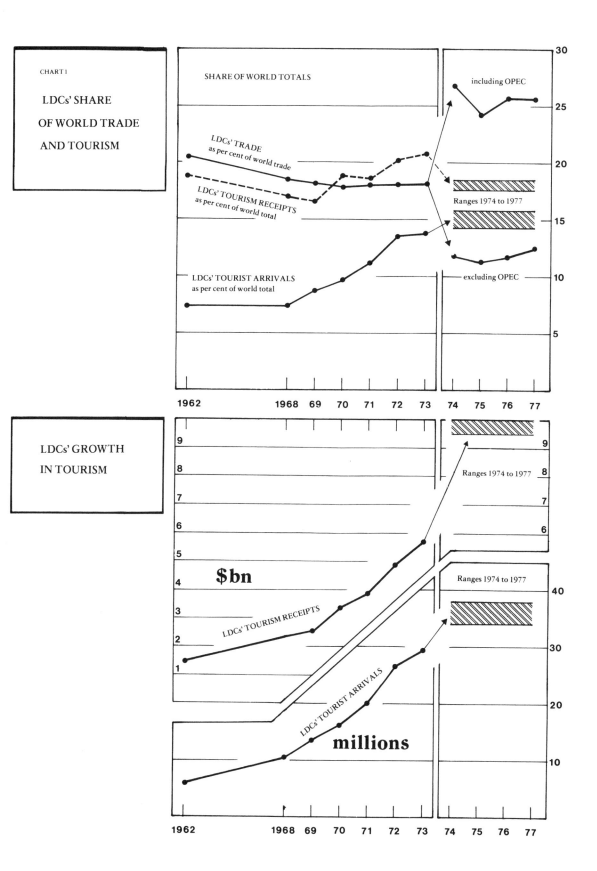

CHART I

LDCs' SHARE
OF WORLD TRADE
AND TOURISM

SHARE OF WORLD TOTALS

including OPEC

LDCs' TRADE
as per cent of world trade

LDCs' TOURISM RECEIPTS
as per cent of world total

Ranges 1974 to 1977

LDCs' TOURIST ARRIVALS
as per cent of world total

excluding OPEC

1962   1968 69 70 71 72 73   74 75 76 77

LDCs' GROWTH
IN TOURISM

Ranges 1974 to 1977

$bn

LDCs' TOURISM RECEIPTS

Ranges 1974 to 1977

LDCs' TOURIST ARRIVALS

millions

1962   1968 69 70 71 72 73   74 75 76 77

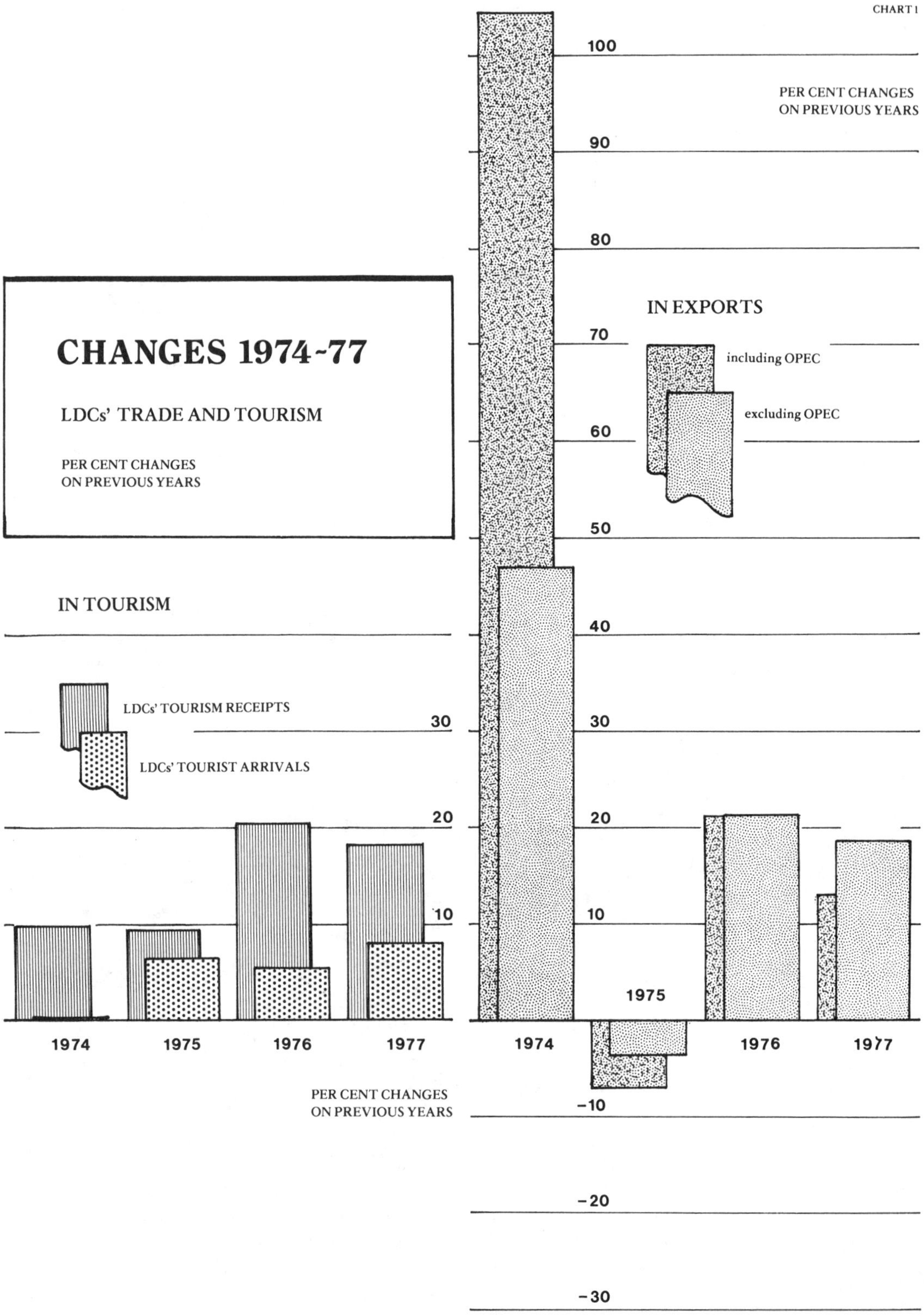

CHART 1
CHANGES 1974-77
LDCs' TRADE AND TOURISM
PER CENT CHANGES
ON PREVIOUS YEARS
IN TOURISM
LDCs' TOURISM RECEIPTS
LDCs' TOURIST ARRIVALS
30
20
10
1974
1975
1976
1977
PER CENT CHANGES
ON PREVIOUS YEARS
100
PER CENT CHANGES
ON PREVIOUS YEARS
90
80
IN EXPORTS
70
including OPEC
excluding OPEC
60
50
40
30
20
10
1975
1974
1976
1977
-10
-20
-30

Factors affecting supply of tourism

Mobility. The greater supply of mass produced motor cars has combined with rising incomes to increase substantially private car ownership. This growth reacts with developing tourism demand in a two way relationship of cause and effect.

Reducing real cost of travel. In the decade prior to 1974, modern transport technology, especially in aviation, served significantly to reduce both the cost of, and time required for, travel. In the last two years, the strong cartel system of fare fixing operated by the International Air Transport Association (Iata) and the largely protectionist system of route allocation determined by the civil aviation authorities of the countries concerned have started to be broken down. This liberalisation has encouraged more non-scheduled services and a greater range of low, special condition fares on certain routes (e g North Atlantic).

Facilities, amenities and promotion. The development of new tourism facilities and amenities, their promotion in travel generating markets, and the new forms of travel (e g package tours) and methods of selling it (e g direct sell) have combined to boost holiday demand.

All of these factors will continue to apply over coming decades, although the reduction in the real costs of travel may be approaching the limit. The "natural" (i e excluding major depressant effects such as the Opec oil price rises of late 1973, or big boosts like the liberalisation of one-stop charters by the US Civil Aeronautics Board (CAB) in September 1975 and the introduction of low budget/standby fares in September 1977) rate of growth of international tourism over the next decade (i e real growth in expenditure) is forecast by Edwards (21f) at 7.3 per cent between 1980 and 1985 and 6.7 per cent between 1985 and 1990.

How are LDCs likely to fare in the coming decades?

Rosenblatt (39) concludes that because "per capita income in the countries that border upon them tends to be low, and the main tourist-generating countries are distant" from them "most developing countries are not in a good position for setting up a major tourist industry in the future".

The balance of evidence, however, suggests that LDCs will at least hold their current shares of world tourism. The natural development of vacation tourism has often been likened to the outward spread of the ripples created by a stone being dropped into a pond. As the consumers of North America and Western Europe look to new destinations, the LDCs of South America, Africa, Asia and Oceania are well positioned to become important receiving countries.

Gray (18) distinguishes between two forms of tourism: sunlust tourism (primarily oriented towards climate, beach and amenities which do not significantly differ in culture or kind from those available nearby) and wanderlust tourism, where the emphasis is on change, different culture, cuisine and a larger, ostensibly educational, element.

LDCs have always attracted the non-institutionalised wanderlust tourists for whom a developed tourist infrastructure is unnecessary, if not a positive deterrent. However, it was to take advantage of the growth in institutionalised, sunlust tourism that LDCs have, over the last decade and a half, encouraged extensive investment in

135

tourism development. LDCs may, therefore, reasonably expect, being located in the main in the outer ripples, to experience a growth at least in line with that of total international tourism demand over the next decade. This expectation is increased by the probability of greater LDC involvement in world trade, thereby ensuring a rise in business travel. As shown by the experience of the last few years, it would be incautious to anticipate any significant expansion of LDCs' market share since the increased personal disposable incomes which will increasingly allow the middle classes to travel to long haul destinations for their vacations will also bring on to the short haul vacation market those lower income groups for whom previously a foreign holiday was not economically feasible. Developed and developing countries are thus likely to share the "natural" growth of international tourism broadly evenly.

Two points should be stressed in connection with a forecast of any significant growth in international tourism to LDCs. First, growth will be centred on institutionalised tourism which will entail LDCs being in closer involvement with the agents responsible for organising travel. The fact that these organisations are nearly all based in the source countries has clear implications for the degree and method of control exercised over their operations by LDC governments. This matter is taken up in Section 4. Secondly, the nature of tourism demand and the influences upon it are so complex (a WTO study lists 133 factors determining travel demand) that LDCs cannot expect a blanket growth rate. Some will fare exceptionally well, others may suffer periods of little growth, dependent upon their performance (in the potential tourists' eyes) across the factors influencing demand.

STRUCTURE OF THE TOURISM INDUSTRY

Chain of distribution

Tourists travel as individuals or in groups. Tourists can either travel independently, purchasing the means of transport and accommodation either directly from the suppliers or via their agents; or they can take an inclusive tour (or package tour), purchasing a variety of services where they are unable to distinguish between the cost of the ingredients. Inclusive tours may be on an individual or group basis.

All tourists, except those individuals travelling totally independently, have recourse to some form of travel organiser. The main economic agents in the tourism industry are:

    i.   passenger transport carriers, i e international airlines, chiefly operated by transnational corporations (TNCs), rail, coach, ship and local transport carriers;

    ii.   accommodation, catering and entertainment establishments;

    iii.   travel agents, i e retailers who act on behalf of hotel companies, airlines, tour operators, shipping lines, etc, taking the part of intermediaries between the tourist and those who supply tourism services, and receiving a commission from the latter;

    iv.   tour operators, i e wholesalers who purchase the individual ingredients of a package of tourist related activities and combine them into a composite product.

These sectors, together with those concerned with the provision of financial services, retailing and information, constitute tourist related activities. The chain of distribution of tourism services is illustrated in chart 1.

Tourism services are owned or controlled in the generating countries

The structure of ownership and control of tourism service wholesaling and retailing militates against the interests of the destination country because, as pointed out in the UN Ecosoc/IUOTO report, "practically all organisations retailing tourism services direct (or wholesaling via travel agents) to the general public in the countries of Western Europe, North America and Japan... are located in these territories. Few organisations, with the exception of scheduled airlines which are cushioned against full competitive pressures by bilateral agreements and pooling arrangements, have attempted to sell travel, in any form, direct to the public, in a state which is neither their native country nor a neighbouring country with similar consumer characteristics (e g the Scandinavian countries)."

There could be a number of reasons for this pattern. First, in order to construct and market tourism products which the public wants, the tour operator (and travel agent) needs a clear understanding of the requirements of prospective consumers which he is more likely to have through living in the same society. Secondly, the main tourist generating markets are, by definition, the richest areas in economic terms, with a stronger and more sophisticated commercial network than other areas of the world. Finally, there is the economies of scale argument. The tour operator in the generating market is usually able to spread his overhead expenses across all the destinations he features - whereas a tour operator from a host country and promoting only its own destinations will have less room for manoeuvrability, particularly if he sells his product in more than one generating market.

The problem is exacerbated by the fact that a significant proportion of the tourism product itself is owned or controlled by foreign organisations. The extent of foreign ownership can be measured and legislated for fairly straightforwardly. Much more difficult to quantify and regulate is the control exercised over the distribution of LDCs' tourism product by foreign airlines, tour operators, etc. Though having little or no financial stake, these organisations exercise a substantial influence on decision taking by means of the structure and terms of contractual arrangements. A foreign tour operator can influence the numbers of package tourists who go to a given destination by means of the programmes he constructs and the promotional assistance he places behind them; and he will, in large part, select which destinations to feature most heavily according to the best deal he has obtained from the recipient country's tourism product proprietors. Similarly, the scheduled airlines of the developed nations play a major role in influencing the numbers of their nationals who travel to a given country stemming from their dominant position as carriers of tourists from the generating markets.

With control firmly vested in the hands of the tourism service suppliers of the tourist originating countries, there is always the possibility of a conflict of interest. For example, a country may decide to increase its promotional activities in order to attract more tourists to fill spare hotel bed capacity. But, unless the airlines agree to increase the frequency of flights or amount of capacity for promotional fare travellers or numbers of charter operations, the country's ambition cannot be achieved. The withdrawal by Pan American of its Caribbean services to its four

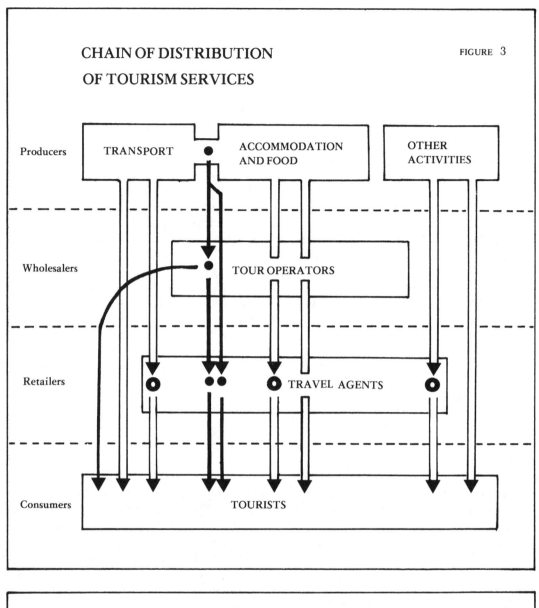

CHAIN OF DISTRIBUTION
OF TOURISM SERVICES

FIGURE 3

Producers — TRANSPORT · ACCOMMODATION AND FOOD — OTHER ACTIVITIES

Wholesalers — TOUR OPERATORS

Retailers — TRAVEL AGENTS

Consumers — TOURISTS

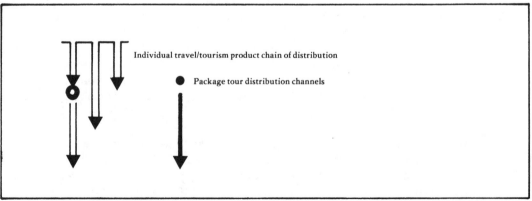

Individual travel/tourism product chain of distribution

Package tour distribution channels

least profitable calls (Guadeloupe, Martinique, Barbados and Bermuda) in April 1975 and Eastern Airlines' decision to cut out five other Caribbean destinations (Aruba, Haiti, Kingston in Jamaica, Curacao and Ponce in Puerto Rico) are examples of this point.

Hotel groups –

Limited locally available capital investment funds have dictated the method of development of the hotel sector in LDCs. Most developed initially on a small scale (30 rooms would have been regarded as a large hotel in the Caribbean 15 years ago) and were family owned and operated. Since the standard of rooms and service in these hotels varied widely, governments introduced grading systems. With limited funds to make the necessary improvements, many such hotels were accorded a low rating. Tour operators, aware of how just one customer's complaints can snowball and seriously affect their own businesses, will rarely include low graded hotels in their tour programmes. The result was that, as demand grew for foreign holidays, there was a shortage of hotels offering the required level of amenities and service. Thus was born the international hotel chain.

There are four main ways in which international hotel chains operate: sole or majority ownership; management contract; lease; franchise. The last three methods apply when the chain has a minority holding or no financial interest in the hotel. Though some of the groups have a direct investment in a number of hotels they operate, the method they prefer is the management contract, which offers a protected return irrespective of the performance of the hotel.

There has been no overall assessment of the degree of foreign ownership and control of hotels in LDCs but the Commonwealth Secretariat, in an unpublished report on international tourism, quotes a World Bank estimate of local ownership of luxury class hotels in Barbados as 23 per cent in 1971 (7). This example may be typical (although a wide range may be expected between LDCs, reflecting the state of development of the local tourism sector) but more important is the fact that the influence wielded by international hotel chains is greater than is indicated by taking a simple percentage of rooms controlled, since their hotel rooms are specifically designed for and marketed to foreign tourists.

– airlines and other transport operators –

Virtually every country has a national flag carrier even if, in some LDCs, they neither own nor operate the aircraft bearing their livery, instead entering into a management and/or technical assistance contract with another airline – invariably of a developed country. For example, British Airways has interests in Air Pacific, Cathay Pacific, New Hebrides Airways, THY Turkish Airlines, Cyprus Airways and Gibraltar Airways. In addition, through International Aeradio Ltd, BA provides technical services at major international airports in the Middle East and elsewhere.

Almost all charter airlines are owned in, and operate from, developed countries. Most developed countries' scheduled airlines operate a subsidiary (e g Lufthansa and Condor) and no LDC has an independent charter airline of significance. The only instances where charter airlines are established in LDCs is when the scheduled airline has a charter subsidiary. There are a number of such examples (for instance, Air India Charters), even if in some of the cases the charter subsidiary has not, as yet, been activated (e g Rotatur – Varig's paper subsidiary in Brazil).

The great majority of tourists are, therefore, transported to their LDC destinations by an airline of a developed country. The largest airline from a developing country, viz Aeromexico, ranks 33rd in the world's airlines.

Of the other commercial transport operators carrying tourists to, and within, LDCs, virtually all shipping and cruise lines are owned in, and operated from, developed countries. Even land transport operators (e g coaches, buses) are likely to be owned within the developed, generating country if the journey planned is one of considerable duration involving travel to several countries (such as a mini tour of Asia or Africa starting and finishing in London).

- and tour operators

Tour operating is a business geared to mass marketing. The destination is, to a large extent, irrelevant. The tour operator designs a programme offering certain standard components and markets it principally on the reputation of his brand name and the assurance of quality which this gives to the customer. And yet, at the same time, the tour operator has a powerful negotiating position (unless demand considerably exceeds supply of hotel beds) because of his ability to influence where tourists spend their holidays.

Despite the fragmentation of tourist demand and relative ease of market entry, there has been a trend over recent years of increasing concentration in the tour operating sector through horizontal and vertical integration. The key to the resolution of why this concentration has happened lies in the fact that the degree of tour operator concentration is far greater in Western Europe than in the USA. The large land area of the USA is clearly one major contributory factor to there being considerably more tour operators in the USA than in European countries. However, there is another important factor. Charter IT programmes have been available in Western Europe for approaching two decades whereas, in the USA, it is only in the last three years or so (since US CAB authorisation of one-stop inclusive tours (OTCs) in September 1975) that such programmes have been offered.

The large number of bodies involved in a charter IT programme necessitates the securing of adequate hotel beds in the destination. Throughout the 1960s, there was considerable competition amongst tour operators for hotel beds in Mediterranean resorts. The most common consequence was for tour operators to enter into longer term contracts for hotel beds, two to five years instead of one year. Combined with the need to obtain aircraft on time charters to secure the most competitive rates, this placed a considerable strain on tour operators' finances. Western European tour operators, therefore, sought to integrate vertically, tying up their own aircraft seats and hotel beds (e g the Court Line group had its own aircraft, the Clarkson tour operating company and hotels in the Caribbean and Spain).

Wright (55) illustrates this point by quoting a study prepared in the late 1960s, which concluded that the costs of entry into the UK charter tour operating business were between £4 mn and £5 mn: half devoted to time charters for aircraft seats; £1 mn to secure hotel beds; and the balance for administration and launch costs. As a result, acquisitions, mergers and cooperative agreements increased in an attempt to build up to the minimum economic scale of operation. This occurred to such an extent that by 1973 in the UK more than 50 per cent of all the inclusive tour holidays were marketed by five companies; and in West Germany, the IT market is virtually controlled by two companies, NUR-GUT[1] and TUI-ITS[2].

---

1 NUR-GUT: Neckermann und Reisen-GUT Reisen. 2 TUI-ITS: Touristik Union International-International Tourist Services.

This trend was not halted until the downturn in demand consequent upon high rates of inflation and recession in the world economy in the 1973-76 period. The collapse of the Court Line in 1974, along with other European tour operators, brought it home to tour operators that they had been operating on far too narrow margins and that the bigger they grew, the greater were the risks. Over recent years, the trend has been for tour operators to move back to shorter term contracts and to minimise their direct investment in the tourist destinations. Further concentration may take place, but principally through attrition and at nowhere near the pace of the 1965-72 period, and vertical integration will spread, though limited to the wholesale-retail sectors in the generating markets.

In the USA, right up until late 1975, the tour operating sector was highly fragmented, with large numbers of wholesalers serving each of the main communities (i e north east seaboard, mid west based on Chicago, west coast, etc) and there were hardly any national operators. This pattern arose because no one company could obtain a marked competitive advantage (the tour basing fares were established by Iata and available to all registered travel companies provided they met the stipulations of minimum/maximum stays, etc). The high capital requirement, large minimum economic scale of operation and price competitive advantages offered by the large volume charter ITs were not available - not, that is, until the last three years, and now there are signs that one or two large tour operators are emerging (e g Caribbean Holidays). Vertical integration is also occurring, with US tour operators purchasing their own aircraft and, in a few cases, leasing or managing hotels in the destination areas. The Commonwealth Secretariat study (7) gives the example of one US tour operator which, in March 1977, owned four aircraft providing a total capacity of 1, 270 seats with plans to expand this by a further 300 to 400 seats. Its operations are concentrated in the Caribbean during the winter and in Europe during the summer.

Another type of tour operator is located in the tourist receiving country. In practice these organisations act as tour operators for local residents on their domestic or overseas travel but, in respect of package tourists from the major tourist generating markets of the developed world, they act solely as land arrangement organising agents for tour operators of the source countries. In respect of destinations which are not large volume resorts, the tour operating principal will use the local companies as middlemen to put together the destination portion of the package. The local tour organising agents have no presence in the major tourist generating markets nor any direct contact with tourists from these markets except insofar as the tourist may independently purchase services (outside the package tour).

Areas of Economic and Social Impact

Tourism has an impact on a wide range of economic and social areas. This chapter seeks to identify these areas and to outline the main pros and cons attributed to them by supporters and opposers of the tourism industry. Special attention is paid to problem areas, particularly the earnings leakage issue and methodologies for the measurement of the net worth of tourism to LDCs.

ECONOMIC FACTORS

Benefits that can accrue-

International tourism is perceived by the governments of many LDCs as an attractive means of economic development for a variety of reasons, including the following.

1. It can aid economic development by earning foreign exchange and reducing balance of payments difficulties. It is a sector which is subject to few trading restrictions, unlike many commodities/products exported by LDCs.

2. It is a growth sector with relatively high price and income elasticities of demand (unlike most primary products).

3. It represents a means of raising the level of employment.

4. It can be an important agent in diversifying the structure of the host country's economy, particularly in the case of those LDCs which are dependent on one or two primary products.

5. It can balance out the regional disparities in income and employment since areas suitable for tourism development are often situated far from the main centres of economic activity.

6. Higher levels of intermediate demand may result from tourists' expenditure both from the provision of accommodation and other services within the host country and, at a step removed, from the locally supplied inputs required by hotels, food producers, etc.

7. It provides taxation revenue for governments.

8. It can serve to promote a better image abroad which, in time, may lead to increased foreign investment.

– but not always do

Not surprisingly, bearing in mind the large differences in LDCs' tourism resources, geographic location, level and structure of economic development and policies with respect to tourism development, there is considerable variation in the extent to

142

which these advantages accrue to LDCs. It is clearly not easy directly to compare countries as disparate as Bangladesh and the Bahamas! Of late, there has been a swing away from viewing tourism favourably. Taking the more successful LDCs as norms, some of the research and literature on other LDCs have indicated a lower than anticipated return from the resources allocated to tourism. This, in turn, has led to a questioning of the economic benefits claimed for tourism and a call to reduce the ownership/control enjoyed by foreign enterprises of the host country's tourism product.

Although there is considerable literature in this field, the results produced are normally incomplete or otherwise unsatisfactory (owing to data limitations) and frequently conflict (owing to the different social and economic structures of the countries under study). This subsection draws on the literature to illustrate the economic costs and benefits of international tourism in the experiences of a wide range of LDCs. The social factors and the implications of foreign ownership/control are dealt with in the two succeeding subsections.

FOREIGN EXCHANGE

Tourism earns foreign exchange -

Virtually all LDCs suffer periodic, sometimes chronic, shortages of foreign exchange (FE) which constrain their capacity to purchase goods and services for investment and other needs. Commodity trade, which is the principal FE earner for most LDCs, has not provided a revenue growth to match the increase in the imports bill. Import substitution and local processing can provide a means of saving or earning FE but many LDCs run into the problem of limited domestic markets or restricted access to foreign markets. In this context, tourism's advocates see it as a prima facie sector for encouragement by the governments of LDCs. Demand (and expenditure) is growing faster than global inflation rates; there are few trade barriers; and FE is earned more conveniently than from manufactured goods since the customer brings himself to the point of sale at his own expense and takes immediate delivery of the services.

- at a cost

There are, however, drawbacks. Tourism receipts data (such as in Tables 1 and 2) are in gross terms. From these totals must be subtracted the costs of a number of items (leakages) required to service tourism.

1. The import cost of goods and services consumed by non-resident visitors. This includes not only direct imports but also the import component of goods produced in the tourist receiving country for sale to the tourist.

2. The import cost of capital goods for tourist amenities such as hotels, vehicles and infrastructure.

3. FE payments to foreign factors of production (interest, rental and profit from foreign capital invested in the tourism sector, commission to foreign travel organisers such as tour operators and travel agents and the repatriated portion of the wages paid to foreign specialists - generally in the hotel sector - employed in LDCs).

4. Expenditure for services abroad, e g promotion and publicity, personnel training programmes.

These represent the FE cost of establishing and operating a tourism sector, but before a country's tourism account can be calculated consideration must be paid to any tourism investments held by the country overseas and expenditure by its own residents on tourism abroad.

The extent of FE cost of the tourism sector varies widely between the different types of LDC and over time. The leakages depend on the particular pattern of tourist demand and the host country's ability to produce the capital, intermediate and consumer goods demanded. The limited volume, high spending tourist generally requires a standard which LDCs are unable to meet with locally produced goods. The simpler (and larger volume) the tourists' requirements the more likely is the LDC host country to be able to produce them locally and reduce the import leakage of FE. Of course, just because a country needs a high level of imports to serve the tourism sector need not imply that it is less capable of generating value added than an industry requiring fewer intermediate imports. Determination of the amount of value added that is generated is a combination of the level of demand and the input structure of the industry. Varley (52) cites the example of the duty free trade in places like Hong Kong and Singapore which operate on the principle of high volume sales and low margins.

The structure of ownership and control in the industry also affects leakages. Hotels operated by the international chains are fitted and furnished normally with standardised equipment imported from the parent company's central store. To the extent that substitute supplies of similar goods are available locally, this policy produces an FE leakage which could be avoided.

Transfer pricing can also serve to reduce the net FE earnings from international tourism. For example, expenditures made by tourists in their home country for goods and services to be supplied in the destination country may not be transferred to the tourist receiving country if the facility to be used is foreign owned or, alternatively, the expenditure may be understated as part of a multinational tax minimising strategy. Further control of FE movements is made more difficult by the spread of credit cards and travellers' cheques since such transactions can easily be made via foreign bank accounts without the necessity of going through local banking channels.

Finally, governments themselves may affect their countries' tourism earnings. In order to attract investors in tourism facilities, governments may grant concessions in the form of exemption from, or rebates of, customs duties and/or profits taxes, subsidies such as low interest loans and the provision of public utility services at less than full cost.

It should be noted that FE leakage does not occur just once at the time of the purchase of the specific product. It happens at each successive round of business transactions as the multiplier works its way through the economic system. There are also a number of complex issues leading to increased leakage. Two instances: first, the "demonstration" effect (discussed later in this section) results in increased demand from local residents for imported goods; and, secondly, the increased demand from local residents (brought about by the tourists' expenditure) may not be capable of being fully satisfied from domestic production resulting in increased imports to fill the gap.

144

Gradual realisation on the part of LDC administrations that these types of FE leak-age are occurring has led to a questioning of tourism's role in aiding the economic development of LDCs. There are two key questions which LDCs need to resolve.

1. Does investment in tourism produce greater net benefits than if it were to be put into alternative sectors?

2. Which form of tourism development will produce the greater net benefits: low volume, high per caput gross receipts but also high leakage, or large volume, low per caput gross receipts and low leakage?

Measuring the import content of tourism earnings

To answer these questions, LDCs must measure the import component of their gross tourism earnings and the full FE cost of the currency earned by the tourism sector. Both types of analysis are complex and, consequently, only in the case of a few LDCs has a thorough attempt been made to prepare full examinations. Further the assessment of the full cost in FE of the currency earned needs to cover a considerable period of time. Consequently, those studies which have been made tend to concentrate on the import component of gross tourism earnings.

To assess the level of the import content, not only must the sectoral composition of tourism earnings be known, but the reliance of each sector on imported inputs to cater for such expenditure has to be discovered. This is a complicated task be-cause domestic suppliers rely on other sectors and on imports to meet their needs, so the origin of all inputs has to be traced to enable import contents to be distinguished. These difficulties have meant that not all the studies undertaken have been drawn up on the same basis and care must be taken in comparing the results. Many studies do not take account of the leakages at subsequent stages of transaction, i e imports to satisfy the higher living standards demanded by visitors, expatriate labour remittances abroad.

The Unctad report indicated that 78 per cent of Kenya's tourist receipts represented net FE earnings on current account (the remaining 22 per cent is accounted for by the direct import content of tourist receipts and the direct payments made to non-resident owners of factors of production). Erbes summarises the results of other surveys:

"For Tunisia, the import content of goods consumed in the hotel trade is estimated by the Commissariat Général au Tourisme at 14 per cent of the gross FE earnings of this branch... In the Bahamas, the import content of the tourism sector as a whole in 1968 was estimated at 79 per cent of the total purchases in that sector... 43 per cent of the gross receipts went on imports of consumer goods."

The comparable figure to the 43 per cent for the Bahamas for other countries varies widely – around 60 per cent for Fiji, 50 per cent for the Virgin Islands, 45 per cent for Hawaii, 30 per cent for Hong Kong, 24 per cent for Israel, 22 per cent for Kenya (as noted above), 15 per cent for Tunisia and Trinidad and Tobago, 10 per cent for Greece and 2 per cent for Yugoslavia.

Other studies confirm the wide variation between LDCs of domestically available materials, expertise and productive capacity. The net percentage of gross tourism earnings accruing to LDCs calculated in the few studies undertaken differs considerably. Mauritius, for example, retains only 10 per cent of gross earnings (21h) owing to its need to import most materials and products and make large payments to foreign tour operators and hotel owners residing abroad. The position is slightly better in Caribbean island economies, where Archer concludes from his work in Bermuda that the net receipts of FE from visitors falls within the range 50 to 70 per cent (2c) while the more self-sufficient LDCs fare even better.

The full scale of realised net earnings proportions of gross tourism earnings can be summarised as follows:

10 per cent:	totally import reliant (e g Mauritius)
10-50 per cent:	heavily import reliant (e g less developed Caribbean and South Pacific islands)
50-70 per cent:	imports of luxuries and a few necessities (e g better developed Caribbean islands)
70-90 per cent:	imports principally for luxuries (e g advanced manufacturing sector with good resources - Kenya, Tunisia, Greece, Yugoslavia, etc).

The import content of capital investment in hotels and in the basic infrastructure needed to service tourists may be somewhat higher than these levels, particularly in the least developed LDCs which are not able to supply many of the necessary materials and goods from local production. UN calculations show, however, that these initially high FE losses can normally be recouped within two years, so the effect on the balance of payments is short term only.

Examples of studies measuring the full FE cost of the currency earned by tourism are rare and limited in coverage. Erbes reports that, in Tunisia, in 1968, 51 per cent of FE attributable to the hotel industry was represented by the cost in FE. This compares with the 14 per cent import content of goods consumed by Tunisia's hotel sector noted above. Between 1964 and 1968 the FE cost of the hotel sector fell from 83 per cent to 51 per cent. However, as the 'demonstration" effect gives rise to pressure for the extension of tourist behaviour patterns to the host country's populace, leading to increased imports, the FE cost will follow a trend similar to the law of diminishing returns, i e high at the outset, decreasing in the next phase and then increasing once again.

INCOME

Measuring the income effects of tourism

There is considerable controversy in the literature and among researchers as to the income effects of tourism. Much of the problem can be traced to inadequate base data and a multiplicity of methodologies. There are a number of possible approaches to measuring the effect of tourism on a country's national income, with the more complex also embracing consideration of many of the other economic factors. Discussion is limited to the merits and disadvantages of the three basic methods of appraisal (excluding the sort of commercial evaluation undertaken by private sector or by specialist tourism consultants) - the multiplier, cost benefit analysis and structural analysis - and the result of a number of case studies. Appendix 9 contains brief summaries of specific methodologies for multiplier and social cost benefit analysis.

Multiplier method

Tourists' spending is received as revenue by hoteliers, shopkeepers, restaurateurs, excursion organisers, etc. This is the initial impact. In the first round of trans- actions, this income is used to purchase a wide range of goods and services (from new stocks to labour), to meet financial obligations (e g interest, rent) and to retain as profit. A portion of these purchases are imports and some of the financial obliga- tions are to foreign organisations. This, therefore, leaks out of the economy.

The money which is retained within the country creates further economic activity - the second round. The recipients of the spending by the hotelier, shopkeeper, and so on dispose of the money by purchasing goods and services, etc, in the way the initial recipients did. Again, an amount leaks out of the economy. At the same time, owing to the increased employment created by the tourism sector, personal incomes rise, consumer expenditure increases and local business turnover grows. This process continues with diminishing effect until the value added which is gener- ated becomes virtually zero.

The relationship between an initial injection of tourism expenditure and the subse- quent generation of value added is the tourism multiplier. Taking the income finally generated as ΔY, and the initial injection of expenditure as ΔE_i, the multiplier is given by the expression $\Delta Y / \Delta E_i$. The multiplier has been the technique most often used, and misused, by countries - developed as well as developing - to measure the impact of tourism. Varying methodologies have produced widely different results, some of which have been misleading for reasons such as that the figures refer to output rather than income multipliers or that the researchers have failed to remove import leakages from income figures.

A study in the eastern Caribbean produced a multiplier value of 2.3 but, as pointed out by Archer, this had resulted merely from adding together the nominal values of a number of transactions and failing to allow for import leakages. "They had in effect multiplied the multiplier." (2b) Bryden's work in the same region produced a much lower tourism income multiplier of 0.88 in Antigua in 1963. His research used an inter-industry transaction matrix, where the Keynesian multiplier was the weighted average of the individual sector multipliers. Assuming that inputs from agriculture are wholly imported and that the input structure of hotels will change as occupancy levels rise, the multiplier reduced to 0.58 (5).

The magnitude of the impact made in a country by tourism expenditure depends upon the diversity of its economy and the extent to which the tourism sector is integrated into the national economic system. The income multipliers in Table 4 demonstrate that in Caribbean countries the amount of income created per tourist dollar is within the range of 0.58 to 1.195.

The nature of a country's economy determines a country's position within this range. Where tourism operations are largely divorced from the rest of the economy (e g Antigua), tourism's contribution is principally through the payment of wages and salaries and the further local spending which this generates. Where local industries can supply a greater proportion of the tourism sector's requirements (e g Dominica) the multiplier is correspondingly higher. Archer concludes that "even in the larger developing countries, it is very unlikely that tourism multipliers can be much in excess of 1.4. The comparable values in Canada, the UK and Eire, for example, lie between 1.7 and 2.0". (2d)

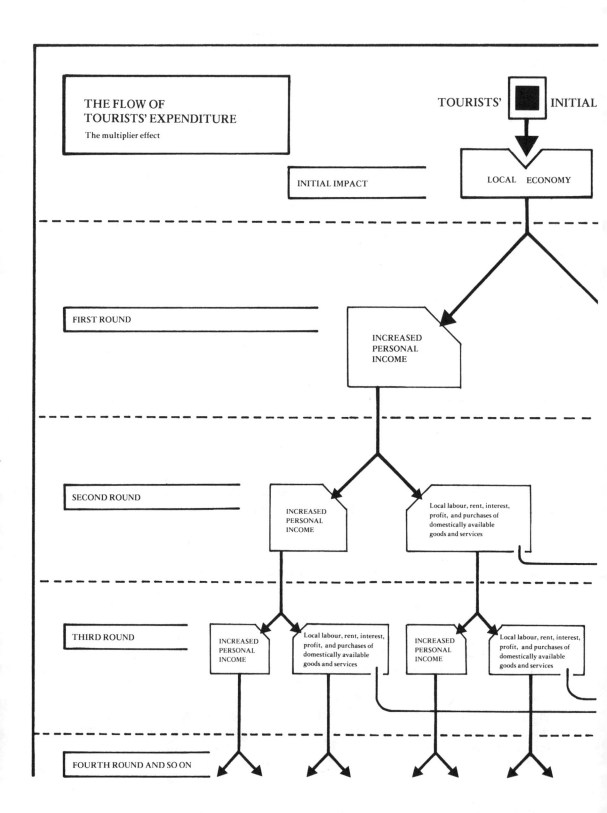

THE FLOW OF
TOURISTS' EXPENDITURE
The multiplier effect

TOURISTS' INITIAL

INITIAL IMPACT

LOCAL ECONOMY

FIRST ROUND

INCREASED
PERSONAL
INCOME

SECOND ROUND

INCREASED
PERSONAL
INCOME

Local labour, rent, interest,
profit, and purchases of
domestically available
goods and services

THIRD ROUND

INCREASED
PERSONAL
INCOME

Local labour, rent, interest,
profit, and purchases of
domestically available
goods and services

INCREASED
PERSONAL
INCOME

Local labour, rent, interest,
profit, and purchases of
domestically available
goods and services

FOURTH ROUND AND SO ON

148

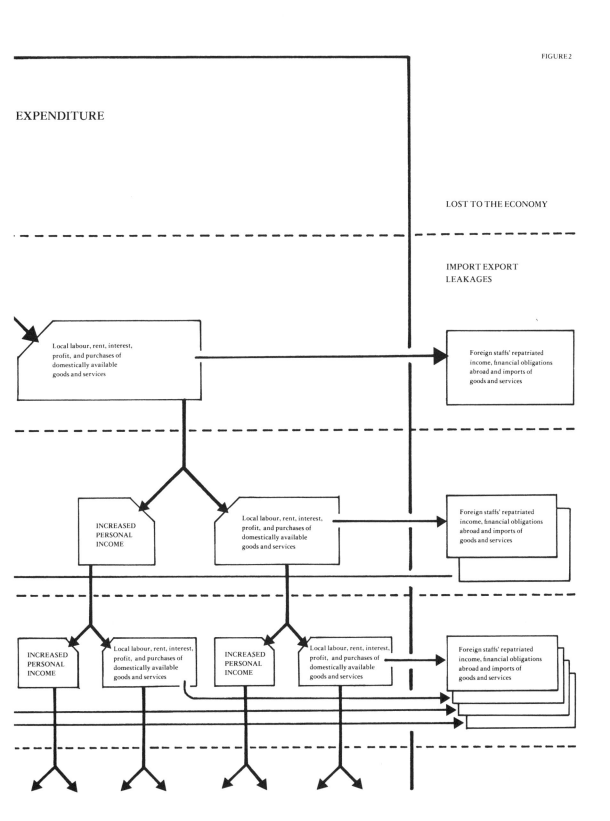

FIGURE 2

EXPENDITURE

LOST TO THE ECONOMY

IMPORT EXPORT
LEAKAGES

Local labour, rent, interest, profit, and purchases of domestically available goods and services

Foreign staffs' repatriated income, financial obligations abroad and imports of goods and services

INCREASED PERSONAL INCOME

Local labour, rent, interest, profit, and purchases of domestically available goods and services

Foreign staffs' repatriated income, financial obligations abroad and imports of goods and services

INCREASED PERSONAL INCOME

Local labour, rent, interest, profit, and purchases of domestically available goods and services

INCREASED PERSONAL INCOME

Local labour, rent, interest, profit, and purchases of domestically available goods and services

Foreign staffs' repatriated income, financial obligations abroad and imports of goods and services

149

Table 4

Tourism Income Multipliers

Country	Multiplier
Dominica	1.195
Bermuda	1.099
Eastern Caribbean	1.073
Antigua	0.880
Bahamas	0.782
Cayman Islands	0.650
British Virgin Islands	0.580

Source: Adapted from Tourism Multipliers:
The State of the Art, Brian H. Archer.

The use of multiplier analysis for small LDCs has been under criticism because it assumes a widespread unemployment of resources and, therefore, a perfectly elastic supply of goods and services. For economies operating without spare resources, multiplier analysis can only legitimately ignore price changes if the increase in the components of demand represent an insignificant proportion of demand disaggregated by the relevant tourism sectors of the economy. This assumption is unlikely to be true for small economies. Bryden (5) argues that, even if sufficient resource capacity exists, many of the factors are likely to have other uses, i e their opportunity cost will be greater than zero. Thus, the overriding failing of tourism multipliers is that they do not, as many have been led to believe, measure the actual, or potential, benefit which the expansion of tourism provides over the longer run. In order to assess the real worth of tourism it is essential to make some assessment of the real cost to society of devoting resources to tourism and a comparison with the benefits which would accrue if these resources were allocated to other uses.

Cost benefit analysis (CBA)

Where there is active or potential competition for a country's resources and factors, the best framework currently feasible for evaluating the income effects of tourism is probably the cost benefit approach. In CBA, the services of factors of production are valued at their opportunity cost (i e the marginal value product of their next best use). This technique enables an answer to be provided to the question whether tourism will generate more FE, more employment, higher earnings to factors of production or higher government revenue, than other sectors of the economy.

Two interesting examples of the use of CBA in evaluating tourism are Mitchell's work in Kenya (30b) and a study in Hawaii produced by Mathematica (28). Mitchell found that given an import content at most equal to that of import substitution industries, the tourism sector in Kenya earns more FE than import substitution industries save. Measuring the value of tourism for the Kenyan economy in terms of the wealth of the individual (the present value of consumption), Mitchell found that this was positive even with a discount rate of 30 per cent.

The Hawaiian study sought to identify the best type of tourist in CBA terms. Four characteristics of visitors were examined, namely length of stay, number of persons in travelling party, daily and total visit expenditure. Three explanatory variables were built in as determinants of visitor behaviour - age, income and region of origin of visitor. The highest benefit-cost ratios were obtained for middle aged, high income tourists, for they spent relatively large amounts per day, and their parties normally comprised couples rather than one person. The least worthwhile visitors had low incomes, were aged over 50 or under 30 and had a longer than average length of stay. The report suggested the imposition of an airport tax to discourage these categories.

Net present value or internal social rate of return. Whether or not tourism creates greater net benefits to society than other forms of development is a function of the nature of the country's economy and the practicable, alternative forms of developments. Of course a country may often choose to promote several forms of development, even though one or more of these may offer relatively lower net benefits, in order to minimise dependence on any one sector.

The net benefit to the citizens of a country from any project can be measured in two ways:

i.   the NPV (net present value) to society, i e the current value of the estimated future benefits to the country;

ii.   the social yield or internal social rate of return (IRR), i e the average annual rate at which the benefits accrue to society.

A positive NPV is insufficient condition alone for project approval. This is because, owing to the possibility of failure to identify the best alternative use of resources, the NPV of some projects may be overstated.

For this reason and the fact that the NPV provides no indication of how close a project is to the margin of acceptability, the more appropriate approach to the evaluation of tourism projects is the internal social rate of return. In general, projects offering social yields in excess of the target yield (which in most countries is likely to be between 10 per cent and 12 per cent) are eligible for selection. Examples of research undertaken using the internal social rate of return include Forbes's study on the Trinidad Hilton which produced an IRR of between 12 per cent and 17 per cent; on the other hand, IRRs have been as low as 1 per cent, indicating that further tourism development creates socially inefficient use of resources. Alternative projects within the tourism sector can also be evaluated in this way. For example, destinations which suffer from a marked seasonality of their tourist flows can use this approach to determine whether resources would be better employed in providing for, and encouraging, additional tourism in the peak season or in developing and promoting the country as an all year round holiday destination. In other words, will the net benefits to be gained by concentrating the available resources to serve extra peak season tourists outweigh those to be obtained from increasing hotel occupancy rates in the shoulder and low seasons? The country's pricing structure is a key factor in this type of evaluation and a number of countries (including at least one LDC) are undertaking complex pricing model studies to assist in the determination of these allocation problems.

The social cost benefit analysis approach itself has its critics, who argue that it is not an application of a scientific theory where predictions can be checked against actual performance, but a system whose validity depends upon the appropriateness of its assumptions rather than the quality of its predictions. While certain reservations may be made about the value of the method in general, its use for the appraisal of tourism projects presents particular problems. Varley (52) notes that there are significant external effects in both production and consumption and that considerable economies of scale can arise where the successful running of the industry depends on high fixed costs in specialist services and infrastructure. The value judgments which have to be made appear to permit methods to be easily manipulated to produce the desired results.

Lal (23) concludes that adoption of the Little and Mirrlees approach to project appraisal (see Appendix 9) will nearly always produce successful results for tourism projects. This is because if tourism is compared with projects in, say, the manufacturing sector the latter receive extensive government protection, thereby inflating market prices.

Structural analysis

The aim of a structural analysis is to identify long term changes in economic structure that will accompany growth. Little authoritative work has, as yet, been carried out in respect of the structure of the tourism economy but as tourism becomes more dominant in economies so the need for such analysis becomes greater. The major dependent variables in cross-country analyses of structural economic characteristics have been identified by Chenery and Syrquin (6) as:

   i.   accumulation processes (investment, government revenue, education);

   ii. resource allocation processes (structure of domestic demand, production and trade);

   iii. demographic and distributional processes (labour allocation, urbanisation, demographic transition, income distribution).

One study worth comment is Renaud's analysis of the effect of the economic growth brought about by tourism on the structure of production and consumption (37). Patterns of change were classified in one of three ways - pro-trade biased, anti-trade biased or neutral to trade. The influence of tourism growth on the traditional agricultural sector was examined. This showed that the development of the tourism sector had not brought about any stimulation of agricultural output. Renaud concludes that the rapid expansion of tourism in Hawaii "simply generates a switch from one export led growth based on agriculture to one based on tourism without the possibility of a simultaneous expansion of both sectors. Overall, the growth of the islands has been pro-trade biased and the increased level of local output has not been accompanied by a strong increase in internal integration!" (37)

Varley (52) notes that progress in applying structural analyses to tourism will depend on the identification of specific patterns of development in a quantitative framework. The four main patterns of development over recent years have been:

   i.   primary specialisation;

   ii. balanced production and trade;

   iii. import substitution;

   iv. industrial specialisation.

As tourism increases in significance in an economy so there occurs a services specialisation in the economy's growth basis. However the role of tourism in a country's development has varied widely and further research looking at patterns of development on an inter-country basis is necessary before the usefulness of structural analysis of tourism can be properly evaluated.

EMPLOYMENT

A labour intensive industry?

Faced with a high level of unemployment in most LDCs, governments are concerned to establish activities that will provide regular, productive jobs. One of the main arguments advocating the establishment, or expansion, of a tourism sector in LDCs is that tourism, as a service activity, creates a high level of job opportunities. The sector, it is argued, is labour intensive and the principal type required is semi-skilled and unskilled - the very type in abundant supply in most LDCs.

Others, however, do not accept this view totally. Bryden contends tourism's special advantages in generating employment, "especially when the whole gamut of investments required to establish a tourism sector are taken into account, including relatively capital intensive and tourist-specific infrastructure"(5).

Employment created by tourism

Tourism provides both direct and secondary employment. Direct employment (i e jobs resulting from, and dependent on, the sector) includes accommodation, shops, restaurants, bars, night clubs, transport operators and government administration of tourism. Secondary employment (i e jobs in sectors supplying the tourism sector, or the activities benefiting from expenditure generated by it) embraces the construction, agriculture and fishing, manufacturing and processing sectors.

From the limited amount of data available, direct employment generated by tourism ranges from as little as 1 per cent of the economically active population in a country like Mexico where tourism's contribution to national income is relatively small (although amongst the highest for an LDC in absolute terms) to as much as one third of the labour force in small island economies.

The volume of secondary or indirect employment generated depends on the degree of linkage between the concerns meeting final tourist demand and the producers. Varley (52) notes that the higher the degree of integration and diversification in the economy, the higher the amount of indirect employment generated. Conversely in the underdeveloped regions of LDCs the volume is low. He notes that in Fiji this occurs because the major linkages developed by hotels are with the large centralised wholesale sector rather than with rural farmers.

Nonetheless the volume of secondary employment generated can exceed the number of direct tourism jobs. Archer reports that in Bermuda in 1975 tourism created 7,000 direct jobs in hotels, shops, taxi firms, restaurants, bars, night clubs, etc. and, in addition, "the multiplier effects of tourist spending accounted for a further 14,000 jobs". (2d) It should be noted, however, that the majority of this secondary employment, which caters largely for household spending, would persist in the absence of tourist spending though at a much lower real level of remuneration.

Labour intensity

A more pertinent question than the numbers of jobs created by tourism is whether or not tourism is more labour intensive than other sectors of the economy. Labour intensity can be measured in two ways: cost per job created; or employment-output ratio, i e the number of workers employed in relation to tourism's contribution or value added to national income.

Whichever of these yardsticks has been adopted, the studies which have been undertaken have generally (though not universally) supported the view of tourism's opposers, namely that tourism is not significantly more efficient in creating employment than other sectors. The principal reason is the often highly capital intensive demands tourism makes on the infrastructure of an economy (see page 160 Infrastructural costs).

A number of studies have been made of labour intensity, though assumptions and conditions built into the calculations differ and due caution must be taken in comparing results. The results are conflicting.

Mexico
: An investment of $80,000 in 1969 created 41 jobs in tourism, 16 in the petroleum industry, 15 in metal trades and 8 in the electricity industry.

Morocco
: Addition of an extra hotel bedroom creates direct employment for 40 workers plus some secondary employment. (24)

Tunisia
: The cost per job created over the second half of the 1960s was found to lie between 7,000 and 10,700 dinars ($13,300-$20,300). This was higher than the cost per job created in the Tunisian manufacturing sector, which was about 6,700 dinars ($12,700) in the same period. High grade hotels in Tunisia in 1969 recorded capital/output ratios of 10.7 (i e 10.7 units of fixed assets were needed to produce one unit of value added.

Kenya
: The cost per workplace created in running hotels in Kenya in 1972 varied between K£2,201 and K£4,179 (average K£3,304) as against K£1,123 for the manufacturing and repair sector, while in Tanzania it varied from T£3,125 to T£4,750 (13). Another study calculated that K£10,000 value added by tourism generated 14 jobs, compared with 13 jobs in the manufacturing sector and 35 jobs in agriculture.

Yugoslavia
: Investment in the hotel and catering trade creates more new jobs than investment in industry - 6.5 new jobs per 1 mn Yugoslav dinars of fixed investment compared with 2.6. However, over the years 1958 to 1967 a capital/output ratio of 3.1 was obtained for all hotels and 3.8 for seasonal hotels, which compares unfavourably with capital/output ratios of 2.5 for manufacturing and mining industries and 2.8 for agriculture.

Israel   During 1965, fixed assets per employee amounted to I£25,000 for hotels and I£23,000 for excursion companies. These amounts are higher than in industry (I£17,000) but lower than in agriculture and transport.

The examples quoted above indicate only the average cost per job created in investment terms. Consideration must also be paid to training costs, differences in labour productivity, etc.

Erbes describes three phases in the build-up of an LDC's tourism industry:

"In the first phase, the average cost per job created will be comparatively high to start with. The country has none of the facilities to meet the requirements of the modern tourist and must install a high proportion of luxury hotels; it lacks experience and organisation skills in this area, and it is obliged to make additional and often enormous exertions in regard to infrastructures. During the first phase, the average cost per job created is bound to be high. (The capital/output ratio is also high because there is still no assured large-scale clientele.)

In the second phase, there is likely to be some reduction in the cost per job created, owing to the installation of less expensive establishments to cater for a more "ordinary" clientele, greater technical experience and better organisation, and the expansion of the non-hotel branch, where investment per job is probably lower. (Similarly, the capital/output ratio is likely to decline, for the same reasons and because there is now a larger clientele.)

It is not possible to arrive at definite conclusions about the capital costs of jobs created in the hotel industry in comparison with other sectors. The Yugoslav example does indicate... that investment in the hotel and catering trade creates more new jobs per million Yugoslav dinars than investment in industry... but the Tunisian example points to an opposite conclusion, as does the case of Israel...

All we can say... is that the average cost per job created in the tourism sector as a whole, and a fortiori in hotels mainly serving the international tourist flow, does not appear appreciably lower than in the manufacturing sector as a whole. This may be followed by a third phase in which the capital cost per job created may rise again because of the higher cost of land, the heavy engineering costs incurred as less favourable sites have to be used, the need to improve standards of comfort with the mounting costs of the added amenities involved, the higher building costs and so on; not to mention the increased infrastructure costs, which are likely to rocket as the tourism sector assumes greater importance in the national economy, both because of the geographical extension of the communications networks and because of the higher capacity expected of them to meet the growing demand of the tourism sector." (14)

One area of debate currently engaging many LDC governments, and which has an impact on the cost per job created amongst other factors, is whether the design, methods of construction and operation of the conventional international tourist style of hotel are an appropriate technology. Large, luxury hotels generate more employment per room and higher employment/output ratios than smaller, lower quality units. However, the costs per workplace created are also higher than for the smaller hotel. If a policy of developing smaller units of good, though below luxury, quality is combined with the adoption of designs drawn from the local culture and the use of indigenously available construction materials, the import leakage will be lower. Furthermore, small units lend themselves more readily to owner-ship and operation by residents. This train of thought has recommended itself to a number of LDCs including Barbados, which is developing a holiday village with several locally owned small units situated in close proximity to one another drawing on a central marketing and reservations system and common recreational facilities provided by a government development agency. Thus control is kept within the hands of Barbadians. This approach faces problems, which require careful research and planning if they are to be surmounted. The hotel must include sufficient familiar features in its design and guarantee the requisite standards of facilities and service to capture the appropriate level of market demand. With an unfamiliar concept and ownership vested locally, the effort needed to convince the foreign tourist (and travel trade) of these factors will automatically be greater.

Regional development

Another benefit claimed for tourism is in generating employment and income in the less developed, often outlying, regions of a country where other opportunities for development are limited. The introduction of tourism activities into such areas can have a proportionately much greater effect on the welfare of the residents than the same activities might have on people living in the more developed parts of the same country. In such areas there are many subsistence farmers or fishermen producing principally for their own consumption, selling their excess at the local market. The impact on their household income from involvement in tourism of just one member as a waiter or cleaner would be quite substantial.

India is an example of a country following a declared policy of investing in tourism in economically backward regions which offer little alternative attraction for indus-trial investment. Through the autonomous public sector organisation, the India Tourism Development Corporation (ITDC), development is encouraged in the poorer regions of the country (Kovalam in the SW, Goa on the west coast and Srinagar in the north).

Similarly in Kenya, where the tourism sector was initially based on the attraction of its wildlife and its capital, Nairobi, the government has now backed the develop-ment of beach resort tourism at a number of previously undeveloped coastal regions. A K£48 mn resort complex is being constructed at Diani, 18 miles south of Mombasa. The resort will provide 26 hotels with 6,500 beds and a full range of tourist infra-structure and facilities. A new town of 40,000 to service the resort is planned; and, by 1994, jobs for 11,000 should be available.

Again there are dissenting voices which question whether an alternative allocation of resources other than to tourism could not achieve the same results at similar costs. Bryden puts the case: "If the region in question is both non-agricultural and non-industrial, then there is unlikely to be either the requisite infrastructure or the requisite labour force, and the development of tourism in that region is likely to require both heavy infrastructural costs and relocation of labour." (5)

Balance of supply of, and demand for, tourism employees

In addition to considering whether tourism's labour intensity has a better performance than that of other sectors, it is important for LDCs to ensure that the supply and demand of human resources for their tourism sectors are in efficient equilibrium. If the balance is not achieved there can be major detrimental effects to the country's balance of payments and income. The difficulty of maintaining this balance is heightened by the wide difference between the high and low season of tourism activity which afflicts many LDCs.

Examples where tourism growth was allowed to take place without control from central government and where, in consequence, the tourisn sector's requirement for staff outstripped the pool of labour available (in optimal economic terms) have occurred in Bermuda and St Lucia. In Bermuda, owing to the absence of a master plan prior to the 1970s, the rapid expansion of tourism was unrelated to the labour supply. This led to galloping wage inflation as employers outbid each other for the limited pool of labour. Combined with the tourist boom this served to push up the cost of land and the rate of inflation. St Lucia depended for many years on its exports of bananas to assist its balance of payments (in 1969 it earned £2.5 mn from this source). Flight of labour from the land to the tourism sector, attracted by the higher wages and glamour, left the task of banana cultivation to the land owners and their families, with a resultant loss in productivity and land utilisation. Meanwhile, much of the food served to the tourist is imported so a significant proportion of tourist expenditure - supposedly replacing the banana as a FE earner - is lost. The problem is aggravated because the peak of the tourist season coincides with banana harvesting time.

There is also the possibility of structural unemployment. At the construction phase the amount of employment generated by investment in tourism plant may be greater than that generated by the accommodation sector itself. If capacity becomes overexpanded and hotel investment dries up, there will be serious structural unemployment unless a compensatory investment demand emerges from outside the tourism sector. This is a particular danger in smaller economies where the construction sector is a major employer and depends heavily on the demand for hotel construction.

Seasonality makes LDC governments' task of controlling the supply and demand of tourism employment more difficult. One or both of two actions may be taken by tourism sector employers as a consequence of the disparity of tourist demand.

1. The laying off of a proportion of staff during the low season. The UN Ecosoc/IUOTO report (49) states that lay-offs usually total around 25 per cent and are drawn from the lowest paid, least skilled workers. If hotels retain key staff during the low season, despite their being underemployed, in order to ensure continuity and maintenance of service standards, cost structures may become uncompetitive (even though fixed costs are the largest proportion of hotel costs). If, on the other hand, staff from all layers are laid off in the low season, morale declines and along with it service standards. These are just the sort of considerations being fed into the pricing model studies referred to earlier.

2. Staff may be imported from other parts of the country or from overseas
    to increase temporarily the labour supply in the high season. The conse-
    quence of importing staff is that the demand for land for housing increases
    and wages are frequently lost to the area if they are remitted home.
    Further, where the imported labour is of a different colour, etc, from the
    resident labour force, there can arise social tension.

Productivity

Tourism is criticised for encouraging LDCs to move straight from an agricultural
society to a service one, omitting the intermediate stage of an industrial phase.
The argument is that such a pattern retards development because the service
sector, and specifically tourism, has a poor productivity performance. Sir George
Young (57) outlines the case, maintaining that if a country's labour force is drawn
into a service sector with a low record of productivity, below average earnings
(although this point applies more to developed, than to developing, countries), low
value added, a high turnover of staff and significant seasonal unemployment then
it is likely that economic growth will be slower than if labour was not so enticed.
He quotes the case of the UK (although the proportion is unlikely to be lower in
LDCs) where 60 per cent of the tourism sector's labour force is unskilled (including
kitchen staff, waiters and bar staff).

The UN Ecosoc/IUOTO report (49) concludes that tourism's use of unskilled and
semi-skilled labour may prove to be an eventual disbenefit, since if tourism grows
to become a dominant part of a country's economy the possibility of improving the
skills of its workforce will be excluded.

Of course, the definition of what constitutes a skill is arguable. Diamond (11)
points out that in a country like Turkey (and the argument would be equally true of
many LDCs) where 50 per cent of the adult population is illiterate, the ability to
speak a foreign language represents a skill.

Creation of income disparities

There has been a general tendency for income levels in the advanced sectors of the
economies of LDCs to be much higher than seems appropriate for countries with
labour surpluses. This occurs because of pressures for employees in the advanced
sector to receive incomes that match or relate to the highest levels of pay, most
often set by international comparison. This phenomenon manifests itself in tourism
(although it applies to all imported industries) where the wage levels paid by hotels,
particularly those owned by foreign international chains, to their staff tend to be
higher than those paid in agriculture and other forms of non-tourism employment.

Self-reliance

Apart from the difficulty of wide variation in seasonal demand for employment,
LDC administrators and tourism sector employers face the problem of limited
availability of managerial and technical (chefs, hotel administration, etc) staff.
The consequence is that labour is brought in from outside to fill these vacancies
with a resultant drain on the economy - this can occur either from one area to
another within a country or by means of importing from another country.

Unesco reported that in Agadir (Morocco) most hotel employees came from Tangier, Rabat and Casablanca before the government started to take measures to encourage local recruitment. The report comments: "Originally the aim of developing a tourist industry was to provide jobs that would keep workers in their own region or country, but it is quite likely to have the opposite effect. In most cases, LDCs have neither the institutional nor the financial resources to set up their own training centres for managerial staff and lower level employees. Training is, therefore, conducted on the job, which means that the regions already equipped with hotels must supply the managerial and supervisory staff. " (1e)

The ways in which LDCs have tackled the problem of training tourism sector staff is discussed on page 212 (Training). The problems do not end with the provision of training schemes. A problem afflicting many LDCs (though not just in the field of tourism but equally in medicine, engineering, etc) is the emigration of middle level staff.

"The seasonal nature of the tourist hotel industry means that higher level staff, if they have the opportunity and the necessary expertise, try to obtain work with hotels catering for business travel, which have the advantage of offering steady employment. In the LDCs, hotels of this type are usually owned by international chains; it is therefore easy for the most capable employees to go on to work abroad in other hotels belonging to the chain, where the pay is higher... The drain of qualified staff also occurs at the hotel training school level... a large number of trainees (as high as 30 per cent) never return to their own country. " (1e)

Conclusion

The foregoing analysis illustrates the complexity of the employment aspect of tourism development in LDCs. As noted later in this section, there are also social impact problems caused by employment arising from tourism, for example increased prostitution. What is clear is that tourism cannot be blindly advocated as the cure for unemployment problems in all LDCs, any more than any other sector is the cure. It undoubtedly contributes significantly in providing jobs. However, the degree to which it is suitable for government support, with a view to job creation, at the expense of investment in other sectors must be assessed individually for each LDC, taking account of the country's resources, state of development, political and social framework, etc. To guide LDCs in this evaluation both on a basis of international comparison and in relating tourism performance to that of other sectors within a country, more detailed evidence of tourism's employment generating performance, capacity and effects would be of major assistance.

GOVERNMENT COSTS AND REVENUES

Expenses that can be incurred by governments

Governments are financially involved in the tourism sector in a variety of ways, some only partly recognised and rarely catalogued in full. Revenue comes principally in the form of taxation, e g direct taxes on tourists levied generally at airports or accommodation establishments and indirect taxes levied on goods and services consumed by tourists or on profits achieved by the providers of those goods and services.

The main categories of expenditure incurred by governments in the tourism sector are:

i.   development, administration and control, e g research, advertising and promotion, training schemes, administrative staff;

ii. operation of certain tourism facilities, e g national airline, state hotels, game parks, local tour operating agencies;

iii. infrastructural costs (including utilities);

iv. grants and incentives designed to attract tourism development in specific regions, times of year, etc.

There can also be a wide range of costs arising from the indirect effects of expansion in the tourism sector.

The amount which governments spend on developing and running their tourism sectors is a matter for individual assessment taking account of the aims they establish. The same principle applies to direct government operation of specific tourism facilities. If a government identifies a weakness in the development of the tourism sector (for example inadequate trained staff or overseas promotional activity) it may choose to step in; similarly if private sector investment is inhibiting the growth of tourism, the government may elect to fill the gap. Governments also operate facilities which involve the exploitation of the country's wildlife or culture.

Infrastructural costs

The two cost areas to governments which involve most debate are infrastructural costs and the provision of grants and incentives. Infrastructural costs bear most heavily on the state. To be able to cater for tourists from the major generating markets of Western Europe and North America, an LDC needs to provide infrastructural services that are comparable with those of the home country. Yet precisely one of the principal characteristics of LDCs is their lack of such infrastructure.

Consequently, investment on infrastructure specifically for the tourism sector is much more likely to be needed in LDCs than in developed countries. Erbes (14) distinguishes between general infrastructure (basic public utilities such as water, transport, power, sewerage, etc, which may not be available prior to the development of tourism) and specific infrastructure (the connection to, and expansion and improvement of, the general infrastructure necessitated specifically by the growth in tourism). Whilst it is easy to separate out and cost the latter, a judgment is necessary to estimate the amount of general infrastructure which a country would provide in the absence of an active tourism sector. It is, however, true to record that the poorer the country concerned, the greater will be the amount and, hence, cost directly attributable to tourism. Even for the infrastructure specifically provided for tourism, in economic terms it would not be right to apportion the whole of the costs to the tourism sector since the infrastructure is also available to local residents, e g improved roads to serve tourism resorts in previously remote areas will benefit local farmers.

The UN Ecosoc/IUOTO report (49) concludes that "there can be no general guide...
to the share that infrastructural costs should represent, or have represented, in
tourism development costs...It appears that the real cost of developing new tourism
regions or complexes away from existing infrastructural facilities is sometimes
not fully appreciated". This latter point is borne out by the heavy costs, compared
with other industries, of job creation in the tourism sector noted in the preceding
subsection.

The costs of grants and incentives

Once the decision is made that tourism is desirable for national economic development, it is necessary to attract the expertise, capital and access to markets that
are required to foster the sector. For LDCs, this has often meant looking overseas.
In order to attract the desired foreign skills and finance, LDC governments have,
in many cases, adjusted the investment climate and conditions to attract investment.

The main categories of concession are described in detail in IUOTO's Sources and
Conditions of Financing for Tourist Development Projects (56y). These are:

i.   tax exemptions/reduction on imported equipment, machinery,
      materials, etc;

ii.   reduction in company taxation by means of favourable depreciation
      allowances on investment or special treatment in relation to excise.
      sales, income, turnover, profits or property taxes;

iii. tax holidays (limited period);

iv.   guarantee of stabilisation of tax conditions (for up to 20 years);

v.   grants (up to 30 per cent of total capital costs);

vi.   subsidies (guaranteeing minimum level of profit, occupancy, etc);

vii. loans at low rates of interest;

viii. provision of land freehold at nominal or little cost or at low or
      peppercorn rents;

ix.   free and unrestricted repatriation of all or part of invested capital,
      profits, dividends and interest, subject to tax provisions;

x.   guarantees against nationalisation or expropriation.

There are many problems inherent in giving incentives or grants but these are no
greater (and in one or two cases are actually lower) than those for manufacturing
industries. One of the basic difficulties is that investment allowances tend to
encourage capital intensive activities, while most LDCs suffer from a surplus of
labour. In the tourism sector, this problem is less marked than in manufacturing
because there is less scope to replace labour with capital.

A danger of open ended commitments to allow duty free or easy import of materials and equipment is that they may act as a barrier in subsequent attempts to establish domestic production facilities for such goods. Governments must, therefore, take care to gear such concessions in accord with longer term policies.

The phasing out of tax concessions is difficult. The UN Ecosoc/IUOTO report states that "there are some instances where, as a result of becoming liable to taxation at the end of a tax holiday, investors have reacted to the sudden change in profitability by reducing their interest in the project, by withdrawing from it or running it down... The likelihood of there being such a drastic change in profitability is reduced where the tax holiday is carefully phased to fulfil its real function, that is to tide the investor over the early period of heavy outlays, and perhaps low receipts, as the business gets under way". (49)

Over generous subsidy arrangements may effectively shift much of the risk back on to the government. Sir George Young quotes an extreme example in Sicily: "The government gives each tour operator $133 for each charter flight on all off-season programmes and a 10 per cent grant for main season programmes. In addition, the operator gets 13 per cent of hotel profits if his programme includes hotel accommodation." (57)

The provision of loans can offset some of the economic benefits expected from the tourism sector. While it is normal for those receiving such credit assistance to provide a substantial part of the investment funds themselves, they do not have to bring funds into the country. Yet one of the reasons for encouraging foreign investment may be a shortage of capital in the country, so granting credit may serve to deprive other sectors of the economy of funds. On the other hand, the lack of such credit assistance could mean that the investment required in the tourism sector is not made.

The problem with providing land (or even permitting foreign enterprises to purchase land) at key sites of tourist potential is that any subsequent government development plan cannot be implemented. Mexico's cure for this problem is to ban foreign ownership of land within 50 km of the coast or frontier.

Concessions can be a valuable tool in helping a country's tourism sector to develop, but there is a danger that the balance of the benefits granted may be tilted excessively in favour of the investor, often foreign. The UN Ecosoc/IUOTO report's conclusion is that "while incentives are provided in order to attract investment, it is rarely clear, when investment is duly forthcoming, just what contribution the incentive has made to the investment decision. Studies carried out into incentives in a number of countries and for various sectors suggest that the impact of such concessions in promoting new investment may have been overestimated". (49)

The World Bank notes the additional problem of incentives being established on the basis of matching or outdoing neighbouring countries: "...too often tax incentives have been applied indiscriminately, regardless of the local or foreign origin of capital; the level of supply and trend of demand; the size, category or location of the accommodation; the obvious need for periodic amendments." (54b)

INFLATION

Tourism can put up prices

The expansion of international tourism in LDCs and its seasonal nature create an increased demand both for imported goods (e g foreign brands of spirits, cameras, watches, even basic items for the holidaymakers such as suntan lotion, tissues, etc), and for local products (e g handicrafts) and factors of production (e g land and labour - see the example of Bermuda on page 157). Shop prices rise and the cost of factors of production, particularly land, is likely to be bid up. Sir George Young quotes the example of a parcel of land of 736 sq m in San Agustin in the Canaries rising over 17 times in value from £1,512 in 1963 to £27,000 in 1971. (57) To the extent that the resident population is adversely affected by the resultant inflation, this can be considered an additional cost of tourism development.

ECONOMIC DEPENDENCE ON TOURISM

LDCs with little industrial development potential are most dependent on tourism

Tourism, as already pointed out, is income and price elastic and so responds more than proportionally to changes in these variables. At the same time, tourism is subject not only to regular seasonal fluctuations but also to irregular swings brought about by changes in world political and economic conditions; changes in consumer tastes; uncertainty of a sector in which there is a dominance of foreign capital.

Assured economic growth for a country which is dependent upon tourism can there-- fore be extremely problematical. On the other hand, tourism is an export industry which complements other exporting sectors and so adds a greater stability to FE earnings. Although "fashionability" will continue to afflict tourism, the probable continued long term growth in tourism will result in almost all countries increasing their tourism receipts. Finally, though it is clearly desirable for LDCs to avoid dependence on foreign capital, "these disadvantages apply to any industry developed on the basis of foreign capital and... tourism may be at less of a disadvantage here that other industries in view of the fact that technological limitations to local owner-ship would appear to be less significant". (5)

Taking 52 countries (44 LDCs, chosen largely on the basis of the availability of the necessary data but also to give a contrast between different types of country, and eight developed tourist country benchmarks), their tourism receipts[f] as a proportion of visible exports (i e goods) are shown in Table 5. Bryden defined a tourism country as one where tourism receipts exceeded 10 per cent of visible exports (5). Using this standard, 22 of the 52 countries examined fall into this classification. All the Caribbean region countries examined (with the exception of Trinidad which has a high oil export income), three of the six Central American countries (though none of the seven South American countries), four of the ten African countries, two of the 13 Asian countries and the sole example from Oceania qualify as tourism countries, with a high degree of dependence on tourism.

---

1 Using tourism receipts as a measure is, of course, subject to the problem that no account is taken of the import leakages which occur to a degree which varies from 10 to 90 per cent according to type of country concerned.

Bryden used a second criterion for identifying tourism countries: where 5 per cent of national income is accounted for by tourism receipts. This cut off indicates that twelve of the 52 countries examined qualify as tourism countries - three Caribbean islands and Bermuda, only Panama amongst the Central and South American countries, only the two North African countries of Morocco and Tunisia from Africa, three of the 13 Asian countries, Fiji and Malta.

The ten countries to emerge as tourism countries from both formulae are:

	Tourism revenue as a % of:	
	Visible exports	National income
Bahamas	15.9	63.5
Barbados	87.4	24.0
Bermuda	454.8	60.9
Cyprus	19.2	6.5
Fiji	60.0	11.4
Malta	28.3	13.2
Morocco	31.0	6.0
Panama	46.3	6.8
Puerto Rico	12.7	6.0
Tunisia	34.0	7.3

Significantly, with the exceptions of Panama, Morocco and Tunisia, these are all islands with little in the way of industrial development possibilities. Furthermore, Morocco and Tunisia have terrains, climates and resources which limited their means of development, while Panama is unique because of the Canal Zone.

Only Malta of the developed country benchmark countries qualifies as a tourism country in both formulae, and its inclusion as a developed country using the UN definition (see Appendix 7) is through ease of statistical presentation rather than because of its state of economic development which would more properly list it as an LDC. Of the remaining developed countries, which are all widely accepted as tourism countries, only Greece, Yugoslavia, Israel (all of which under a definition specifically related to level of economic development might well be termed LDCs) and Spain earned tourism receipts which constituted more than 10 per cent of the value of visible exports; none had gross tourism earnings which contributed more than 5 per cent of national income (Greece being the highest at 3.9 per cent).

Tables 5 and 6 illustrate how heavily dependent on tourism are small islands or other countries with limited resource development potential; it also shows that LDCs with great but largely unexploited tourism resources (e g many South American, African and Asian countries) can increase their tourism earnings several fold before dependence becomes a cause for concern.

In most of the LDCs which are currently heavily dependent on tourism revenue, there is also a heavy reliance on primary exports (for example sugar) and a high degree of foreign participation in the modern sector. It is argued, therefore, that the structure of production is not evolving in a way that will lead to greater self-sufficiency because production is geared to primary products (and tourism) for export to developed countries. The economic development of LDCs in this situation is, therefore, subject to commodity price fluctuations and the incomes of developed countries. Further, the foreign influence leads to increased demand for imports (from the local population) and can reinforce an inequitable distribution of income.

Table 5

Tourism Revenue Compared with Visible Exports, 1977

North America & Caribbean	Exports of goods ($ mn)	Gross tourism revenue[a] ($ mn)	Tourism revenue as % of exports of goods	Balance of payments account[b] ($ mn)
Bahamas	2,589	412	15.9	67
Barbados	95[c]	83[c]	87.4	-57[c]
Bermuda	42[c]	191[c]	454.8	-101[cd]
Dominican Republic	716[c]	91[c]	12.7	-264
Haiti	111[c]	28[c]	25.2	-13[c]
Jamaica	660[c]	106[c]	16.1	-303[c]
Puerto Rico	3,346[c]	424[c]	12.7	-2,086[c]
Trinidad & Tobago	2,370[c]	87[c]	3.7	204[c]
Central America				
Costa Rica	815	54	6.6	-220
El Salvador	751[c]	18[c]	2.4	22[c]
Guatemala	794[c]	85[c]	11.3	-8[c]
Mexico	4,781	867[e]	18.1	-2,068
Nicaragua	542[c]	25[c]	4.6	-66
Panama	268[c]	124[c]	46.3	-195
South America				
Argentina	3,930[c]	110[c]	2.8	125[c]
Brazil	12,045	55	0.6	-4,849
Chile	2,182	97	4.4	-448
Colombia	2,378[c]	146[c]	6.1	341[c]
Ecuador	1,385	36	2.6	-268
Peru	1,360[c]	118[c]	8.6	-1,193[c]
Venezuela	9,669	261	2.7	-2,053
Africa				
Egypt	1,993	746	37.4	-814
Ghana	970	11[f]	1.1	-42
Ivory Coast	1,642[c]	21[c]	1.3	-206[c]
Kenya	1,138	121	10.6	58
Libya	10,384	8	0.1	2,905
Madagascar	248[c]	3[c]	1.2	-24[c]
Morocco	1,247[c]	386[c]	31.0	-1,397[c]
Sierra Leone	129	4	3.1	-45
Tanzania	548	11[f]	2.0	-11
Tunisia	949	323	34.0	-534
Asia				
Bangladesh	476	2	0.4	-287
Cyprus	304	60	19.7	-88
Hong Kong	9,626	786	8.2	-831
India	5,573	350	6.3	-38
Iran	24,356	153	0.6	5,082
Malaysia	6,507	39	0.6	1,541
Pakistan	1,117	60	5.4	-725
Philippines	3,075	301	9.8	-829
Singapore	7,724	300	3.9	-556

(continued)

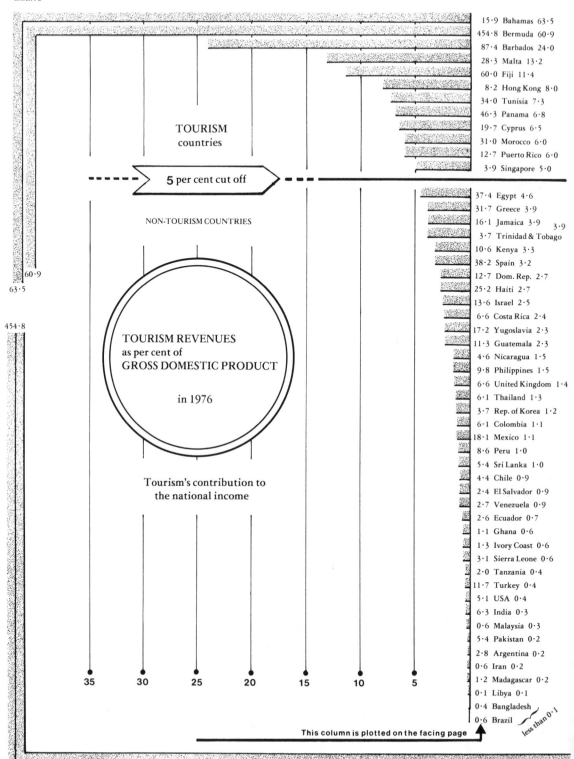

CHART 2

TOURISM
countries

5 per cent cut off

NON-TOURISM COUNTRIES

TOURISM REVENUES
as per cent of
GROSS DOMESTIC PRODUCT

in 1976

Tourism's contribution to
the national income

15·9 Bahamas 63·5
454·8 Bermuda 60·9
87·4 Barbados 24·0
28·3 Malta 13·2
60·0 Fiji 11·4
8·2 Hong Kong 8·0
34·0 Tunisia 7·3
46·3 Panama 6·8
19·7 Cyprus 6·5
31·0 Morocco 6·0
12·7 Puerto Rico 6·0
3·9 Singapore 5·0

37·4 Egypt 4·6
31·7 Greece 3·9
16·1 Jamaica 3·9
3·7 Trinidad & Tobago 3·9
10·6 Kenya 3·3
38·2 Spain 3·2
12·7 Dom. Rep. 2·7
25·2 Haiti 2·7
13·6 Israel 2·5
6·6 Costa Rica 2·4
17·2 Yugoslavia 2·3
11·3 Guatemala 2·3
4·6 Nicaragua 1·5
9·8 Philippines 1·5
6·6 United Kingdom 1·4
6·1 Thailand 1·3
3·7 Rep. of Korea 1·2
6·1 Colombia 1·1
18·1 Mexico 1·1
8·6 Peru 1·0
5·4 Sri Lanka 1·0
4·4 Chile 0·9
2·4 El Salvador 0·9
2·7 Venezuela 0·9
2·6 Ecuador 0·7
1·1 Ghana 0·6
1·3 Ivory Coast 0·6
3·1 Sierra Leone 0·6
2·0 Tanzania 0·4
11·7 Turkey 0·4
5·1 USA 0·4
6·3 India 0·3
0·6 Malaysia 0·3
5·4 Pakistan 0·2
2·8 Argentina 0·2
0·6 Iran 0·2
1·2 Madagascar 0·2
0·1 Libya 0·1
0·4 Bangladesh
0·6 Brazil   less than 0·1

60·9
63·5

454·8

35   30   25   20   15   10   5

This column is plotted on the facing page

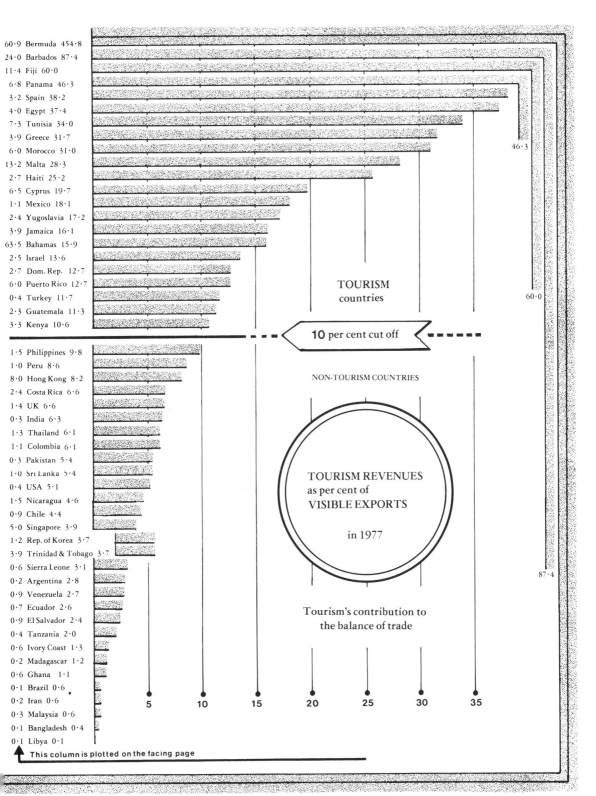

TOURISM
countries

10 per cent cut off

NON-TOURISM COUNTRIES

TOURISM REVENUES
as per cent of
VISIBLE EXPORTS

in 1977

Tourism's contribution to
the balance of trade

60·9 Bermuda 454·8
24·0 Barbados 87·4
11·4 Fiji 60·0
6·8 Panama 46·3
3·2 Spain 38·2
4·0 Egypt 37·4
7·3 Tunisia 34·0
3·9 Greece 31·7
6·0 Morocco 31·0
13·2 Malta 28·3
2·7 Haiti 25·2
6·5 Cyprus 19·7
1·1 Mexico 18·1
2·4 Yugoslavia 17·2
3·9 Jamaica 16·1
63·5 Bahamas 15·9
2·5 Israel 13·6
2·7 Dom. Rep. 12·7
6·0 Puerto Rico 12·7
0·4 Turkey 11·7
2·3 Guatemala 11·3
3·3 Kenya 10·6

1·5 Philippines 9·8
1·0 Peru 8·6
8·0 Hong Kong 8·2
2·4 Costa Rica 6·6
1·4 UK 6·6
0·3 India 6·3
1·3 Thailand 6·1
1·1 Colombia 6·1
0·3 Pakistan 5·4
1·0 Sri Lanka 5·4
0·4 USA 5·1
1·5 Nicaragua 4·6
0·9 Chile 4·4
5·0 Singapore 3·9
1·2 Rep. of Korea 3·7
3·9 Trinidad & Tobago 3·7
0·6 Sierra Leone 3·1
0·2 Argentina 2·8
0·9 Venezuela 2·7
0·7 Ecuador 2·6
0·9 El Salvador 2·4
0·4 Tanzania 2·0
0·6 Ivory Coast 1·3
0·2 Madagascar 1·2
0·6 Ghana 1·1
0·1 Brazil 0·6
0·2 Iran 0·6
0·3 Malaysia 0·6
0·1 Bangladesh 0·4
0·1 Libya 0·1

46·3
60·0
87·4

5 10 15 20 25 30 35

This column is plotted on the facing page

This bar is doubled to show it at the same scale as the rest of the plots

167

Table 5 (continued)

Tourism Revenue Compared with Visible Exports, 1977

Asia (continued)	Exports of goods ($ mn)	Gross tourism revenue[a] ($ mn)	Tourism revenue as % of exports of goods	Balance of payments account[b] ($ mn)
South Korea	10,046	370	3.7	8
Sri Lanka	747	40	5.4	132
Thailand	3,453	211	6.1	-1,099
Turkey	1,752	205	11.7	-3,325
Oceania				
Fiji	125[g]	75[g]	60.0	-9[g]
DEVELOPED COUNTRY BENCHMARKS				
Greece	2,522	980	31.7	-1,341
Israel	3,389	461	13.6	-581
Malta	237[c]	67[c]	28.3	64[c]
Spain	10,485	4,003	38.2	-1,205
UK	56,593	3,760	6.6	634
USA	120,556	6,164	5.1	-15,251
Yugoslavia	4,881	841	17.2	-1,602

a Gross payments made in the country visited; excluding international transportation receipts. b Goods, services and transfers. c 1976; June 30, 1976, for Puerto Rico. d Goods only. e Data relates to tourists to the interior; in addition, short stay visitors crossing over the US-Mexico border spent $1,506 mn in 1977. f Estimates based on data for part year. g 1975.

Sources: World Travel Statistics 1977, WTO, for tourism revenue; International Financial Statistics and UN Monthly Bulletin of Statistics for exports and balance of payments.

Table 6

Tourism's Contribution to National Income, 1976

North America & Caribbean	GNP per caput[a] ($)	Gross tourism revenue per caput ($)	Gross tourism revenue per caput as % GNP per caput
Bahamas	2,500	1,588	63.5
Barbados	1,400	336	24.0
Bermuda	5,500	3,351	60.9
Dominican Republic	694	19	2.7
Haiti	220	6	2.7
Jamaica	1,310	51	3.9
Puerto Rico	2,200	132	6.0
Trinidad & Tobago	2,090	81	3.9

(continued)

Table 6 (continued)

Tourism's Contribution to National Income, 1976

Central America	GNP per caput[a] ($)	Gross tourism revenue per caput ($)	Gross tourism revenue per caput as % GNP per caput
Costa Rica	1,064	25	2.4
El Salvador	503	4	0.9
Guatemala	600	14	2.3
Mexico[b]	1,130	13(38)[b]	1.1(3.3)[b]
Nicaragua	761	11	1.5
Panama	1,055	72	6.8
South America			
Argentina	1,900	4	0.2
Brazil	1,100	1	0.1
Chile	960	9	0.9
Colombia	540	6	1.1
Ecuador	621	4	0.7
Peru	700	7	1.0
Venezuela	2,070	18	0.9
Africa			
Egypt	310	12	4.0
Ghana	230	1	0.6
Ivory Coast	730	4	0.6
Kenya	220	7	3.3
Libya	5,000	5	0.1
Madagascar	210	0.5	0.2
Morocco	360	22	6.0
Sierra Leone	200	1[c]	0.6
Tanzania	150	1	0.4
Tunisia	735	53	7.3
Asia			
Bangladesh	85	0.5	0.1
Cyprus	1,157	75	6.5
Hong Kong	2,090	167	8.0
India	132	0.5	0.3
Iran	1,700	4	0.2
Malaysia	840	3	0.3
Pakistan	180	1	0.3
Philippines	360	5	1.5
Singapore	2,470	124	5.0
South Korea	641	8	1.2
Sri Lanka	214	2	1.0
Thailand	358	5	1.3
Turkey	980	4	0.4
Oceania			
Fiji	1,117	128[d]	11.4

(continued)

Table 6 (continued)

Tourism's Contribution to National Income, 1976

	GNP per caput[a] ($)	Gross tourism revenue per caput ($)	Gross tourism revenue per caput as % GNP per caput
DEVELOPED COUNTRY BENCHMARKS			
Greece	2,322	90	3.9
Israel	3,288	83	2.5
Malta	1,533	203	13.2
Spain	2,663	88	3.2
UK	3,550	51	1.4
USA	6,996	27	0.4
Yugoslavia	1,540	37	2.4

a National income at market prices; data relate to 1976 unless otherwise stated. b Figures in parentheses include expenditure by short stay border excursionists. c 1977. d 1975.

Sources: The World in Figures for GNP and population data; World Travel Statistics 1977, WTO, for tourism revenue.

THE COMMERCIAL PRACTICES OF FOREIGN ENTERPRISES

LDCs need foreign knowhow rather than foreign capital

As already indicated, LDCs are heavily reliant upon foreign capital and expertise in their tourism sector development. The commercial practices adopted by foreign organisations in respect of their operations in, and dealings with, LDCs create both economic and social effects. The purpose of examining these practices separately is to answer the question: are LDCs right, from an economic viewpoint, to welcome the contribution made by transnational corporations (TNCs),i e can it be shown that TNCs have a special advantage in supplying tourism services and do not exploit these advantages solely to their own benefit?

Before tackling the arguments for and against foreign participation in LDCs, there are some preliminary questions which should be answered. Do LDCs need foreign partners at all in the development of their tourism sectors? Why has the situation developed where foreign organisations play such an important role in LDCs' tourism sectors? The answer is not because of a shortage of investment funds (which are available from government, local private sector and international agencies). It is the proprietary knowledge and expertise possessed by the foreign based hotel groups, tour operators, etc, which make LDCs dependent on them. The tourism product (which embraces the provision of facilities, coordinating them, designing and selling attractive holiday packages, transporting tourists between their sources and destinations and ensuring the local performance is to the standard required by tourists) is, in many ways, more difficult to supply than exported commodities or goods because of its perishability. If a consignment of cocoa or textiles is delayed a day or two, there is generally little concern; if a planeload of tourists is similarly delayed, the repercussions may be substantial. Social or political disturbances (at least short of a revolution) do not make much difference to the export of goods; but such events may serve virtually to eliminate tourism for quite a period (for example, Portugal during the period of its political and social restructure in 1974/75).

There is no doubt that the foreign based hotel groups, airlines and tour operators can do much to help LDCs get over these problems, through coordination of travel arrangements, confidence boosting publicity, etc. If it can be proved that the TNCs do not exploit these special advantages solely to their own benefit and that they bring some economic benefit to LDCs this might well justify their welcome.

In the next few pages the pros and cons of foreign TNC involvement in LDCs' tourism sectors are debated, based on past research in the field. Whilst emphasis is laid on the deleterious effect of the commercial practices of international hotel groups, airlines and tour operators and the proportion of expenditure of tourists using their services on trips to LDCs which is lost from the LDC tourist receiving country, a number of points should be noted. First, the extent to which these revenue "distortions" are a function of the foreign TNC is not always clear or even proven; second, that the costs and benefits of foreign hotel groups, airlines and tour operators are frequently interdependent and it may not be easy to eliminate or reduce costs; and, third, that whatever the loss of tourists' revenue from operations using foreign TNCs, the key consideration should be whether or not the foreign organisations use available resources more efficiently than other users.

HOTEL GROUPS

How foreign participation works

As indicated in Section 2, international hotel chains prefer to exercise control over resource allocation in host countries through franchise or management agreements rather than through ownership. In LDCs, the management contract is more common simply because the level and quantity of expertise to operate hotels of international standard is not available within the LDCs. The Hilton chain states its policy as being "in the business of designing and operating hotels, not buying and owning them". Neither is it their policy to franchise or to share management responsibilities. Hilton sells its capacity in "creating, designing, developing, managing and marketing hotel services". (20)

There are two main types of management contract.

   i.   based on turnover (typically 2 to 4 per cent with the higher rate covering instances where the marketing, as well as the management, function is contracted to the hotel chain) plus an incentive commission related to profits (after depreciation and amortisation of equipment but before tax, interest and building depreciation);

   ii. based on a share of profits (20 to 25 per cent is the normal range) plus small, pre-specified percentages of the turnover to cover fixed charges and the replacement of assets.

While a management contract related to turnover plus commission normally runs between five and ten years, one based on profit sharing is usually a good deal longer, around 20 years.

International hotel chains bring a number of benefits to LDCs which most LDCs are unable to provide from internal resources. These include:

 i. the provision of trained staff, experienced in working in differing economic, political and social environments and accustomed to dealing with tourists;

 ii. access to an international computer reservations system;

 iii. centralised purchasing (leading to guaranteed supplies and higher quality and lower price than could be obtained by a local hotel).

It should also be noted that there are concomitant costs, e g the loss of local control over decision making (through the TNC's policy of centralisation) in respect of resource allocation. Hilton's policy demonstrates this point: 'The lines of action flow up and down from the president through the area vice presidents and divisional directors to the general managers of each operating hotel, who are never left by themselves to make vital decisions without the counsel and guidance of this highly professional group of hotel experts, available immediately in any phase of hotel operation." (20)

Do international hotel groups usurp LDCs' sovereignty?

The charges levelled against international hotel groups are numerous but the evidence available is too confusing to enable definitive conclusions to be made for or against their participation in LDCs. At the most extreme level is the charge which can be made about all TNCs irrespective of the sector in which they operate, that international hotel chains usurp the sovereignty of LDCs. Certainly hotel groups (and international airlines) are in a position where they can choose whether or not to integrate their operations with national plans and there have undoubtedly been examples where strategies have been pursued contrary to such plans. The circumstances under which such undermining actions are most possible occur when the TNC has no direct financial stake in the LDC. The trend noted earlier for international hotel groups to prefer to run hotels under management contracts or franchises rather than have a financial holding facilitates this practice.

Is their technology inappropriate?

A second charge made against international hotel chains is that the technology brought to LDCs is inappropriate. This argument has been touched upon earlier (see page 34) and involves consideration of whether or not the tourism plant of an LDC should be designed in a style familiar to its potential customers and furnished and equipped to provide the level of creature comforts believed to be required by the majority of tourists from the generating centres. The issue is far wider than initially appears to be the case and embraces consideration of what type of tourism product the LDC should provide, i e whether the maximisation of FE, provision of employment, etc, is the principal aim, in which case the flexibility to move outside the requirements of the tourist generating market is fairly small, or whether tourism development is seen as being essentially compatible with the social and economic aims of the LDC, in which case a tourism product relying heavily on indigenous designs, materials and staff may be more suitable, albeit with a far

172

reduced level of custom. Finding the answer to this problem is currently taxing many LDCs. They need to know how many fewer tourists and, more important, jobs and reduced FE earnings, will be generated given the latter policy; and do these outweigh the social benefits of lessening the dilution of the country's traditional society, culture, and so on.

This brings us back to the problem of inadequate skilled staff available in LDC tourism administrations. There is insufficient knowledge of generating market requirements and preferences and a lack of the requisite skills both to assess the value and cost of technology and to identify better alternative sources and methods of transfer. These shortcomings, combined with the fact that data may be difficult to obtain (much of it having to be provided by the foreign TNCs), make it extremely difficult for LDCs to resolve this issue.

<u>Do they import too much?</u>

A third complaint made by LDCs about TNC hotel groups is their excessive reliance on imports. The UN Ecosoc/IUOTO study surveyed LDCs and reported that LDCs considered that there were a number of instances where foreign owned or operated hotels imported excessive amounts of food, hotel furniture and furnishings. Hotel chains pursuing a standardisation policy were particularly criticised. Central purchasing departments, situated outside the LDC, are also viewed with suspicion, the feeling amongst LDC administrations being that "whilst such arrangements may lower costs to the purchasing hotel in the short run, they may also inhibit the development of local industries, particularly in the agricultural sector, as well as increasing the import content of tourism". (49)

For their part, the international hotel chains refute these charges, claiming instead that they use local materials, products and food supplies wherever possible and even serve to stimulate local furniture and furnishings operations through their demand.

The UN Ecosoc/IUOTO (49) study attempted to analyse the import content of constructing, equipping and operating a hotel in an LDC. Clearly this greatly depends on the resources and economic and industrial structure of the country concerned, but the consensus view was as follows:

	Cost component analysis (%)	Import content (%)
Construction & capital equipment	87.5 to 92.5	50 to 80
Furniture & furnishings	4 to 6	10 to 50
Hotel operating equipment	4 to 6	20 to 70
Overall	100	45 to 80 (average 60)

Varley (52) produces comparable figures for Fiji - it fares well on construction and capital equipment (54 per cent imported) but less well on furniture and furnishings (52 per cent imported); virtually all (90 per cent) of the operating equipment required is imported. In neither of these studies, however, is there clear evidence to show that, where the developer is a foreign enterprise, this results in higher imports than if the hotel had been developed by a local concern.

With respect to hotel operating costs, the UN Ecosoc/IUOTO report states: "In terms of the division of hotels' revenue according to the proportion which is retained within the country of location and that which is lost in the form of imported materials, expatriate staff, etc, there is wide variation, depending on location of ownership, and degree of the host country's self-sufficiency in trained hotel staff, maintenance equipment, food supplies, etc. The worst situation is that of a developing country which retains less than 25 per cent of its hotels' gross revenue." (49) Then, in the only direct comparison between locally owned and foreign owned hotels, the report states that in the case of one LDC which has already achieved mass tourism status (Tunisia), there is a greater dilution of earnings for foreign owned hotels.

Ownership	% of operating revenue retained locally
Domestic	80
Foreign	60

Are their employment and training programmes adequate?

Failure to employ sufficient local management and inadequate or inappropriate training programmes is the fourth charge made against international hotel chains. Despite legislation designed to oblige foreign hotel groups to expedite the transfer of skills and management posts to local personnel, LDCs believe there is considerable evasion of this responsibility by the TNC hotel groups.

All international hotel chains have a core team of expatriate management staff - a typical pattern reported by UN Ecosoc/IUOTO is three in a 100 room hotel, five in a 250 room hotel and eight in a 350 room unit. Furthermore, in the early days of operation at least, foreign hotel chains employ more management (usually expatriates) in a hotel in an LDC than in a comparable unit in a developed country. The hotel groups claim that this is necessary in order to provide adequate training and supervision of local staff. As a proportion of the wages and salaries bill, hotel chains estimate that expatriate staff account for between 15 and 20 per cent of the total, although they are at pains to point out that a considerable proportion of this will be spent locally and contribute to local value added.

The international hotel chains all pursue a publicly stated policy of training local staff. The complaint of LDCs is that the schemes for training local personnel for management posts are inadequate (in terms of speed and volume) and inappropriate. One way of circumventing the former problem has been for LDCs to stipulate as part of a management contract with an international hotel chain running for, say, ten years that within three or five years the whole of the management (or all except the general manager) must be local citizens. The accusation of the inappropriateness of training programmes is founded on the centralised policy-making of the international hotel chains. The training programmes undertaken by the hotel groups are designed to induce the local managers and employees to behave consistently with parent company policy, rather than considering the individual country's interest. This appears to be a valid point - certainly the Hilton International group regards its trained managers as a company resource movable from country to country, rather than as being limited to their native countries - but this is in line with the training policies of TNCs in other sectors, and a major change in the balance of power between the LDCs and TNCs will be necessary before significant changes are likely to be enforceable.

CHART 3

IMPORT CONTENT IN SETTING UP HOTELS IN LDCs

Per cent of total. Based on mid-point ranges
from a   UN ECOSOC/IUOTO Report

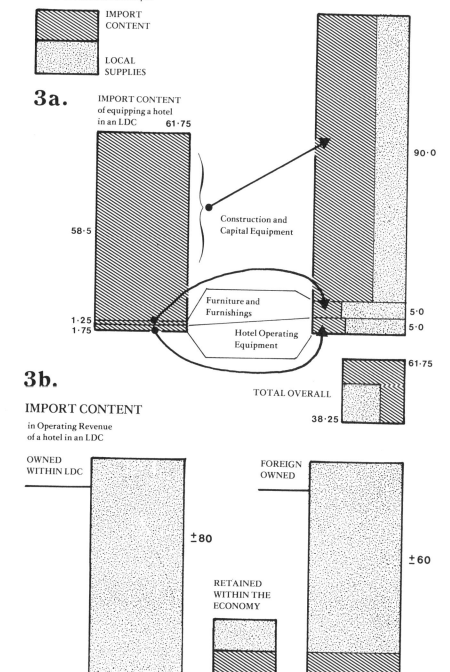

IMPORT
CONTENT

LOCAL
SUPPLIES

3a.

IMPORT CONTENT
of equipping a hotel
in an LDC   61·75

90·0

58·5

Construction and
Capital Equipment

Furniture and
Furnishings

Hotel Operating
Equipment

5·0

5·0

1·25
1·75

3b.

61·75

TOTAL OVERALL

38·25

IMPORT CONTENT

in Operating Revenue
of a hotel in an LDC

OWNED
WITHIN LDC

FOREIGN
OWNED

±80

±60

RETAINED
WITHIN THE
ECONOMY

IMPORTS

±40

±20

Accusations of profiteering are unproven

A fifth area of suspicion about the practices of international hotel chains relates to profits and transfer prices. There is almost no evidence to support any LDC accusations of excessive profiteering through overspecifying equipment, furniture, etc, for units in LDCs supplied from the group's central stores, or as regards the manipulation of the prices of goods and services transferred between subsidiaries. Again, the deficiency of skilled personnel in LDCs to undertake this type of analysis and the fact that the requisite data have to be obtained from "the accused" make such evaluation extremely difficult.

Wages too high?

The sixth (and somewhat paradoxical) charge made against international hotel chains is that they pay their local staff too highly, immediately bringing about social tensions and disrupting the local labour market by creating large wage inequalities compared with other sectors. This will eventually erode any comparative advantage a specific LDC might have had in terms of cheaper labour as the process of wage bargaining spreads the "imported" wage levels to other sectors of the economy. The reason the international hotel chains pay relatively high wages is that they want to attract the best quality staff to enable a service to be provided to the foreign tourist which will enhance the LDC's reputation and image in his eyes. The hotel groups also claim that their payment of good wages serves to improve standards in training, education, health, etc. Furthermore, the only way in which the accommodation sector will become increasingly self-sufficient is if more citizens of LDCs set up their own hotels, prerequisites for which are adequate skills and funds. The surest way of obtaining these is by working for a period with an international hotel chain.

Conclusions

No definite conclusion can be drawn from the available evidence as to whether TNC hotel chains are worthwhile to LDCs, although the knowledge gulf described earlier makes it imperative for some (probably substantial) involvement with international hotel chains if an LDC wishes the tourism sector to play a significant role in its economic development (both China and Cuba have recognised this and are consequently negotiating with foreign hotel groups to assist in the development of their hotel sectors).

Clearly considerably more research is essential before firm conclusions can be made, but two points do emerge.

1. In the cases where the operations of international hotel chains have been least satisfactory to the host LDC, the great majority have involved corporations without any financial investment in the hotel. This is significant (and perturbing) given the increasing trend for TNCs to operate hotels under management contracts and franchises.

2. The negotiating position of LDC host countries is stronger in the hotel sector than in industrial sectors, because the design, building, equipping, furnishing and operating phases can be disaggregated into a number of contractual arrangements, while the "package deal" approach is more normal for TNCs in the processing and manufacturing sectors.

AIRLINES

Do pooling arrangements benefit developed countries?

Air tariffs are agreed in traffic conferences of Iata   subject to the approval of the
governments concerned.   The fares agreed are then incorporated into <u>bilateral</u>
<u>agreements</u>, which take one of two forms.   The most common is where the airlines
are left largely free to decide, on commercial grounds, the frequency and capacity
of the services they offer.   The other type of agreement is one in which a particular
government (in order to protect its own small national airline) controls the number
of flights and passengers which foreign airlines may fly to/from its country.

While Bermuda type agreements allow (mainly) free competition between the desig-
nated airlines of the two governments, in practice the airlines concerned usually
also enter into an annual <u>pooling agreement</u>.   This is designed to ensure a fair reward for input (i e the capacity and flight schedule operated, promotional activities
undertaken, technical services offered, etc).   Pooling agreements can vary from an
arrangement to provide reciprocal technical services to a division of all revenue
earned and costs incurred on a route.

Probably because the airlines are extremely secretive about the precise terms of
pools, suggestions have been made that the terms discriminate against the LDC
airline (relative to its costs of operating the route) when an agreement is made with
an airline of a developed country.   It is difficult to make a judgment on this point
because the two countries are unequal partners - most of the traffic on routes between developed countries and LDCs will be generated in the former and tourists
will prefer to travel by the developed country's airline (as a result of its greater
promotion and prestige).   Given totally unrestricted competition, the LDC airline
would obtain only a very small share of the market on most routes between developed
and developing countries.   A pooling agreement offers a somewhat higher share but,
unless it is a full revenue and costs pool, it may still be the case that the LDC airline
is in a disadvantageous position in relation to its operating costs.

The US government is resolved to deregulate the world airline industry.   This has
been manifested by its pushing for much more open competition in the recently
renegotiated bilateral agreements with the UK, West Germany and Israel, a ban on
its airlines entering into pooling agreements and a threat to Iata   (the airline's
fare setting and regulatory body) by requiring it to "show cause" why the US Civil
Aeronautics Board should not impose its anti-trust laws on the world's airlines,
finding that their membership of Iata's   fares fixing conferences were contrary to
the public interest.   If Iata does become greatly weakened, a natural consequence
will be less extensive pooling agreements.   LDC airlines must, under such circumstances, be the biggest losers and are resisting the US government's moves to remove their protective umbrella.

Revenue from foreign airline operations

Two aspects of foreign scheduled airline operations (servicing and expatriate staff)
result in a drain on the economies of the countries·in which they operate.   "Few
developing countries have the servicing plants necessary for the current generation
of passenger aircraft and so potential FE earnings from servicing a foreign airline's
planes are lost.   Approximately five expatriate staff are used by scheduled airlines
in major overseas stations".   (49)

Charter operations. The UN Ecosoc/IUOTO report states that a host country receives only 7 to 9 per cent of the airline's revenue (in the form of landing fees, fuel costs, passenger handling) if the airline is a charter operator of another country. If fuel is excluded, this proportion may fall as low as 2 to 3 per cent. Little of charter package tourists' air fare expenditure, consequently, accrues to LDC destinations and many have expressed doubts about the desirability of encouraging extensive foreign charter operations. LDCs can limit or ban charter programmes (e g Brazil, Israel until 1977, Bermuda) but this might result in lower revenues from a smaller volume of tourists.

Resolving this dilemma requires answering another difficult question; is the volume of spending by charter tourists on local goods and services greater or lower than that of those tourists who might, in the absence of charters, travel on the LDC's airline? Answering this is made more difficult by the fact that it will differ from country to country, reflecting the type of tourism resources, promotional activities, scheduled airline operations, etc. Whilst the general rule appears to be that charter flights are fundamental to the development of large scale or mass tourism, there are exceptions. For example, Bermuda has developed a major tourism sector with limited reliance upon charter operations.

TOUR OPERATORS

As noted earlier   , LDCs are apprehensive about the power foreign tour operators have because of their knowledge of consumer requirements and control of the distribution system.

Contracts with hotel groups

Foreign tour operators enter into low rate (discounts off rack of up to one third), group size related, contracts for hotel space in destinations featured in their tour programmes. The conditions of these contracts, in terms of who bears the greatest risk, reflect the relative negotiating strength of the two parties - is it a buyer's or a seller's market? The system adopted by the large tour operators is that, approximately two to three months before each programmed tour departure, the tour operator will confirm the exact group size, thus determining the rate which will apply, and will relinquish the remaining originally reserved rooms. Normally there will be no penalty for not filling these rooms, although penalties are levied on some of the smaller tour operators for failing to achieve minimum occupancy levels.

Hoteliers find they are unable to replace this lost custom in the two to three months from notice of cancellation when market demand is weak (and it should be noted that there is no evidence that LDC hoteliers fare worse under such circumstances than those in developed country resorts). As a consequence, there is a tendency to double book or double allocate rooms during the planning period, which may be a year in advance. If demand is strong, the incidence of two parties arriving for one room may be considerable, leading to widespread consumer and tour operator dissatisfaction.

Clearly the negotiating position can vary widely between different countries and from year to year. In popular resorts with limited hotel capacity, the tour operator may find it extremely difficult to obtain room allocations and the terms are likely to favour the hoteliers. A laudable move to try to lessen this pendulum effect and to eradicate the need for hoteliers to double allocate rooms is the proposal by the Spanish tourism authorities to introduce a standard hotel booking contract form to be used by the country's hoteliers in their dealings with overseas tour operators. If the form, however, reduced the tour operators' bargaining position (by, for example, binding tour operators to their room allocations), the action would need to be taken on a regional basis (at least) to be successful.

Payment methods may be to host countries' disadvantage

The prepayment in his home country by the tourist for a package tour can lead to various abuses in the transfer of monies to the tourist receiving country (e g a credit may be issued in the generating country for use by the local tourism enterprise's owner, thereby enabling him to evade FE control regulations). Similarly, certain tour operators give their customers vouchers to purchase meals, tours, etc, but there is no guarantee that the local supplier will cash them in the tourist receiving country. A third example is where the supplier of the tourism services in the receiving country is financially linked (e g through vertical integration) to the tour operator, in which case payments and receipts may simply be book entries at manipulated prices.

All of these concerns apply equally to developed and developing tourist receiving countries. Furthermore, there is little concrete evidence that any of these feared violations of FE regulations have taken, or do take, place. This is another area in which detailed research is lacking.

LDCs' lack of control over tour operators

LDCs criticise tour operators on the following scores:

   i.   drawing up tour programmes without consultation with the NTO of the developing country;

   ii.   encouraging travel agent retailers not to distinguish between destinations through paying commission as a set amount (rather than a percentage of retail price) per booking;

   iii.   lacking any responsibility for promoting particular destinations but instead using destinations to sell package tours;

   iv.   presenting an inaccurate image of destinations in their brochures;

   v.   employing tour guides of their own country and threatening to drop the destination from their programme if the host country government insists on local guides.

All of these issues reflect the nature of the tour operating business, which is indeed selling tours rather than specific destinations, and are a function of supply/demand. It should be noted that there is little specific discrimination against LDCs - the same points are made by all destination countries.

Revenue from package tourists accruing to LDCs

The proportion of tourists' gross expenditure which adds local value to the tourist receiving country depends, amongst others, on the following:

    i.   geographic location (and proportion of total expenditure made up by transportation);

    ii.   type of airfare and locus of ownership of airline;

    iii. type and locus of ownership of accommodation used;

    iv.   socio-economic characteristics of tourists;

    v.   catering arrangements (pre-arranged or self-catering).

Taking a two week package tour arrangement with full board included, the UN Ecosoc/ IUOTO report looked at the levels of dilution of tourists' expenditure which might occur in different types of destination and using different means of transportation.

For a country like Spain (a developed, mass tourism country, short haul from any Western European generating market) between one third and two thirds of the tourists' prepaid inclusive tour expenditure would accrue locally and contribute to local value added (the variation is caused principally by the type of air travel arrangement used and the locus of ownership of the hotel stayed in).

Taking an LDC like Tunisia, but with otherwise the same characteristics as Spain, the proportion of expenditure contributing to local value added is lower - between one third and one half (although since the bulk of tourists travel on foreign owned charter airlines the average proportion realised is much nearer the lower end of this scale).

Taking a long haul LDC such as India, the proportion falls again to between one fifth and one half. This further fall is because of the increased importance in the tour cost of the air fare element which is subject to a greater foreign component than the land element.

The report estimates that package tourists' expenditure on incidentals constituted an additional 70 to 80 per cent of the prepaid tour price in the case of short haul destinations but only an extra 30 to 50 per cent for long haul destinations (reflecting the higher air fare component). Before deducting imports from these incidental expenditures, an average two thirds of a tourist's total expenditure (prepaid and incidentals) accrues to a short haul destination, a proportion which declines to between 40 and 50 per cent for a long haul destination. Gross expenditure on incidentals constitutes up to three quarters of the short haul LDC's receipts from the package tourist, and up to two thirds in the case of long haul LDCs.

The picture must cause concern to all LDC administrations. If, simply for illustrative purposes, it is assumed that one half of tourists' purchases of incidentals is lost to pay the import cost of such items, then the net proportions of total expenditure accruing to the destination are:

    Short haul: 38.5-51 per cent
    Long haul: 28.5-48 per cent

Clearly tour operator TNCs pursue a number of practices which militate against the interests of LDC (but also most developed country) destinations. Most such practices are pursued because the supply/demand balance favours the foreign tour operator. As in most other areas, inadequate detailed evidence exists to present positive conclusions but it is clear that, until LDCs, individually or collectively, tilt the balance in their own favour tour operators' practices will not significantly change.

SOCIAL AND CULTURAL FACTORS

Tourism's social and cultural impact has only recently been recognised

In this section, we outline some of the major issues surrounding the social and cultural impact of international tourism, although it must be emphasised that it is not always possible to separate these effects from the purely economic.

Interest in the sociology of tourism is comparatively recent, the first articles appearing in the mid 1960s, while serious academic recognition of the importance of tourism's impact on society and culture has only dated from the early 1970s. The growth of mass tourism appears to have prompted this interest but still, to date, no definitive methodology has been established (possibly because it has been economists rather than sociologists who have opened up this area of research). But it is now widely recognised that tourism development brings about many of the same characteristics of social change as the various forms of industrial development.

Tourism in LDCs inevitably involves the introduction and spread of Western social and cultural values. Tourism's opposers argue that it has an impact similar to that of the mass media which Marshall MacLuhan blames for turning the world into a "global village" (27). Until the development of sophisticated communications methods enabled the spread of the mass media throughout the world, different societies lived in more or less closed circles with their own civilisations and value systems. Increased knowledge of other societies (particularly in LDCs about Western Europe, North America, etc) leads to adoption of some of their values and a growing uniformity of the different societies. Tourism, it is argued, works in a similar way (though more direct since there can be physical contact). With the development of low cost, fast air transportation, these agents of change can be easily introduced into previously isolated societies.

Tourism's advocates do not accept the diagnosis that tourism breaks down social and cultural differences, believing instead that individual cultures can withstand increasing exposure to each other. Within its statement of "fundamental aim", the WTO sees tourism as a means of contributing to "international understanding, peace, prosperity and universal respect for, and observance of, human rights and fundamental freedom for all without distinction as to race, sex, language or religion" (extract from the "fundamental aim" of the WTO). The opposing viewpoint is that tourism is responsible not only for creating a uniform society but also for all sorts of social and cultural (as well as economic) problems, grouped under the umbrella accusation of neo-colonialisation.

With such a wide disparity in the views of tourism's impact on society, it is perhaps not surprising that, as yet, there is no cut and dried method for making the necessary evaluation. In this section of the report, a number of case studies are drawn on in

DIVISION OF TOURISTS' EXPENDITURE

CHART 4

on a 2 weeks, full board inclusive tour to an LDC
in revenue units — based on UN ECOSOC/IUOTO *Report*

SHORT HAUL

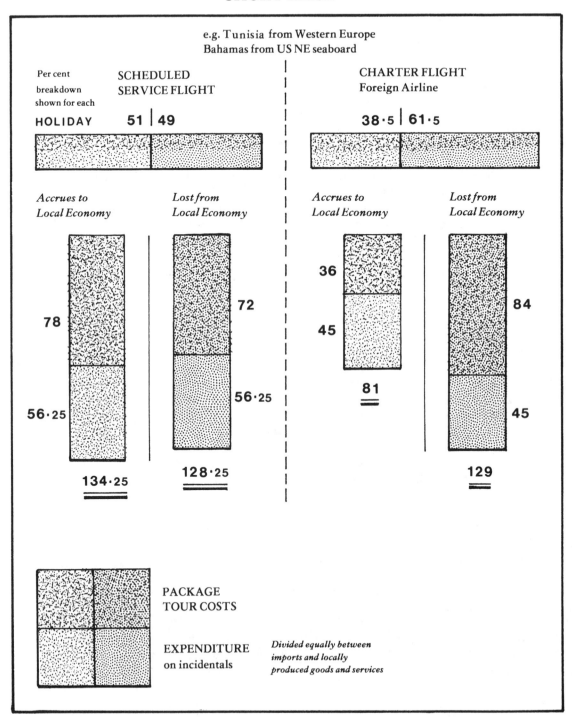

e.g. Tunisia from Western Europe
Bahamas from US NE seaboard

Per cent breakdown shown for each

SCHEDULED SERVICE FLIGHT

CHARTER FLIGHT
Foreign Airline

HOLIDAY   51 | 49   38·5 | 61·5

Accrues to Local Economy   *Lost from Local Economy*   *Accrues to Local Economy*   *Lost from Local Economy*

78   72   36
56·25   56·25   45
       81
134·25   128·25   129
                45   84

PACKAGE TOUR COSTS

EXPENDITURE on incidentals   *Divided equally between imports and locally produced goods and services*

182

LONG HAUL

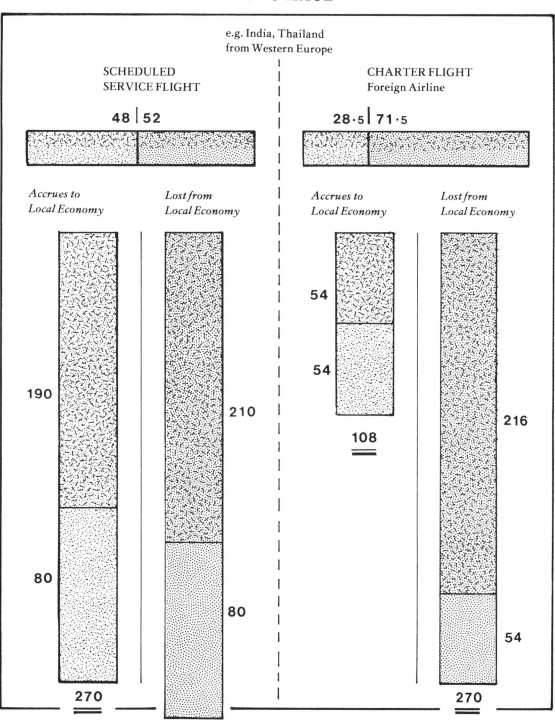

e.g. India, Thailand
from Western Europe

SCHEDULED
SERVICE FLIGHT

48 | 52

Accrues to
Local Economy

Lost from
Local Economy

190

80

270

210

80

290

CHARTER FLIGHT
Foreign Airline

28·5 | 71·5

Accrues to
Local Economy

Lost from
Local Economy

54

54

108

216

54

270

order to present examples of social and cultural impact attributed to tourism. The purpose of this approach is not to draw any specific conclusions as to whether or not tourism does have a certain impact but to identify a number of possible hypotheses to which future research should be directed, e g the saturation level concept (see page 197).

There are different types of tourist (not only from different cultures and socio-economic strata but also with different requirements of their overseas travel) who can be expected to exert influences on host countries which themselves differ considerably. Attention is paid initially in this section to the identification of these main tourist types, and the range and sequence of reactions of residents of tourist receiving countries to foreign tourists is outlined. Then follows an exploration of the theory that the degree of adverse reaction on the part of host country citizens is directly related to the volume of tourism. The ways in which tourism has been claimed to affect the structure, socio-economic and socio-cultural aspects of the societies of tourist receiving countries are then examined and a final subsection looks at the impact on the environment.

TYPES OF TOURIST

Classifying tourists:-

Types of tourist differ according to their expectations and, to a certain extent, on how much they are willing (and able) to spend. Apart from vacationing tourists to which this discussion is principally devoted, tourists take various forms including those of businessmen, diplomats, conference/convention delegates, students, sportsmen and persons travelling for reasons of health, religion and family. A number of tourism taxonomies have been suggested. Some are based on the tourists' interests (ethnic, cultural, historical, environmental, recreational); others on the frequency and style of travel; yet others have tried to separate tourist types according to a blend of their socio-economic backgrounds and holiday preferences. All typologies suffer from one or more of the failings of being tentative in nature, overlapping or being non-discrete.

The choice of tourism types in this report has been dictated by the need to separate tourists according to the different impacts they create on the residents of the host country. There are a number of important variables: the extent to which the tourist is interested in immersing himself in the host country environment; the time spent by the tourist in the host country; and the type of host country resident which the tourist meets (and the purpose of the meeting). Cohen (9) suggests that the key is whether or not the tourist is "institutionalised" (i e using programmed services of airlines, travel agents, tour operators, etc). He has designed a typology appropriate for the purposes of this section. He takes the two segments (sunlust, wanderlust) identified by Gray further by dividing sunlust tourism into organised and individual mass tourism segments while wanderlust tourism is subdivided into categories he terms the "explorer" and the "drifter".

- the organised mass tourist -

The holidays taken by the organised mass tourist are characterised by minimal involvement with the people of the country visited or their culture because of the use of hotels and other facilities developed specifically for the tourist. This type of tourist does not expect to forgo many of the leisure features to which he is accustomed; he wants to experience "the novelty of the macroenvironment of a strange place from the security of a familiar microenvironment" (9). Typical mass tourist resorts in LDCs are Acapulco (Mexico), Nassau and Freeport (Bahamas) and Sousse (Tunisia). Visits will be structured and generally of short duration (long weekend to two weeks).

- the individual mass tourist -

The only difference from the organised mass tourist of the individual mass tourist is that travel is arranged independently rather than as part of a group. The resorts/ countries visited, expectations and duration of trip are largely the same as for the organised mass tourist.

- the explorer -

The explorer type is not institutionalised, but frequently acts as a trailblazer for the mass tourist who follows in his wake as new tourism destinations are developed following publicity from individual visits. Their experience of host countries, as they step out of their "environmental bubble" (9) is often great but it is generally gained in the role of spectators not willing to adopt permanently any of the characteristics. Visits will be largely unstructured and of longer duration than the mass tourist.

- the drifter

The drifter is also non-institutionalised and may also act as a pioneer for the mass tourist in some instances. Drifters have very different expectations, often being intent on leaving familiarity behind and experiencing other cultures fully. They look at the host society "from the dustbin" (9) and seek to achieve a quite different level of contact with the societies of the countries they visit from any of the other types of vacation tourist. The "alternative tourist" often shuns air transport, instead using road or rail on overland tours of Asia or Africa. As with the explorer, visits will tend to be of long duration (several weeks), enabling more contact with and (at least as a general rule) more understanding of the host community.

RESIDENTS' REACTIONS TO TOURISTS

How tourists and residents meet

Any meeting between tourist and host is characterised by its transitory nature, by constraints of time and space, and by relationships that are unequal and lacking in spontaneity. There may also be barriers of communications (language) and culture (lack of empathy).

As already noted, the drifter and the explorer are likely to look for and appreciate the life style of the countries they visit and actively to seek to mix with the local population. On the other hand, the institutionalised tourist neither wants, nor is able (because of the structure of his pre-arranged package), to mingle with the resident community. Because of the large numbers involved and the travel trade's desire to control their movements and to process as many tourists as quickly and smoothly as possible, the people that the institutionalised tourist meets play specific, functional roles, e g waiter, tour guide, curio dealer. This produces an impersonality of contact and distorted views of each other by both host and tourist.

For the institutionalised tourist, one country is much like another. The packaged, standardised culture (shops, dances, tours of sights) presented to him soon leads to a blurring of the distinguishing features of unfamiliar cultures. It does not matter in which country beaches, sunshine, and friendly tourist minded people are found; what matters is that these factors exist and that the price is low. This impersonality of the institutionalised mass tour is further reinforced by the nature of tourist accommodation - large hotel chains built on Western lines with Western cuisine only partially adapted to take account of local foods in order to add a touch of the exotic. And many tourists in large resorts are virtually confined to tourist ghettos.

For his part, the host increasingly sees the tourist as a stereotype. Tourists seem to come from a system where untold riches abound because they are conspicuous spenders. This reaction is particularly marked in LDCs because the income gap between tourist and resident is exaggerated. In addition to creation of a false impression in the mind of the host country's inhabitants, it can also lead to situations where the hosts seek to take maximum economic advantage of tourists. There may well be a phase in the development of institutionalised tourism where this is inevitable and the tourist then becomes aware of what is happening to him and reacts by withdrawing his demand for services. The host-tourist relationship is also strange in that for the tourist his holiday is a once a year occasion which he has been looking forward to and which he intends to get as much out of   as possible, whereas the host sees a new set of tourists every week or two, all acting similarly and indistinguishable one from another.

Once tourism is established, residents' reactions change -

Human relationships are never static. The valuations of tourism held by residents of receiving countries change over time. Tourism usually began without any formal planning and was welcomed by the citizens of the host country because of the economic benefits it brought and human curiosity. In many cases, however, this enthusiasm waned as the numbers of tourists increased, facilities became overstretched, the local populace became economically dependent on tourism and the realisation occurred that the resident population no longer controlled (or was even consulted about) tourism's development, but was being used merely as an agent by the foreign travel organisers.

The tourist in this sense becomes the focus of resentment against impersonal forces to which the local population has no access. The resentment against the tourist as a symbol of continuing national dependence on foreigners can be exacerbated by a more fundamental dislike based on the socio-economic and cultural history of an area (e g the Caribbean). Resentment also occurs when full realisation occurs of the wide gap between the consumption patterns of the tourist and the standards of living of LDCs, where poverty is widespread and a relatively small proportion of the local population shares the benefits of tourism. This creates higher, but unrealisable, expectations leading to frustration.

Extremes of these two stages in the attitudes of local residents towards tourists can be illustrated by the studies of Schawinsky in Guatemala (43) and Varley in Fiji (52). In the eyes of their Guatemalan hosts, Schawinsky found that the tourist created:

exposure to new experiences;

increasing independence vis-à-vis the religious and family environment;

confidence in technology;

an awareness of the advantages of leading a life of one's own choosing;

a craving for training and the acquisition of vocational skills;

active participation in various groups;

the need for information.

At this stage of the development of Guatemala's tourism sector, therefore, the feelings of the host nation were positive, tourism appeared to present exciting new opportunities although it was already evident that major social changes were inevitable.

Varley's research in Fiji revealed a quite different set of attitudes. He quotes from a leaflet distributed by a major hotel in Suva to its guests, warning about the types of harassment and malpractice that can be expected and advising how they should be dealt with:

"Another disturbing matter which guests find offensive and annoying is the growing practice by a group who gather around the entrance of the hotel and throw a lei or a necklace of flowers around a guest's neck and then demand payment of anything from 10c to $3.00. They will even carve your name on the handle of a wooden knife and then demand that you pay between $10.00 and $15.00 for it; and incidentally the same knife can be purchased in the Suva markets for probably less than a few dollars.

Most guests find these practices most disturbing and even frightening and we suggest that you do not encourage these people in these practices. If they place flowers around your neck, it is suggested that you remove them and hand them back or drop them on the ground and walk on, even although you may be abused. It is also suggested that you think carefully before giving money to the growing group who beg you to contribute to their "school funds". A suggestion from you that you will call a policeman will sometimes frighten them off but they are usually most persistent.

Fiji welcomes you as a friend and the government of Fiji and the management of the hotel deplores these menacing practices and tactics and hopes that you will refuse to be exploited and taken for a "sucker" by these people by ignoring them, no matter how plausible and pitiful their tales of woe and distress may sound. It is also suggested that you hold your handbag tightly when surrounded by these unwelcome individuals and that you do not walk in unlighted streets after dark unaccompanied. Your door should be kept locked and windows closed when leaving your bedroom. Take the same precautions here as you would in any large city."

– and resentment grows

A number of attempts have been made to trace the sequence and time scale of these changing valuations. For example, Doxey(12b) constructed an index of the level of irritation ("irridex"). Here the fundamental belief is that irritation resulting from contact between tourist and host cannot be completely avoided and will ultimately destroy tourism unless kept under review and proper control. Doxey's "irridex" covers four levels of expression of reactions on the part of the host population:

  i.   <u>euphoria</u> – initial phase, both visitors and investors welcomed;

  ii. <u>apathy</u> – transition to this stage varies in length, depending on the speed and amount of development – gradual formalisation of contacts – tourists seen as stereotypes and taken for granted;

  iii. <u>annoyance</u> – host population begins to express doubts;

  iv. <u>antagonism</u> – overt expression of irritation – all social and personal problems attributed to the tourist.

The causes of irritation are numerous and are interrelated – social, economic, cultural and environmental – all of which point to the need for integrated planning of tourism. Some of the variations giving rise to the irritations are, according to Doxey:

  i.   fear that hosts are being treated as second class to tourists;

  ii. fear of threat to local values and culture;

  iii. loss of access to facilities (crowded transportation, private beaches);

  iv. dislike of tourists' dress (particularly that of women) and behaviour.

Despite these theories it is abundantly clear that the reasons why misunderstanding of, or by, tourists may lead to resentment on the part of some of the host population is imperfectly understood. That 'his is so can be demonstrated by citing examples where such irritation has not occurred. The Balinese, for example, have accommodated tourism, the institutionalised variety, too, into their way of life and culture without such problems. They distinguish between different types of audience – religious, local, foreign vacationer – and tailor the performance to each. The speed and intensity of the development of irritation on the part of the host community is almost certainly linked to the values and cultural background of the hosts. Other factors serving to slow this process down may be where tourism is only a supplementary (rather than sole) income source and tourist attractions have an independent, different meaning for the host.

It is clear, therefore, that although mere numbers of tourists do not by themselves constitute the reason for the speed and intensity of the development of resentment on the part of local residents, the findings of most researchers into the effect of increased interface between tourists and hosts is that there is a point at which irritation grows rapidly. What circumstances bring about this situation is far from clear, but it appears that they are complex, embracing, amongst others, aspects such as contrast of life styles and cultures, socio-economic disparities between tourist and host, land mass of receiving country, historical background, language, structure of economy and level of dependence on tourism, and so on. The saturation level concept is considered further on pages 197 to 200.

THE DEMONSTRATION EFFECT

Contact with tourists can change values and attitudes in the host country –

The effects dealt with so far have arisen from direct contact between tourists and residents of the tourist receiving country. It is claimed, however, that there exists an indirect impact of tourism caused by the mere presence of tourists where this results in the tourists' values being transferred and adopted by the host population. The term used to describe this is the demonstration effect (acculturation) and its validity rests on the theory that the local population seeks to imitate the consumption patterns and levels of the tourists. Where the local population is able to realise this pattern of imitation, this may serve to reduce the level of domestic savings and increase imports which, in turn, may result in a lower level of domestic output.

The term implies two effects:

i.   impact on the value system and the attitudes of the host population;

ii.   changes in dress, accommodation demands, eating habits and demand for consumer goods that are induced in host populations by the desire to imitate tourists.

To have these effects, of course, the tourist must be a model worth emulating. It is likely that in the early stages of tourism development host peoples do seek to imitate the tourists, if only because the tourist is a symbol of financial superiority. Young people are particularly susceptible and attempt to imitate dress, language and habits – all of which probably seem an exciting alternative way of life. Older members of the local population, this view continues, may react differently – at the outset they may experience a feeling of inferiority that sets off a process of imitation but, if the weaknesses of the tourist system are later recognised, then detachment may develop. This process can take ten years according to Nettekoven who studied it in Tunisia (33).

It is, however, far less certain that the tourist is the model on whom value changes are based. There is one line of argument which suggests that it is in fact the means of attaining values, rather than the values themselves, that have changed. This school of thought puts up the local leaders as the models rather than the tourists. The tourists are not the motivating force but only the channel or medium for transmission of new ideas. The real transmitter and source of information is urban industrialised society and tourists are simply one channel (others being advertising, mass media and films) for this information. All these channels serve to focus the information signal on the residents of the community so that local mediating agents (e g national leaders, or foreigners residing in the community) can act as effective models for learning. The "demonstration effect" is thus indirect, achieved through mediation[1].

---

1 The impact of tourism is far more evident in socio-economic terms (e g improvements in hygiene, health, education, technology, producing methods, changes in hours of work, adoption of different forms of architecture, food habits, etc)

- but sometimes to its benefit

It is also relevant to pose the question: are changes in values and the methods of attaining them necessarily harmful to the local population? Clearly, the answer is not always. Many species of wildlife (e g elephants in East Africa) would have soon been exterminated without tourism; and there are many other examples where tourism has heightened local awareness of natural resources and cultural heritage. (Even here, however, tourism can play a negative role - many elephants are killed only for the export ivory market and religious monuments desecrated because of the ready tourist market for the ornaments.)

Another area in which the change in values induced by tourism may be beneficial is its introduction into parts of developing countries where the economy is weak, and where, because of outside influences, the people are already questioning the validity of their traditional values, rules and structure. Under these circumstances tourism will inevitably bring some sort of new system: the basic questions about this new system will be whether it maintains enough of the old system for long enough to avoid serious social disruptions, and to what extent individuals can adapt to the new system.

Much will depend on the type of tourism introduced, for example, enclaves such as are planned at Cayo Sabinal in Cuba are deliberately designed to prevent too much contact and consequent social disruption. Semi-integrated tourism is also less likely to cause social disruption. On the other hand rapid development of mass tourism facilities without proper planning and control can have serious disruptive effects.

Other factors to be taken into account are political - particularly relevant in LDCs. Nettekoven (33) has suggested that an individual distressed by his country's economic backwardness compensates by either adopting Western behaviour wholeheartedly or rejecting it completely, depending on whether he blames his own politicians or those of foreign countries. In this instance the role of tourism is subsidiary.

Thus there is considerable unresolved argument about the actual amount of demonstration effect, the way in which it achieves its impact and whether or not the influence is good or bad for the societies affected.

SOCIO-ECONOMIC IMPACTS

Tourism changes the structure of LDCs' societies

Whether or not the development of a sector to handle institutionalised tourists serves to change a society's values (or means of attaining them) and whether or not any changes are good or bad for the society, there can be no argument that the socio-economic impact of tourism can serve to bring about profound changes in the structure of the host country society. In regions with an active and well diversified economy tourism has no special socio-economic effects, but major changes are inherent in the introduction of tourism into LDCs. When this happens it can result in developed and backward regions existing side by side, modern production techniques alongside traditional techniques, and behaviour normal to an industrial society juxtaposed with behaviour normal to a traditional society. This causes major changes and stresses within the socio-economic fabric.

Movement away from traditional forms of employment

The economic consequences of tourism in respect of employment have been already examined. Employment in the tourism sector also has a major social impact. In most LDCs subsistence agriculture or fishing are the main means of livelihood. With the introduction of tourism the local population becomes wage earning and the social status, for example of a farmworker who becomes a hotel worker, changes completely. The meaning of this social change has apparently been neglected in the literature although it represents the most serious change that societies can undergo. A fisherman can similarly undergo a dramatic change in his way of life and consequently his attitudes. Tourism may have two effects - his material position may be improved because of a new market for his fish or alternatively he may use his traditional boat to "entertain" the tourists by fishing. The latter brings him into direct contact with tourists and means a change of status for him - he still fishes but is now part of the show!

While a job in tourism may be preferable to subsistence agriculture, there is some argument about the value of the jobs created. Once the decision has been made to develop the tourism sector in an LDC and, for the reasons noted on page 20 , the system becomes externally dominated, the local population is likely to be employed in low skilled, low paid jobs (e g waiter, busboy, maid, gardener, kitchen helper). "Layering" occurs, with the levels of employment reflecting the economic powers of the country. This also makes it difficult for the lower ranks to achieve promotion up the scale. Despite this, there is evidence (e g Finney (in Noronha - 54c) found in Tahiti that wage labour such as in tourism is an "exciting, clean and modern way to earn one's living". Even the lowest paid find the most menial jobs in hotels more congenial (and better remunerated) than working on the land. The St Lucia example of a movement away from banana cultivation to tourism (see page 157) is a good illustration of this point. On the other hand, tourism produces, as well as many low paid, low skilled jobs, a range of "lower middle" occupations like taxi drivers, cooks, supervisory and office jobs in hotels, entertainers, boat operators, skilled craftsmen and artists. These in turn provide opportunities for promotion and the growth of small businesses.

The major concern of an increasing dependence on tourism as a form of employment in LDCs is the unemployment implications (which would most hurt those who have little in the way of alternative employment possibilities) brought about by a sudden shift in demand.

Labour force migration

As discussed above in the section on the economic aspects of tourism, tourism can bring about migration of the labour force. Esh and Rosenblum (15) found that in the case of the Gambia staff of four hotels used primarily for institutionalised tourists were divided as follows:

43. 4 per cent	resident in areas close to the hotels
19. 2 per cent	moved to area before the hotels opened
33. 5 per cent	moved to the area after the hotels opened but not specifically for employment at the hotels
17. 0 per cent	moved to the areas specifically for employment in the hotels.

A major cause of migration is, of course, the very building of tourist facilities. These are placed in the most scenic areas, be they coastal or mountain, and will often cause displacement of the local population, particularly at the institutionalised stage of tourist development. Other tourist related activities such as overfishing to feed the tourists will cause the local population to move.

The worry about the migration of the labour force is that it can serve to break down relationships and responsibilities to the detriment of the society. Of course tourism is not alone in creating migration of the labour force and the collective evidence from studies of migration caused by all forms of industrial development suggests that ties with the extended family are maintained notwithstanding migration to an urban environment. Esh and Rosenblum (15) found, for example, that the Gambian who migrates from an inland village to work in a coastal resort hotel maintains his family responsibilities.

The seasonality of tourism affects employment

The seasonality of tourism can have important social effects: it can mean either that employment must be supplemented by other work or that the tourism worker is un-employed in the off-season with attendant social problems. In some areas it is possible for hotel employees to return to their traditional employment, for example agriculture in the cases of Turkey, Morocco and Yugoslavia. In fact the Yugoslavs move whole communities, including the police force, down to the coast during the summer months and back to the inland farming areas when the season ends. How this affects the social structure of the communities is unknown but the transition to and from a traditional life to one catering for tourists must cause major strains. In Turkey a positive effort has been made by the government to counteract seasonal unemployment and at the same time to encourage local arts and crafts. Credit facil-ities are made available to enable otherwise unemployed workers to make handi-crafts and so on during the winter months and pay their debts when their goods are sold during the summer tourist season.

Economic independence of young people and women

Most tourism jobs will be filled by the younger people of the host nation. This gives them a financial **independence** which they would not otherwise have had, economic power is transferred from the older to the younger generations and a generation conflict is often created with the young looking at the traditional occupa-tions of their parents as inferior.

Tourism can have a particular effect in the role of women in a society. For a start it often gives them a chance to be paid for work which was traditionally considered to have no economic value, such as cleaning and washing. More dramatically it can bring about economic independence and changes in lifestyle which can have far-reaching effects socially. For instance, the ability of women to buy their own clothes, jewellery, etc, in Hawaii had such an effect on the male ego that it caused an increase in stomach ulcers! (22)

It has also been suggested that tourism employment increases the incidence of divorce. Prior to employment opportunities brought about by tourism, the life of women in LDCs revolved around the home and their contacts were limited mainly to relatives. A wider exposure to other people, it is claimed, serves to increase the likelihood of extra-marital involvements and to "liberate" the previously held attitudes. There are also claims that tourism creates undesirable side effects such as increases in prostitution, illegitimate births and crime. The evidence is, however, inconclusive. Often, of course, tourist resorts in LDCs such as Bali, Tahiti and the Seychelles were initially promoted as "Gardens of Eden" and "Islands of Love", taking advantage of the local customs where, as in the Seychelles, "the conventional Western regimentation of sexual relations does not apply. Illegitimacy is common, causes little scandal..." (47a).

Tourism alters land values and ownership

The consequence of using land for tourism development is that its value rises (sometimes massively, see page163) and ownership generally passes into the hands of the most economically powerful nationals and foreigners. At the early stage of tourism development, the local owners profit by selling land previously considered to be of little value. The principal concern for governments is not that the value escalation does not benefit the local community but that local owners are deprived of their land through shortsightedness encouraged by misleading representations on the part of the prospective purchasers. Land control boards monitoring what lands may be sold (and, in some cases, to whom and at what price) have been the solution in, amongst other places, Fiji. Such bodies can ensure that land is not used for tourism development if there is a better alternative use.

SOCIO-CULTURAL IMPACT

A double edged effect

Many LDCs would have no basis for the development of a tourism sector without their indigenous culture. Most tourists want to experience, albeit at a safe distance and in a packaged form, the cultures of the countries they visit. Tourism has a twofold effect on culture: on one hand it can help to preserve cultural values, i e the ones that have a specific value to the tourist as well as the host such as religious buildings, archaeological sites, and tribal dances; on the other hand culture can be debased by tourism as in the development of the "plastic arts", cheap copies of indigenous artifacts, etc (also known as airport art).

Art and handicrafts

There is consensus that tourism has assisted in the revival of the art and handicrafts sector, resulting in the preservation and diversification of items produced and a growth in jobs. Of course the type of art that tourism encourages is often the mass produced "plastic art" and it has been suggested that mass tourism, with its demand for souvenirs, encourages the entry of fakes, and lowers the quality and standards of art. In practice, in LDCs with well developed tourism sectors the "art" available typically ranges from the traditional through pseudo-traditional to wholly introduced forms.

The first type are those works which are made by the society for religious or secular use within the society or for traditional trade. The second category, which includes airport art, is usually mass produced by people with no knowledge of the traditional culture. The third category, which grows up in response to tourists' demands, is the work of individual creative artists. The role of the tourist vis-à-vis art and handicrafts probably lies somewhere between depriving that nation of its treasures and encouraging art preservation.

The tourist has also, however, encouraged the development of pseudo traditional (particularly airport) art, forgeries and altered art forms to fit the requirements of the tourist, for instance the reduction of ceremonial masks and shields to suitcase size. On the positive side, tourism has helped to preserve and promote art forms that may otherwise have died. (This also has a socio-economic benefit through job retention, even creation, as in Morocco where not only might the art of carpet weaving have disappeared but also between 40,000 and 50,000 artisans are kept in employment through tourism).

There are also examples where local communities have been able to adapt items of serious social importance to the needs of tourists without making a total mockery of them. The "kachina" (a wooden figure depicting a supernatural spirit mediator between the Pueblo people and their gods) is modified for sale to tourists by removing the significant symbols. The religious significance is retained but tourists' requirements are also satisfied.

Archaeology and architecture

On the whole there is evidence that tourism, when introduced into LDCs, has a beneficial effect on archaeology. According to Sessa (44) the cultural heritage that determines the attractiveness of a country to tourists encourages the authorities to protect it. In this way, tourism has been responsible for stimulating numerous cultural salvage operations. An additional benefit is that the local residents are made aware of their cultural originality.

Unesco, the UN agency which sponsors many cultural restoration and preservation programmes, follows the principle that if a monument has retained its religious, political or social function, it is necessary to ensure continuity of that function or to find another use for it. In this way, tourism finds a new purpose for many threatened monuments while enabling restoration of the cultural heritage to be self-financed. Unesco has carried out various studies for governments on preservation programmes for historic monuments and so on; for instance it put forward recommendations on the preservation of historic monuments in Kathmandu Valley to the government of Nepal in 1968. Unfortunately, shortage of funds and trained personnel has prevented the full implementation of this programme and many of the lesser monuments have been lost.

There is no such clear cut consensus on the benefits of tourism for local architecture. Indeed, the imported designs and layouts used in the hotels catering for mass, institutionalised tourism often overwhelm local styles of architecture. Added to this is the fact that the local population is often understandably likely to view a concrete or corrugated iron building as a more desirable symbol of advanced society that a traditional hut.

There have been some encouraging signs of attempts to relate hotel architecture to indigenous culture, notably in Africa and the Caribbean. In Tunisia for example many of the new hotels are low and spreading, built around courtyards in the manner of the traditional Arab caravanserai. Another method of developing a hotel style appropriate to the local environment is by the conversion of existing buildings - on the Yugoslavian coast an entire village has been converted into a hotel complex without any alteration of its external appearance. In Isfahan the Shah Abbas Caravanserai was converted into a hotel and in India (e g Rambagh Palace) and Java the palaces of the sultans have been similarly converted.

The holiday village has been talked about for many years in Caribbean tourism circles and, as noted on page 156 there are important social and economic as well as cultural benefits from this type of development since the emphasis is on the use of local designs and indigenous materials.

Commercialisation of culture

Commercialisation or "commoditisation" of culture applies to a phenomenon that takes place with the institutionalisation of tourism when aspects of local culture (such as ceremonial dances) are monetised. What the local population formerly did as a matter of spontaneous obligation, or ritual, is now performed for reward, and often results in the revival of ceremonies which may have been forgotten or abandoned. Even mock weddings are arranged in Tunisia to cater for tourist demand.

A number of consequences deleterious to the resident community are said to result from this development of an artificial folk culture.

1.   The value of the ceremony to the host population is lessened (and the fabric of the society consequently weakened) because the ceremony is moved from the sacred to the secular.

2.   The choice of the parts of local culture to be commercialised is made by the foreign tourist (or, more accurately, tourism organiser) rather than by the host population.

3.   The artificial ceremonies present a narrow and outdated picture of local culture, an impression which is heightened in LDCs because of the minimal contact between institutionalised tourist and host.

A bizarre example of what can go wrong is reported by Turner (47a). At an arts festival in Papua New Guinea in 1972, when the warriors of Okapa discovered they had not been given first prize for their performance of native songs and dances, they attacked the audience of tourists with bows and arrows. It took the combined efforts of the attendants (riot police in disguise) and the tourists to drive the warriors back into their jungle homeland. This demonstrates the danger of exploiting tribal societies which are unable to understand the motivation of tourism.

Another tourism pressure which serves to reduce the religious significance of ceremonies is the use of flash cameras.

A vivid description of how the commercialisation of local culture can harm both tourism and host is provided by Wenkam in respect of Hawaii: "The hapless tourists...are herded into hotel dining rooms like cattle, fed several meagre samples of Hawaiian food and some American fillers to keep them satisfied - all on paper plates - drink some watered down rum out of plastic cups, then are sung to, and laughed at, by talent-deficient entertainers who imitate Tongan fire-walkers and Tahitian hip-shakers while piously claiming to preserve Hawaiian culture."
(1f)

Yet commercialisation of local culture need not necessarily be detrimental to the host community. As noted on page 188 the Balinese distinguish between audiences. When there is primarily a tourist audience, there is a minimum attendance stipulation for the performance to go ahead; for an audience attending for religious purposes, there is no question of cancellation.

Reproduction of lifestyle and culture

Ethnic models or reconstructions of aboriginal lifestyles may be a useful way to satisfy tourists' desires to "see how the natives live" without direct invasion of their privacy. The Polynesian Cultural Centre at Laie, Hawaii, is such a model. It attracts an average 3,000 visitors per day and employs 800 workers with a payroll of several million dollars per annum. The centre is locally an important economic institution but also provides additional indirect economic benefits through the employment of students from distant Polynesian islands, thereby facilitating their education at a nearby university campus. The centre consists of seven reconstructed Polynesian villages, each depicting the aboriginal culture of a different people. Mc-Grevy (29) outlines five requisites for the development and successful operation of a model culture:

i.   a suitable inventory of available, conservable cultural assets;

ii.   a labour force to demonstrate and conserve them;

iii.   initial funding for the project and, ultimately, the establishment of a sound, continuous fiscal base;

iv.   a tourist market willing to pay for a quality product;

v.   a sense of educational mission.

SUMMARY

Drawing together the arguments and examples of this brief survey, it is clear that the evidence for and against a number of hypotheses put forward on the social effects of tourism is inconclusive.

Does tourism create irritation and resentment?

It is the development of mass, institutionalised tourism which creates the circumstances in which a rift occurs between tourist and local resident. The only form of contact between the tourist and the host population is formal and standardised leading to incomplete and stereotyped views of one another; and ownership and planning control of tourism facilities moves increasingly out of the hands of the local population. The speed of the spread of resentment is not solely related to tourist numbers but involves the specific country's socio-economic and cultural background and the distribution of political and economic power.

Does tourism change the values of society?

Tourists appear to be the channel for transmission of new ideas rather than the motivating force itself. The "demonstration" effect is not as strong as many observers have claimed. Furthermore by increasing local residents' awareness of natural resources and cultural heritage and by being introduced in backward areas where the residents are already questioning local values tourism can have a beneficial effect.

Does tourism change the internal structure of society?

By providing economic independence for young people and women, by changing the traditional forms of employment and by encouraging migration of the labour force, tourism does have a significant impact on the internal structure of society and stresses may be caused. However, there is no strong evidence to suggest that relationships and responsibilities within the host country society break down or that tourism is responsible for a major increase in prostitution, crime, divorce, etc.

Does tourism freeze socio-economic strata?

For the hypothesis that tourism freezes the socio-economic strata in the destination country to be proven it would be necessary to show that those tourism employees drawn from the lower socio-economic strata are somehow locked into tourism and that there is no opportunity for advancement or improving status. This might be true to a certain extent but it is by no means universal and tourism also generates many lower middle jobs and opportunities for self-employment.

Does tourism encourage the bastardisation of art?

There are numerous examples where tourism has had a detrimental effect on art and culture but there are also many instances where the local society has managed successfully to cater for tourists' requirements without loss to its own religious and cultural values. There is no rule of thumb which can be applied.

More analysis and planning needed

It is clear that our knowledge of the social, socio-economic and socio-cultural effects of tourism is superficial. There is no known set of conditions when particular effects will occur. All that can be stated is that the effects will be specific to the historical, cultural, political, social and economic conditions of a country, whether tourism is institutionalised or not, the speed of its development and the size of the host population. The key to improved future understanding and control of tourism's social effects (discussed in detail in Section 4) lies in wider application of:

i.   social cost benefit analysis examining the differential social impact of alternative methods of economic development and alternative forms of tourism development;

ii.   "therapeutic" planning - not necessarily for tourism alone - with local participation.

TOURIST SATURATION

The density of tourism

As noted earlier, the volume of tourism is one of the several factors leading to resentment towards tourists by local residents of tourist receiving countries. Bryden states that "tourism density, which is to some extent related also to dependence, is an indicator of the degree of confrontation between tourists and indigenes and...this confrontation gives rise to resentment of tourists" (5).

197

Few countries, developing or developed, have paid close attention to considering the optimum level of tourists before saturation occurs. The inadequacies normal in tourism data collection and compilation already referred to would, in any case, make a useful analysis impossible. Sir George Young advocates that "instead of simply stating the number of tourists, or the number of nights they spend, that number is expressed as a percentage of residents, or of the number of resident nights. Another example of using this approach would be to calculate tourist densities by expressing the number of tourists per square mile". (57)

Table 7 contains such an analysis for 75 states (68 LDCs and seven developed tourist country benchmarks) for which usable data are available. It is interesting that countries associated with mature tourism sectors - Spain, the UK and the USA - do not come out at the top. Ten LDCs have a higher tourist nights per 100 population ratio than Spain. These ten - Aruba, the Bahamas, Barbados, Bermuda, the Seychelles, Macao, the Cook Islands and French Polynesia - all have relatively small populations. Taking the other parameter - tourist nights per square mile per annum - twelve LDCs record a greater density than the highest of the three main developed country benchmarks - the UK at 1,483 annual tourist nights per square mile. These twelve - Aruba, the Bahamas, Barbados, Bermuda, the Cayman Islands, Martinique, Montserrat, Puerto Rico, the Seychelles, Hong Kong, Macao and Singapore - all have small land masses.

<u>When does tourism stop having beneficial effects?</u>

No precise research has been undertaken to indicate cut-off levels for tourism density, principally because the available data do not permit such assessment. An analysis such as is presented in Table 7 must be regarded as a preliminary step only because there are several drawbacks to the data and the way they are used:

i. they represent an annual pattern, rather than distinguishing between peak and low seasons when tourist density will be higher and lower respectively;

ii. they relate to each country as a whole, rather than the specific tourist centres within those countries where tourist density is much higher;

iii. they ignore the long stay expatriate (whose socio-cultural impact is nonetheless significant).

Furthermore, as noted earlier, it is not simply the density of tourist flow which defines the optimum level of tourism. Consideration must be taken of the full range of socio-economic and cultural factors. To date there has been little examination of the relationship between the volume of tourism and these social and economic costs and benefits. The most probable relationship seems to be a curve where, at a certain level at any given time, depending on the items fed into the model and the methods of measuring them, a point of diminishing average returns will occur - as illustrated in Figure 5.

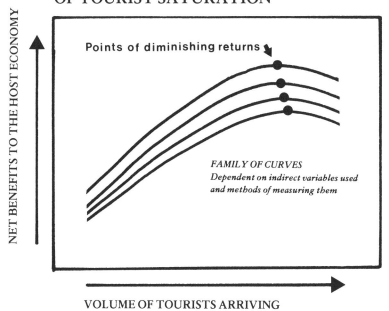

PROBABLE CURVE PATTERN OF TOURIST SATURATION

FIGURE 5

NET BENEFITS TO THE HOST ECONOMY

Points of diminishing returns

FAMILY OF CURVES
*Dependent on indirect variables used
and methods of measuring them*

VOLUME OF TOURISTS ARRIVING

The point of diminishing returns if only economic factors are considered will clearly be different from the one where social impacts are assessed. Two useful approaches would be to assess the level of tourism at which adverse social impact occurs (i e resentment on the part of local residents) and the absorptive capacity of a given location and at a given time (i e total number of visitors, taking account of the requirements of different types of tourist, capable of being adequately served by the available local skills and facilities). The difficulty of estimating absorptive capacity is that it is only fully useful if tourism is the sole economic means of development – otherwise factors such as the socio-economic differences between tourist and host, the distribution of benefits, questions of control of investment and management of tourism facilities, and type and location of accommodation have to be included in the assessment. However, the calculation of absorptive capacity would constitute a good first step.

Haites (19) has attempted to calculate the optimum ceiling of tourism, after which adverse social impact occurs. His paper indicates the following index of adverse social impacts, the basic elements in the formula being the number of tourists (t) and the host country's population (p), area in sq km (a) and per caput income in $ (c):

$$S = \frac{t}{p^{.19} \times a^{.36} \times c^{1.79}} \times 10^4$$

where S is the level at which adverse social impact occurs. He found that of 71 countries examined, the average value was 189 in 1970. The highest (i e worst) values were Rwanda (456), Grenada (326), Lebanon (275), Barbados (259) and Malta (225). Portugal had a value of 201 while the remaining 65 countries recorded scores of sub-200.

In order to calculate the level of tourism at which adverse social impact occurs it is necessary to represent the equation as follows:

$$t = \frac{S \times p^{.19} \times a^{.36} \times c^{1.79}}{10^4}$$

The method of calculating this equation is:

$$\log t = \log S + .19 \log p + .36 \log a + 1.79 \log c - 4$$

THE ENVIRONMENT

Environmental problems result from mass tourism

Tourism pollution is a concept which enters into most discussions on the impact of tourism. It is a real problem and is generally being inadequately handled. Basically tourism's effects on the environment rise in direct proportion to the volume of tourists (in the same way that the more people walk across the carpet, the sooner it becomes threadbare). Non-institutionalised tourism has little impact on the environment, it is mass tourism – the sheer volume of numbers – which has a major effect through the development of tourism facilities (e g hotels) and infrastructure (e g airports), in the desert, on mountains, by rivers and lakes, and so on.

Examples of the deleterious effects of tourism development on the environment abound all over the world. The great problem seems to be the administrators' lack of awareness and understanding of the likely impact of tourism development and growth. For example, little attention was paid to the problem of a rise in saline water following the use of hitherto untapped groundwater in such places as Djerba in Tunisia, the Bahamas and French Polynesia.

Economic greed is another factor which leads administrators to turn a blind eye to the problems of pollution. During the initial phase of a tourism development the apparent benefits (e g increased employment opportunities, foreign exchange, etc) outweigh any possible future problems arising from harm to the environment. With the arrival of mass tourism, however, environmental aspects become highly important because of the danger of destroying the very features for which tourists travel to the country concerned.

Environmental effects can be direct or indirect. The construction of a large high rise hotel on the beach front has a direct impact on the landscape. For example, Wenkam notes that "The claim is made that the best view of Waikiki is from the roof of the Sheraton-Waikiki Hotel, because from there you cannot see the hotel" (1f). And it can have more subtle indirect impacts, for instance the former residents of beach front villages may be driven back into previously unsettled areas in the hinterland where their activities may break down the vegetable cover and cause soil erosion, etc.

Table 7

Tourism Density, 1977

Country	Mid-1976 population ('000)	Tourist[a] arrivals ('000)	Ratio of tourist arrivals per 100 population	Area (sq miles)	Tourist nights ('000)	Ratio of tourist nights per sq mile	Ratio of tourist nights per 100 population
North America & Caribbean							
Aruba	62	151	244	75	1,042[b]	13,893	1,681
Bahamas	211	965	458	4,404	6,720[bc]	1,526	3,185
Barbados	247	269	109	166	2,293[bc]	13,813	928
Bermuda	57	441	774	21	2,236[d]	106,476	3,923
Cayman Islands	14	67	479	100	329[d]	3,290	2,350
Dominican Republic[e]	4,835	260[f]	5	19,332	1,922[f]	99	40
Haiti	4,670	96[f]	2	10,204	721[f]	71	15
Jamaica	2,057	265	13	4,411	2,294[b]	520	112
Martinique	369	136	37	425	833	1,960	226
Montserrat	13	13	100	39	142[bg]	3,641	1,092
Puerto Rico	3,213	1,474[g]	46	3,423	6,487[bg]	1,895	202
Trinidad & Tobago[e]	1,067	159	15	1,980	700	353	65
Central America							
Costa Rica	2,018	328	16	19,656	1,146[b]	58	57
El Salvador[e]	4,123	278	7	13,173	889	67	22
Guatemala	6,256[h]	445	7	45,452	1,779[b]	39	28
Mexico	64,590[h]	3,247	5	763,944	36,369[b]	48	56
Nicaragua[e]	2,233	207	9	57,145	1,472[i]	26	66
Panama	1,719	326	19	28,575	2,566[d]	90	149
South America							
Brazil	112,240[h]	635	1	3,288,000	8,421[cd]	3	8
Chile	10,660[h]	297	3	285,133	3,563[d]	12	33
Colombia[e]	25,050[h]	522	2	439,992	3,655[b]	8	15
Ecuador	7,305[h]	202	3	275,855	1,009[d]	4	14
Peru[e]	16,580[h]	264	2	482,258	3,538[d]	7	22
Venezuela	12,390	652	5	352,144	5,219	15	42

(continued)

Table 7 (continued)

Tourism Density, 1977

Country	Mid-1976 population ('000)	Tourist arrivals ('000)[a]	Ratio of tourist arrivals per 100 population	Area (sq miles)	Tourist nights ('000)	Ratio of tourist nights per sq mile	Ratio of tourist nights per 100 population
Africa							
Algeria	17,910	242[f]	1	851,077	1,015[c]	1	6
Benin	3,200	23	1	43,484	55[f]	1	2
Ethiopia [e]	26,680	37	0.1	471,800	222[d]	0.5	1
Egypt	38,067	888	2	386,198	5,594[d]	14	15
Ivory Coast [e]	5,017	122	2	184,174	1,100[d]	6	22
Kenya	13,847	301	2	224,960	4,452	20	32
Libya	2,510	126[j]	5	679,358	302[b]	0.4	12
Madagascar	8,266	18[j]	0.2	241,094	53[k]	0.2	1
Mauritius [e]	895	73[k]	8	720	820[k]	1,139	95
Morocco	17,828	1,427[f]	8	180,000	20,984[d]	117	118
Senegal	5,115	168[f]	3	77,730	711[f]	9	14
Seychelles	59	55	93	156	528[cf]	3,385	895
Sierra Leone	3,110	28	1	27,700	72[b]	3	2
Sudan	18,850[h]	29	0.2	967,500	288[b]	0.3	2
Tanzania	16,070[h]	93[f]	1	362,688	651[b]	2	4
Togo	2,280[h]	60	3	21,600	132[f]	6	2
Tunisia	6,070	1,016[f]	17	48,300	6,197[b]	128	102
Upper Volta	6,170	23	0.4	105,870	100[f]	1	2
Zaire [e]	25,630	25[l]	0.1	905,567	114[b]	0.1	0.4
Zambia	5,138	56	1	290,584	281	1	5

(continued)

Table 7 (continued)

Tourism Density, 1977

Country	Mid-1976 population ('000)	Tourist arrivals ('000)[a]	Ratio of tourist arrivals per 100 population	Area (sq miles)	Tourist nights ('000)	Ratio of tourist nights per sq mile	Ratio of tourist nights per 100 population
Asia							
Afghanistan	19,803	117	1	245,000	1,522[d]	6	8
Bangladesh	80,560	45	0.1	54,501	209[bc]	4	0.3
Cyprus	639[h]	178	28	3,572	1,709[m]	478	267
Hong Kong	4,510[h]	1,756	39	391	6,672[d]	17,062	148
India	610,077	640	0.1	1,262,000	17,600[d]	14	3
Indonesia	139,616	457	0.3	735,270	6,394[d]	9	5
Iran	33,400	691[l]	2	628,000	2,762[b]	4	8
Macao	275	2,788[l]	1,014	6	2,957[n]	492,833	1,075
Malaysia	12,300	1,289	10	127,317	6,703[d]	53	54
Nepal	12,904	129	1	54,362	1,448[b]	27	11
Pakistan	72,368[h]	220[l]	0.3	310,403	3,748[d]	12	5
Philippines	45,030[h]	730[l]	2	116,000	5,914[d]	51	13
Singapore	2,308[h]	1,331	58	291	4,525[c]	15,551	196
South Korea	35,860	950	3	38,025	3,799[b]	100	11
Syria	7,840	681	9	66,046	1,342[b]	20	17
Sri Lanka	13,730[h]	154[l]	1	25,332	1,644[d]	65	12
Thailand	44,040[h]	1,221	3	200,148	5,505[d]	28	13
Oceania							
Cook Islands	18	15	83	93	102	1,097	567
Fiji	580	173	30	7,040	1,488	211	257
French Polynesia	132	91	69	1,544	622	403	471
New Caledonia	135	40	30	7,358	224	30	166
New Hebrides	97	25	26	5,700	209	37	215
Papua New Guinea	2,830	30	1	178,260	262[do]	1	9
Tonga	90	13	14	270	75	278	28

(continued)

Table 7 (continued)

Tourism Density, 1977

Country	Mid-1976 population ('000)	Tourist arrivals[a] ('000)	Ratio of tourist arrivals per 100 population	Area (sq miles)	Tourist nights ('000)	Ratio of tourist nights per sq mile	Ratio of tourist nights per 100 population
Developed country benchmarks							
Greece	9,165[h]	3,961	43	51,182	20,329[f]	397	222
Israel	3,571[h]	894	25	8,050	14,642	1,819	410
Malta	330[h]	362	110	122	3,772[b]	30,918	1,143
Spain	36,350[h]	21,000	58	194,881	111,300[b]	571	306
UK	55,852[h]	11,490[p]	21	94,216	139,700[d]	1,483	250
USA	215,120[h]	18,610	9	3,615,000	130,269[b]	36	61
Yugoslavia	22,230[h]	5,625	25	95,558	29,026[b]	304	131

a WTO/UN definition, i e a visitor staying at least 24 hours or making at least one overnight stay in the country visited and the purpose of whose journey can be classified under one of the following headings: i. leisure (recreation, holiday, health, study, religion and sport); ii. business, family, mission, meeting. Excludes excursionists and cruise ship passengers staying less than 24 hours. b Average length of stay of visitors registering in tourist accommodation applied to all tourists so defined under note (a). c Estimate based on 1976 figure. d Tourist days (as opposed to tourist nights). e 1976. f Figure relates to tourists registering in accommodation establishments. g Fiscal year ending June 30, 1977. h 1977. i Estimate based on 1975 figure. j All holders of visas for less than three months entering the country for reasons other than remunerated activity. k 1974. l Total visitor arrivals. m Average number of days stayed by tourists departing from hotels who stayed on Cyprus less than 30 days applied to total tourist arrivals. n Aggregate of (i) nights spent in accommodation establishments plus (ii) other visitors at one day each. o Estimate based on equal mix of pleasure (average stay seven days) and other (average stay five days) tourists. p Overseas visitors: persons staying less than twelve months for holiday, business or other purposes, including visiting friends and relatives, study, attending sporting events, health and religious purposes; migrants excluded.

Sources: World Travel Statistics 1977, WTO, for tourist arrivals and nights; UN Monthly Bulletin of Statistics, for population; The World in Figures, for population and area.

CHART 5

TOURISM DENSITY 1977

a sample 75 countries

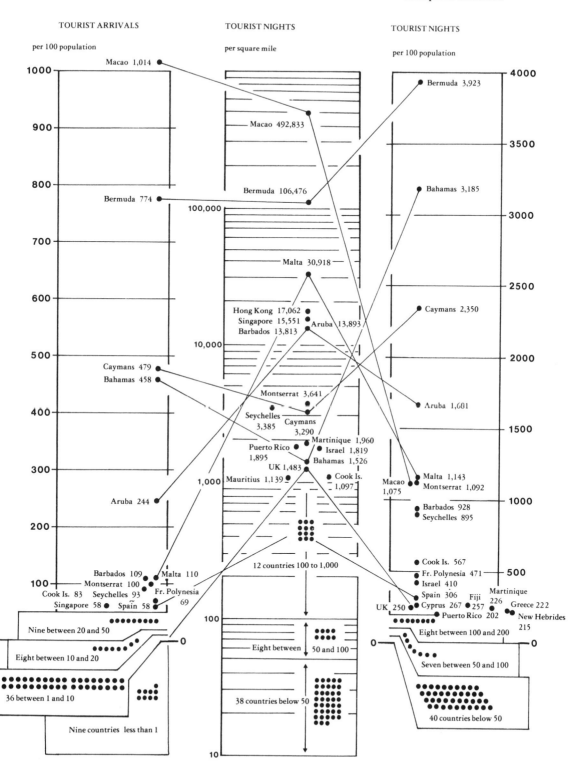

TOURIST ARRIVALS

per 100 population

TOURIST NIGHTS

per square mile

TOURIST NIGHTS

per 100 population

Macao 1,014

Macao 492,833

Bermuda 3,923

Bermuda 774

Bermuda 106,476

Bahamas 3,185

Malta 30,918

Hong Kong 17,062
Singapore 15,551
Barbados 13,813
Aruba 13,893

Caymans 2,350

Caymans 479
Bahamas 458

Montserrat 3,641

Seychelles 3,385
Caymans 3,290

Aruba 1,601

Martinique 1,960
Puerto Rico 1,895
Israel 1,819
Bahamas 1,526
UK 1,483
Mauritius 1,139
Cook Is. 1,097

Aruba 244

Macao 1,075
Malta 1,143
Montserrat 1,092

Barbados 928
Seychelles 895

12 countries 100 to 1,000

Cook Is. 567
Fr. Polynesia 471
Israel 410

Barbados 109
Montserrat 100
Cook Is. 83   Seychelles 93
Singapore 58   Spain 58

Malta 110

Fr. Polynesia 69

Spain 306
UK 250   Cyprus 267   Fiji 257
Puerto Rico 202

Martinique 226
Greece 222
New Hebrides 215

Nine between 20 and 50

Eight between 10 and 20

36 between 1 and 10

Nine countries less than 1

Eight between 50 and 100

38 countries below 50

Eight between 100 and 200

Seven between 50 and 100

40 countries below 50

205

Wildlife conservation can have detrimental effects

Even actions taken with the best social motivations can have a two-edged effect. The creation of national parks and game reserves, to conserve and protect wildlife, may cause economic deprivations to the local community and/or disruption of another facet of the environment. A good example of the former is Myers's (32) discussion of the dilemma facing Kenyan administrators. The parks and reserves established in Kenya to conserve wildlife and present a spectacle to tourists are located in savannah lands which, given current agro-technology, have only a marginal productivity. The land use costs are, thus, low, but Myers argues that social costs take a number of forms: first, there is the loss of tribal lands; secondly, the growth in the Kenyan population is beginning to result in a spillover from the overpopulated fertile areas into savannah territories; and third, the costs of the conservation of wildlife (e g through the damage caused to crops outside the parks and reserves by protected animals such as elephants) to the agricultural community are much greater than the benefits these people receive from tourism. The choice is fundamentally "people or animals". Myers argues that the benefits of tourism will need to be supplemented through additional economic justifications for safeguarding wildlife. He suggests that this might be achieved through new fiscal strategies and by new institutions so that the developed world, from which most conservation pressure emanates, pays a fairer price for the sacrifices made by the Kenyan community which is being prevented from using its land resources from exclusively competitive activities. Another way in which Turner and Ash (47a) suggest game reserves could be made to benefit the resident community is to permit controlled cash cropping for meat of the overpopulated species which otherwise starve.

The creation of protected reserves can also disrupt the natural balance of the environment. The reserves attract large numbers of visitors to areas which previously were relatively isolated. This upsets the ecological balance; for example, in Guadeloupe and Dominica remnants of tropical rain forest have been set aside as national parks - a laudable idea, but unfortunately since most of the rain forests are already in a state of disequilibrium this valuable resource is likely to degenerate rapidly unless the movement of people is closely controlled (1c).

Tourism as the agent for wildlife conservation is by no means ideal. The very presence of large numbers of tourists disrupts the natural patterns of animal life (far more drastically in fact than did the traditional hunting safari).

Assessing the impact

The range and type of environmental impact are enormous. Understanding of the effects created by tourism is low and few attempts have even been made at suggesting a methodology or yardstick for measurement, let alone for corrective action. WTO has held numerous seminars and discussion groups on the subject but these have always concentrated on specific problems in specific countries. Further, the emphasis of such meetings has often been that of dealing with the social and economic consequences of tourism-caused environmental problems rather than establishing a system for foreseeing (and acting upon such forecasts) the impacts of tourism developments.

The subject is, of course, enormously complex and difficult. There must be a set of values in order to assess the importance and quality of the impact and these values may differ from country to country, such assessment being intimately related to the economic importance of tourism. Worse still this value gap is likely to be most marked between developed and developing countries.

One attempt has been made to establish a framework. Writing in the WTO Travel Research journal (56d), Burmeister identifies five types of impact:

    i.   physiological (air, water and thermic pollution);

    ii.   physical (soil pollution and destruction of landscape);

    iii.   biological (damage to plant and animal life);

    iv.   economic (hotel);

    v.   social and psychological.

He suggests that each proposed tourism development should be assessed, in respect of these five categories of impact, utilising three parameters:

    i.   whether the impact is direct and/or indirect;

    ii.   whether it is short or long term;

    iii.   the degree of importance attached to the impact (i e the value judgment).

The grid put forward by Burmeister and the parameter classifications he considers generally appropriate are reproduced in Table 8. This is unlikely to be definitive in any way but it is the right sort of approach. LDCs will need to take such assessments if they are to avoid major environmental problems such as occur in places like Hawaii where "52 mn gallons of raw sewage are pumped daily into the ocean five miles from Waikiki Beach", where "tourism has become an industry symbolic of scenic trespass, overuse and environmental exploitation" and where leaflets are being distributed by the Hawaii Residents' Bureau (in contrast to the Hawaii Visitors' Bureau) depicting a can of "instant, imitation Aloha in heavy syrup distributed by the friendly skies of Air Pollution Corporation" and pleading "Please don't visit Hawaii until we are able to serve what's left... You can't buy ALOHA. " (1f)

CONTROL AND TRAINING

The conclusion of this report is that the key to improved understanding of, and results from, tourism in LDCs is in an appropriately structured and staffed tourism administration and an adequate supply of trained indigenes in all skills (including management) in the tourism sector. As a backcloth to the recommendations put forward in Section 4 on these issues, this section is devoted to a review of the current structure and standard of control of, and training in, the tourism sector in LDCs.

Table 8

Partial Analysis of the Impact of Tourism on the Host Country's Environment

Event	Economic	Social & psychological	Biological	Physiological	Physical
Hotel	D, S, IM	I, L, LI	D, S, L(?), UI	D, S, IM	D, S, L(?), LI
Airport	D, L, S(?), IM	I, L, UI	D, S, L, LI	D, S, IM	D, S, LI
Night club	D, I, S, LI	I, LI	D, S, UI	D, S, LI	D, S, UI
Highway	D, I, S, LI	I, L, UI	D, S, IM	D, S, IM	D, S, IM
Parking	I, S, LI	–	D, S, UI	D, S, LI	D, S, IM

Key: D – Direct;   I – Indirect;
     S – Short term;   L – Long term;
     IM – Important;   LI – Less important;   UI – Unimportant.

Source: Burmeister, WTO Travel Research Journal 1977.

CONTROL OVER THE TOURISM SECTOR

Tourist organisations can be structured in different ways

Public sector administration and control of the tourism sector varies widely between countries. The usual approach taken by developed countries has been, in the early stages of tourism development, to have a non-governmental organisation as the sector's representative and/or an administrative body. The main reason for this form of representation was that the tourism sector developed normally from private, rather than public, sector enterprise and initiative. Later, as the numbers and types of private sector organisation dependent on tourism grew, the establishment of a national tourism administration was often seen as fulfilling a catalyst role. Thus, with the advent of mass tourism, governments of many developed countries found it necessary to transfer their private tourism organisations into semi or fully governmental bodies (e g the transformation of the British Travel Association into the British Tourist Authority and the Australian Travel Association into the Australian Tourist Commission).

The historical development of tourism in developed countries also had a bearing on its organisation. In many European countries well known cities and resorts established reception services; as tourism increased, travel agencies appeared and tourist organisations at the provincial, county or resort levels were established. These were funded not only by the private sector but also by direct taxes on tourists. The NTOs were established mainly between the first and second world wars and during the rapid growth period of the 1950s. It was a gradual process of integration and centralisation based on guidelines arising from statistical analysis and research from which policies were derived.

In contrast, in LDCs the NTOs were usually established at an early stage in the tourism sector's development and on the initiative of the central government. Provincial and regional organisations came later. There was no grass roots base on which to build a tourism sector but rather a conscious decision on the part of each government to promote tourism because of its economic possibilities. The NTOs of LDCs thus usually play a more dominant role and have many more functions to perform than in developed countries.

NTOs' responsibilities in developing countries are wider

A good idea of the wide areas of responsibility of NTOs in LDCs can be gained from the WTO's survey published in 1975 (56q):

Fields of activity of NTOs in LDCs
(total number of respondents = 73)

Official tourist organisations at national and international levels - 72 NTOs

Research studies, surveys and statistics - 71 NTOs.

Tourism promotion abroad - 71 NTOs.

Tourism planning and development - 70 NTOs.

Domestic tourism planning - 67 NTOs.

Regulation and supervision of tourist enterprises - 69 NTOs.

Facilitation (i e easy entry requirements, etc) - 66 NTOs.

Tourist reception and information - 70 NTOs.

(Tourism vocational training - discussed later in this section).

Preservation, protection and utilisation of historical, cultural and handicraft resources - 65 NTOs.

Ecology and the environment - 57 NTOs.

Schmoll (46e) contrasts the structures and responsibilities of typical developed country (the Netherlands) and LDC (Sri Lanka) tourism administrations. The Netherlands National Tourist Board is responsible fundamentally for marketing and promotion only.

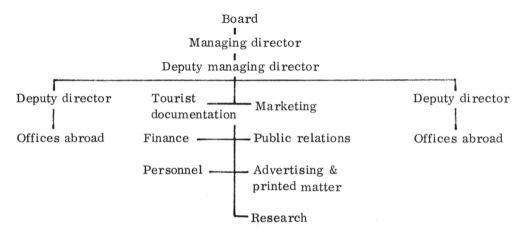

The range/responsibilities of the Sri Lanka Tourist Board (founded in 1966) are more far reaching, embracing training, planning and development as well as marketing and promotion.

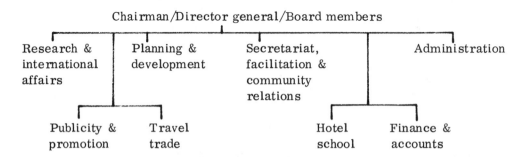

Development of an NTO

The stage and level of tourism development in the country concerned is, therefore, probably a more important factor in the determination of the NTO's organisation structure than the fact that the NTO is a government body.

210

In many countries, the structure of NTOs has evolved over time. Israel is a case in point.

pre-1955   Tourism the responsibility of the Ministry of Commerce and Industry.

1955   Government Tourist Corporation founded in the Office of the Prime Minister, with a board of directors composed of representatives of various Ministries. The corporation's responsibilities were limited to marketing (through overseas tourist promotion offices) and product improvement. Interministerial committees considered specific aspects of tourism.

1957   Tourist Industry Development Corporation founded, responsible for the financing of tourism developments. With rapid growth in tourism, conflicts of interest arose between tourism and other sectors over the priorities to be applied in physical planning and in the allocation of financial resources. Without representation of tourism at ministerial level, its interests either went by default or were subordinated to other sectors, regardless of the actual merits of individual cases.

1963   Formation of Ministry of Tourism (although still retaining the Government Tourist Corporation and the Tourist Industry Development Corporation which was made subordinate to the ministry). Until 1965, the Tourist Industry Development Corporation was the sole public source of investment finance for tourism projects; post 1965 proposals for funds have been channelled, through the development budget, to the Government Tourist Corporation. The Tourist Industry Development Corporation has, therefore, ceased to be the financial decision making vehicle in the development of the tourism sector.

1977   Merging of the Ministry of Tourism into the Ministry of Industry, Commerce and Tourism.

Without the same representation as other sectors at government decision making level, tourism is likely to be considered of secondary priority. Where tourism is not regarded as of vital importance to the economy, this is of little concern; but where tourism is a major component of a country's development plan, it is clearly desirable that it should be accorded equal voice with other sectors.

Finding the requisite manpower skills

Manning of NTOs in LDCs presents serious problems. Because of their wide and disparate responsibilities, there is a requirement for a large number of skills (in contrast with the NTOs of developed countries where marketing is often the only skill required). It has also been argued (8) that if an NTO is a government department then its top executives are recruited from the general civil service and do not look on tourism as a career. Their term does not last more than a few years thus discouraging specialisation. This, coupled with the technical ignorance highlighted earlier, illustrates why LDC tourism administrations rarely seem in touch with the industry and are frequently ignored by foreign tour operators in drawing up their programmes.

The Bahamas seems to have solved the problem fairly successfully. The Bahamas Ministry of Tourism was established in 1964 by a special act of its legislature. Under this act, the Tourism Promotion Act, the employees of the ministry are government officials and the minister of tourism is a member of the cabinet. The officials, however, are not part of the civil service and are not selected by the Public Service Commission. The minister has full powers over the selection of employees, the setting of their salaries according to qualifications and increments based on performance.

This organisation has both the status and authority to represent the interests of tourism effectively at decision making levels and at the same time has the flexibility to hire the necessary specialists at competitive salaries. The Bahamas Ministry of Tourism has, as a result of this policy, had as its director in recent years some of the world's leading tourism administrators (Chib from India, Atkinson from Australia, Wallace from Canada).

It should be stessed that this use of expatriate tourism administrators does not imply that the Bahamas is ignoring the training of nationals to take on these senior positions in due course. Many Bahamaian nationals are being groomed for senior positions by working in the NTOs abroad in order to gain the essential knowledge of consumer characteristics and travel trade operations.

TRAINING

Training is often another responsibility of the NTO in LDCs

In developed countries, training for the tourism sector is integrated into the general education system of the country and provided through both public and private institutions. In LDCs, however, the situation is very different: education is likely to be in its formative stage generally and thus training for tourism is an expensive extra. Although large hotel chains usually provide in-house training for their staffs the bulk of the responsibility for training is likely to fall on the National Tourism Organisation.

Training for the tourism sector falls into three main areas:

    i.   hotel and restaurant - catering staff;

    ii.   tourism services staff;

    iii.   tourism administration, marketing and development staff.

Hotel and restaurant - catering staff

Employees in the hotel and restaurant sector require a more intensive training than those involved in material processes because they are in contact with a varied clientele and have to understand their requirements. Because of this, and the fact that hotels and restaurants account for the bulk (generally around two thirds) of total employment in a country's tourism sector, training schemes are usually comparatively well developed. Nonetheless, Erbes notes: "In a developing country with a vigorously expanding tourism sector, usually free from the tradition of hotel-keeping, installed capacity generally progresses faster than personnel training. At the time when hotel capacity is rising fast, training schools for hotel staff are generally non-existent, or only just being built. Their capacity is very small to start with, and often falls far short of the needs later on. Moreover, at least four to six years' training in the school and on the job are needed to form a high-level manager, two to four years to form a technician or middle manager, and one to two years to form a qualified employee. Attempts to introduce accelerated training methods often give disastrous results, and may lead to the hotel trade in the country concerned acquiring a bad name. Often, however, there is no option; in this eventuality some of the shortcomings can be corrected by further training of the staff during the off-season! "(14)

In addition to hotel training schools, local institutions have, over recent years, established comprehensive training programmes for hotel management. The Bahamas Hotel Training Council, a non-governmental agency, established in 1973 and financed mainly by industry, operates a series of courses which concentrate on practical training rather than theory. A two year diploma course, open to citizens of Commonwealth Caribbean countries, is 80 per cent technical and 20 per cent management. Nine out of ten school students are industry based. The diploma is accepted by certain US colleges and universities towards a degree in hotel administration, counting for 90 credit points out of a total 180 necessary for a US degree.

Another example of a combined Caribbean-US hotel training scheme is a four year degree course divided into three years at the Puerto Rican school and the final year at Cornell.

Apart from local schools and universities, training for this sector can be achieved through:

i. international hotel chains;

ii. workers being sent abroad to an institution (e g many Caribbean hotel employees study at a US university such as Cornell) or in hotels (sponsored by government, employers or as part of a bilateral training agreement between two countries);

iii. ad hoc training programmes organised by international agencies such as UNDP.

One of the most important problems which LDCs must try to avoid in structuring their training programmes is that of staff trained to be, say, waiters or barmen finding that their jobs are dead end rather than a platform for promotion. This problem has been recognised in the Caribbean and is the subject of investigation by the Organisation of American States in association with the Caribbean Tourism Research and Development Centre. There is little evidence of staff starting as waiters or in jobs of similar standing and working their way up to a management position. Since the waiter's job is seen as of low social status and offering little upward mobility, those Caribbean personnel who receive management training are not prepared to start at the bottom and gain experience of all phases of the operation like their counterparts in Western Europe or North America. The consequent lack of practical training often leads foreign hotel groups to retain expatriate management. Investigation is currently being made, involving consultation with hoteliers, trades unions, worker delegates and training experts, as to the types of policies and training procedures needed to increase the upward mobility of the Caribbean's hotel workers.

Tourism services staff

Staff are needed for the selling of tourist services (travel agencies, tour operators, reservation services etc), information and assistance to tourists (guides, hostesses, tour group leaders, etc), wildlife parks and reserves and the public or semi-public tourism authorities (national and regional tourist offices, etc). Training for this sector is obviously more difficult than for hotels or restaurants - there is a much greater variety of skills to be taught, the numbers involved are much smaller and training institutes are therefore less likely to be operated on an economic basis.

While guides are normally trained within the country at a training school (e g India and Cuba), most of the other skills are rarely taught to the adequate quality and quantity within LDCs. This is why foreign tour operators are generally so loth to use local guides for their package tourists. The lack of training in the different requirements and cultures of the principal nationalities visiting a specific country prevents local guides from being able to fulfil adequately the hand holding role required by many mass tourists.

One of the few schools for training wildlife experts is established in an LDC - at Garoua in Cameroon. Organised with the aid of the UNDP Special Fund and bilateral programmes, the school offers courses of nine to ten months for various types of game park employees ranging from public engineers to veterinarians. Programmes include tuition in the promotion, organisation and exploitation of wildlife.

Tourism administration, marketing and development staff

The training for tourism administration, marketing and development can be achieved in one of three ways:

i.   within the tourism administration of the LDC (i e traineeship on the job);

ii.   through WTO's correspondence courses;

iii. by participation at one of the growing number of colleges and universities offering tourism degree or diploma courses (e g McGill in Canada, George Washington in the USA, Surrey and Bradford in the UK).

WTO operates an International Centre for Advanced Tourism Studies which is particularly geared towards LDC students being headquartered in Mexico City on the premises of the Centre for Third World Economic and Social Studies. The centre's study cycles are designed for training post-graduates and retraining people already engaged, or wishing to embark on a career, in tourism. One of its programmes is a correspondence course embracing market research, marketing, forecasting and distribution. The centre's priority is advanced multidisciplinary courses and management and marketing programmes.

Courses of this nature have an important role to play, particularly because of their emphasis on instilling in the participating students the awareness and knowledge

214

of the structure, characteristics and requirements of the tourist generating markets. WTO supports the centre's regular courses by preparing technical handbooks on key subjects such as forecasting, sampling methods, etc.

Another even more far reaching study programme is the three month "post-experience" course on tourism planning offered by the University of Bradford. It is one of the few (if not the only) short course which embraces all aspects of the planning process including consideration of the social as well as the commercial features. It claims to extend to tourism the disciplines used in industrial or infrastructural project planning and its aim is to lessen the gulf between tourism planners and government administrators.

In addition there are, of course, a number of longer term degree courses in tourism. The problem about participating in a two or three year programme of study for students from LDCs is quite simply that of finance. Even participation in a three months' programme is unlikely to cost less than $10,000 per delegate (fares, fees, subsistence). Correspondence courses avoid this problem but present another equally formidable one – that of the communications gap. It is quite unrealistic to expect a newly graduated student from an LDC who joins his country's tourism administration to be able to grasp the workings of the tourism system of the principal tourist generating markets through the sole medium of a correspondence course.

The LDC is thus in a dilemma – it cannot afford to send sufficient delegates to overseas training programmes to ensure the optimal administration of its tourism sector, and home based courses of education will not provide the requisite knowledge of generating markets to enable the job to be done effectively. The answer appears to be twofold: more LDC students to be sponsored by international agencies (or, as a goodwill gesture, by foreign multinationals?) and training programmes operated by tourism experts (under WTO's guidance) to be undertaken in the LDCs themselves.

Organisation of training

According to the WTO's latest survey of the aims, activities and fields of competence of NTOs (Appendix 10), of the 73 LDCs who responded, only ten did not include vocational training within the fields of competence of their NTOs. The questionnaire covered various aspects of the organisation of training and details (extrapolated) given by developing countries were as follows.

In 55 countries NTOs are responsible for the determination of manpower and training requirements.

In 42 countries NTOs are responsible for the granting of fellowships.

In 51 countries NTOs are responsible for the formulation of training programmes for hotel and catering staff, guides, hostesses, recreation staff, etc.

In 47 countries NTOs are responsible for organising vocational training courses, seminars and study cycles.

In 36 countries NTOs are responsible for the establishment of hotel and tourism schools.

In 39 countries NTOs are responsible for the "reception of trainees".

On paper, therefore, it seems that LDCs are well on the way to coping with the vocational training requirements of their tourism sectors. The survey, however, gives no details of the capacity and efficiency of the training provided.

LDC tourism administrations approach the challenge of sufficient, well qualified, staff for their tourism sectors in varied ways. Some look for aid from international agencies to sponsor overseas students, others seek to be self-sufficient by establishing local training schools, yet others enter into bilateral agreements, and many adopt a combination of two or more of these approaches.

Three points can be made which apply to all LDCs.

1. It is necessary for LDCs to forecast accurately their trained staff requirements and establish forms of training capable of producing this level of qualified output.

2. Individual countries must tailor their training approaches to their requirements rather than adopt blanket suggestions from international bodies.

3. The training of tourism sector staff requires large scale financial backing to be successful, the more so in LDCs because of the socio-cultural gulf between tourist and tourism worker.

Some specific proposals to guide LDC tourism administrations in the organisation and execution of the training function are presented in the next section.

Conclusions and Recommendations

In this final section, the facts and arguments presented in the preceding three sections are drawn together in order to suggest guidelines for the future development of tourism in LDCs and the national, regional and international measures needed to improve LDCs' position in the international tourism market.

The recommendations concentrate on ways in which the average LDC may better develop and control its tourism sector to its own maximum benefit. Many LDCs already have implemented such processes. In other LDCs, there are valid reasons why this average solution is not appropriate.

The limited scope of the research programme for this report has necessitated the restriction of recommendations to two areas.

1. Measures which the state, as opposed to private enterprise, should implement.

2. An outline description only of measures which would improve the level and proportion of gross tourism earnings accruing to LDCs. Many of these measures require some financial investment but the quantification of such costs and the comparative costs and benefits of alternative non-tourism sector forms of investment demand individual examination for each country and, thus, falls outside the scope of this report.

GOVERNMENT CONTROL OF TOURISM

The main problems concern tourism objectives and lack of personnel

Government control of tourism development in LDCs varies widely in type and quality. The main problems are interdependent:

i.   the failure of many LDCs to establish their tourism development objectives in terms of the type of tourism they wish to attract;

ii.   the insufficient supply of personnel with adequate knowledge and experience of the structure, characteristics and requirements of the principal tourist generating markets to control and direct the tourism sector's development.

The consequence of these two failings include some, if not all, of the following for nearly all LDCs:

     i.   lack of a clear tourism policy;

     ii.   absence of systematic, phased tourism development plans;

    iii.   contracts and arrangements with foreign organisations where the terms are unfavourable to the LDC concerned;

    iv.   the development of an ill matched mixture of tourism facilities, many of which are unsuited to the resort or country;

     v.   haphazard, even badly directed, tourism marketing strategies;

    vi.   ignorance of the economic and social impact of tourism;

   vii.   ignorance of whether (and to what extent) or not the commercial practices of foreign enterprises militate against LDC interests;

  viii.   little involvement in the distribution of their tourism product to the consumers of tourist generating countries.

The case for a ministry or department with responsibility for tourism

The precise role that the state should play in tourism development in LDCs is the key consideration. The choice is between controlling the tourism sector closely or permitting it to develop in the main through private sector initiative with fairly loose government direction and control. The resolution of this choice is a function of the importance attached to tourism in the country's economic development. If tourism is nominated as a major growth sector, the "hands on" state approach is probably necessary because only governments can ensure that tourism development is designed to achieve a "proper commercial size" (56p), i e the minimum threshold level of accommodation, and only governments (and then only if countries in a region act in consort) can deal effectively with foreign tourism organisations. The choice is less clear cut if tourism is not viewed as a major growth sector, but because tourism is potentially of major economic benefit to LDCs and it can, at the same time, have adverse social impact, the case for extensive state intervention is still strong.

Government involvement in tourism in LDCs may well be required as direct executive participation, for example to establish and operate hotels (e g Indian Tourism Development Corporation), to provide guides at centres of tourist interest (as in Jamaica), and so on. However, the experience of LDCs throughout the world strongly suggests that overall responsibility for the administration, control and direction of the tourism sector should be vested with a single authority - the Ministry or Department of Tourism. The best interests of an LDC ambitious for a well developed tourism sector providing maximum economic and social benefits are served by the following.

1. A Ministry or Department of Tourism should be formed, responsible for the full range of government involvements in the nation's tourism development: planning;

training; facilitation; marketing and overseas travel trade liaison; statistics; regulation and supervision of tourist enterprises; local reception and information; preservation, protection and utilisation of historical, cultural and handicraft resources; ecology and the environment; domestic tourism planning.

2. Equal status to that of other industrial sectors should be accorded to the country's tourism ministry (or department). Only through the granting of such status to tourism can LDCs ensure that tourism development is fully and optimally integrated with that of inter-related sectors such as construction, food and, more broadly, with that of all other sectors in the national plan.

In the remainder of the report, recommendations are presented on the functions to be fulfilled by LDCs' tourism administrations and a broad programme of work for the direction and control of tourism development by them. To overcome the major problem, common to all LDCs, of a lack of suitably qualified and experienced personnel, a three phase approach appears to be best for countries seeking to provide for, and encourage, institutionalised tourism.

1. Consultants should be retained to prepare a national tourism master plan, its specific objectives to be integrated with the nation's overall economic and social development objectives.

2. Foreign specialists (advisers, consultants, on long term contracts such as in the Bahamas) should be appointed to oversee the implementation of the master plan (advisers can be supplied through the UN or under multilateral or bilateral assistance programmes).

3. There should be a scheme (involving local and foreign training) for the creation of a core of qualified experts to constitute the nation's Department or Ministry of Tourism.

PROGRAMME OF OPERATIONS

Tourism administrations face some daunting tasks

The tasks facing LDC tourism administrator are frequently daunting because tourism has been allowed to grow, to a significant extent in most LDCs, largely on an uncontrolled and undirected (or ill directed) basis. The three basic tasks can be expressed simply as follows.

1. Assessment of the country's tourism resource potential.

2. Setting up of procedures to make sure that the maximum benefit may be realised from this potential.

3. Constant checking, on a comparative basis with other sectors and countries, of performance achievement, i e are benefits up to the level expected and adverse impacts kept at a minimum?

The recommendations that follow are grouped in terms of these tasks.

What is tourism's potential?

Policy, planning and strategy
Statistics (first generation) and forecasting.

How is the maximum benefit obtained?

Land zoning
Training
Import substitution
Incentives
Liaison with foreign travel trade
State's direct executive involvement
Foreign exchange controls.

How is the country's tourism sector performing?

Statistics (second generation)
Social cost benefit and structural analysis.

POLICY, PLANNING AND STRATEGY

How to plan tourism development

Tourism development should be undertaken "consciously and methodically and
carefully planned as part of the national development effort" (50). Whilst this is
a truism, the preceding analysis has shown that the lack of adequate manpower and
accurate information has meant that such an approach to development is more often the
exception than the rule. Of course, policy and plans for tourism cannot be laid
down without knowledge of the likely economic and social consequences compared
with those arising from alternative means of national growth. Yet understanding
of these consequences cannot be achieved unless the state establishes a detailed
system for tourism measurement and control. Faced with this conundrum LDCs
can only start with broad outline goals and, over time, refine and develop them
into a fully integrated national development programme. The first priority for
LDCs to be able to advance along these lines is, of course, the establishment of a
system for accurately recording and measuring the level and impact of tourism
(see below).

It is perhaps worth considering what is meant by planning tourism "consciously and
methodically and... as part of the national development effort". Planning involves
a choice - between tourism and other development sectors, between different resorts, between different types of tourism. Planning is not solely concerned with
tourist numbers and the desired foreign exchange they bring with them; it needs
to link tourism development with that of other sectors, such as agriculture and
education; it should even try (though this has rarely been brought about in tourism
plans) to relate tourism development to the more equitable distribution of wealth
within the host country. Tourism planning requires the choice and weighting of
social as well as economic indices. The negative impact of sociological consequences
can thus be reduced by study of the social and cultural patterns of the destination area.

In establishing planning procedures to be followed, it is worth noting the three basic stages in tourism development:

    i.   discovery (by a small number of foreigners);

    ii.   response by local population (local control of facilities and decision making, little change in social structures or values);

    iii.   institutionalisation (control and development decision making passes out of local hands, changes in social structures and values, increase in resentment of tourists).

It is important to realise that the move from the second to the third stage is not inevitable, even if the economic benefits from large scale tourism are needed by a country, but can be controlled. There appear to be three essential elements for the balanced growth of tourism without the third stage being reached. First, the numbers of tourists must not grow at a rate beyond the capacities of the local population to manage and cater for them. Secondly, the country's attractions to tourists (natural resources, events such as fairs, the theatre, and facilities such as hotels and restaurants) should already be in existence to meet local needs so that tourism supplements local demand. Thirdly, planning must be undertaken in cooperation with the local populace. Planning in this way will prolong the onset of the third stage so that the economic benefits from large tourism flows can be realised without deleterious social effects. Such an approach will also allow the tourism sector to be developed alongside other sectors and in close harmony with local culture. It will also facilitate the protection of physical resources and the organisation of training and research programmes. This approach to planning will also enable the correct pace of development of tourism to be gauged, i e the optimal level of tourism flows as discussed on page 197. Of course, the government may well have to take steps to prevent undue foreign infiltration of the tourism sector (see below).

Local participation at all stages appears to be the key to successful planning without social problems, from initial goal selection to direct involvement in the planning and decision making process. In LDCs where the part of the population most affected by tourism is quite likely to be illiterate, the process may well prove difficult and lengthy, but it is nonetheless essential. Sociologists can help by identifying the society's traditional forms of organisation and the methods of decision making.

Plainly, then, the job of tourism planning is complicated. If many developed countries have made disastrous mistakes, how can LDCs be expected to handle it better, particularly since the socio-economic and cultural gulfs between tourist and host are much wider than in developed tourist receiving countries?

Do not rush tourism development

"While the growth of tourism may be temporarily affected by political circumstances such as war or insecurity, its long term growth seems to be secured by powerful socio-economic factors: higher incomes, shorter working hours, the saturation of other forms of consumer spending and cheaper transport." (Gerald Eldin, OECD deputy secretary-general speaking at a 1978 special session on tourism and the environment). Despite the certainty of the long term growth of tourism, LDCs are tempted to rush into tourism development without considering the social and cultural factors discussed earlier - present day politicians will not get much kudos from a tourism sector which reaches its peak in the 21st century (albeit that the social and cultural problems are kept at a minimum in that way) and are under constant pressure from commercial interests to press ahead with tourism development. Yet, over rapid decisions to encourage tourism lead inevitably to loss of local control over the tourism sector, a situation which it is virtually impossible to redress in a democratic society. Worse still, in certain types of country (for example small islands where the absorptive capacity for tourism is finite), unplanned and inappropriate tourism development can impose an economic burden which is unlikely ever to be removed.

Take, for example, the case of the island of Madeira. Traditionally, Madeira has attracted relatively small numbers of high spending Europeans for whom it provided a high quality hotel sector. Without beaches the island was well suited to the elderly clientele it attracted. The fact that the island's mountainous terrain limited its airport to handling short haul jet passenger aircraft presented no problem since sufficient tourists to fill the island's hotels came from Europe on scheduled services. During the early 1970s, the capacity of the island's accommodation sector more than doubled. Expansion was concentrated in luxury, five star hotels, and in high rise units for the growing, low budget, self-catering market segment in Europe. Occupancy rates plummeted as demand could not meet this major surge in capacity, and pressure was placed on the Portuguese government to build a new airport enabling wide body jets to bring US tourists for the new capacity in luxury hotels and charter tourists for the self-catering units. Apart from the fact that low budget, mass tourists are unsuitable for Madeira, which lacks beaches, the economic costs of giving in to this pressure (which arose from unplanned and uncoordinated development) could be high development costs for the new airport, and a much reduced level of average earnings per tourist (as the island's traditional high spending tourists are deterred by the increased crowds and replaced by short stay Americans and low budget Europeans). Any form of systematic planning procedure would surely have restricted such accommodation capacity expansion. The island, which has an area of just 741 sq km (286 sq miles), most of which is uninhabitable mountainside, is seriously considering switching from high spending, low volume to low spending, high volume tourism, precisely the wrong long term approach for an island with such limited absorptive capacity.

This report counsels an exhaustive, analytical approach to tourism development in LDCs. For each proposed resort/area development, following initial resource inventory and outline assessment of market potential, it is desirable that both tourism experts and the local community should be consulted before development plans are drawn up. One such example concerns the southwest corner of Turkey, stretching from Izmir on the Aegean to Antalya on the Mediterranean. Popular with domestic Turkish tourists but virtually ignored by foreign tourists, the region suffers from having only a three month season. A decision was made to develop the region for foreign tourists. Rather than rushing into commissioning of development schemes, the region was the subject of a specially convened conference of tourism experts which concentrated on the fundamentals - policy formulation, product development, the use of research and improved information systems, training programmes and socio-economic impact.

Use foreign consulting assistance - but selectively

The job of tourism planning, in the early stages at least, falls outside the capability of tourism administrations in almost all LDCs (and many developed countries as well). This is why the retention of a foreign consultant to prepare the country's master plan and a foreign adviser to oversee its implementation has been advocated. However, the LDC must stipulate two fundamental requirements which has not been the case with most tourism master plans prepared by foreign consultants.

1. The incorporation and integration of sociological research into the development plan, as part of the social cost benefit analysis approach (if no sociological studies have been undertaken prior to the contracting of the consultant, the organisation of such work could well be included in his responsibilities).

2. The specification of training programmes geared not only to providing sufficient numbers of qualified staff to cater for tourists in hotels and so on, but also to producing a core of local personnel capable of undertaking all aspects of the social cost benefit and structural analyses described below.

Establish a phased and "rolling" planning system

It is recommended that a "rolling" plan should be adopted with separate programmes prepared for a number of different time periods progressively increasing in detail in line with the proximity of the planning horizon. A typical approach might be to draw up a master plan presenting outline plans over a 20 year or longer horizon, a five year development plan and an annual or even biannual programme of action. In other words, tourism should be treated at state level in the same way that any private sector company or corporation might handle its corporate planning.

Turkey again provides a good model. Although its tourism sector is well developed compared with those of most LDCs, it admits to making many mistakes en route (such as developing hotel capacity on the assumption that demand would automatically be generated to fill the beds) and has only recently adopted the following planning procedure. The government has established a broad overall policy for tourism: the development and maximisation of the benefits produced by tourism in line with the overall social, economic and development policy of the country. Its specific objectives are to reduce the balance of payments deficit through tourism revenues, to help solve the country's unemployment problem and to try to reduce the imbalance between regions.

A series of economic, social and physical planning studies are conducted and fed into the three phase development planning process:

   i.   the perspective plan (outline alternatives reviewed within government)

   ii.   the five year development plan (identifying the precise tourism product which the country wishes to develop, establishing targets in respect of tourist flows, foreign exchange, accommodation, tourism facility and infrastructural requirements, manpower needs and training programmes, investment required and sources and conditions of financing, regional development programme, etc);

   iii. annual programmes (laying down details of specific developments, goals, projections, measures, the investments to be undertaken in the public sector, incentive measures to encourage investments and overseas marketing strategies).

STATISTICS (FIRST GENERATION) AND FORECASTING

A major improvement is needed

The poor situation with respect to tourism statistical recording has already been
highlighted. Without a major improvement in the compilation and utilisation of first
generation tourism statistics (i e directly relating to tourist movements), LDC
tourism administrations will not reach a position where they can assess their
country's performance on a comparative basis or plan with assurance for the future.
Neither will they be able to establish whether or not tourism is meeting the economic
objectives established for it. The recommendations presented below stress the
need for comprehensive and standardised collection of tourism statistics with particular emphasis on establishing seasonal, regional visiting, length of stay and
expenditure patterns. They lean heavily on measures suggested by BarOn at the
Esomar seminar (3).

1. The definitions and classifications given in the UN guidelines (reproduced in
Appendix 11) should be adopted as the base by all tourism administrations and other
organisations concerned with the collection of tourism statistics. Where analyses
are made which are more detailed than those presented in the UN guidelines, these
should be drawn up in a way to facilitate international comparison, and where there
are methodological or definitional differences between those adopted in a given
country and the UN guidelines these should be noted and, ideally, quantified (even
if only broadly).

2. A set of guidelines comparable to these are urgently required for domestic
tourism. This is especially important because the determination of future requirements for accommodation, other tourism facilities and manpower must reflect
demand from both international and domestic tourists. Although many countries have
been working on systems for recording domestic tourism flows, their efforts require
the coordination of a body such as the World Tourism Organisation.

3. All countries should aim to publish basic tourist movement data (arrivals and
tourist nights by principal resorts, residents' departures) on at least a quarterly
basis (preferably monthly), to enable more efficient study of current and seasonal
trends. Such data would also facilitate the calculation of a tourism density or
saturation index such as discussed on page 83 onwards.

4. There is a strong need for the creation of data banks of tourism statistics (such
as operated by the Institute of Air Transport). This would help LDCs in particular
to maximise their limited resources by eliminating the need to duplicate research
on, say, generating markets. The LDCs are strongly represented in the WTO which
thus stands out as an ideal medium for the operation of such a data bank.

LAND ZONING

Selecting areas for tourism development

For the state to carry out any form of regional development plan with respect to
tourism it is necessary for the country to be divided into zones, and each zone given
a priority rating. Investment (through incentives or simply by blocking developments
in non-designated zones) can then be directed into the pre-selected priority zones.

224

Zones which are considered likely to have a greater benefit to the nation if developed for agricultural or industrial purposes can then have investment channelled for that type of development.

TRAINING

A number of requirements –

As indicated in the earlier analysis, manpower training is of paramount importance for the tourism sector of LDCs. The UN report, Tourism Development in Developing Countries, highlights the requirements: "Training has formal education, non-formal educational and public educational aspects. Special schools or special programmes in the already established educational institutions are needed for the training of high level professionals. For the training of middle level personnel, both lower level formal educational programmes and non-formal training courses are needed. Training for upgrading the existing personnel is also important. Moreover to ensure the proper functioning of tourism facilities, operational standards should be established and followed up by the responsible governmental agencies. " (51b)

The provision of an adequate quantity of manpower of the right skills is clearly one of the biggest tasks facing tourism administrators. The way LDCs tackle this task varies widely (see page 212), reflecting different social structures. Each country's approach to manpower training must be individual, particularly at the lower levels where people are changing from occupations in areas such as agriculture to tourism. The initial process in the establishment of manpower needs is, however, common to all countries. There are three steps:

i.   to draw up forecasts of tourist flow;

ii.   to examine basic inventory of tourism sector manpower and to calculate additional staff requirements, by type, year and region;

iii. to establish training schemes to produce the required output, these to be tailored to the circumstances and nature of the country's tourism sector.

– and recommendations

This report makes a series of recommendations as to how LDCs should treat training for the tourism sector.

1. LDCs should establish a section or department within the national tourism administration to handle the training function.

2. Trained staff requirements should be forecast regularly and schemes established geared to the phase of tourism development in the country concerned (e g multi-purpose in early phases, specialised in subsequent phases).

3. Self-sufficiency in training staff in all sectors (except administration, marketing, etc, where some overseas experience will remain an important component of the essential education) should be the aim of all LDCs.

4. To this end, LDCs should:

    i.   set up training schools for both service and managerial/supervisory staff;

    ii.   oblige foreign tourist operators to institute their own training schemes for local staff (e g hotel chain management contracts can stipulate minimum trained staff output levels);

    iii.   seek to establish tourism degree courses at universities (probably most realistically on the basis of one per region);

    iv.   establish on the curricula of secondary schools courses on tourism (characteristics, purpose, economic benefits).

5. To help fund the expense of establishing and running such schemes, LDCs could operate:

    i.   a training tax (payable by the tourist);

    ii.   a levy on foreign tourist operators.

6. For NTO staff, LDCs should sponsor participation on selected courses and schemes overseas, e g the WTO workshops (see page 126).

7. Training schemes should be aimed at encouraging the upward mobility of tourism employees and alleviating the problems of seasonal unemployment.

Training related to phase of tourism development

The high cost of mounting training schemes makes it essential for LDCs to adopt a pragmatic approach. Tunisia provides a good example of an LDC tailoring its training methods to the different phases of tourism development. In the early period (1960s), its approach was to make the best of its limited means. It even used a barracks as a hotel staff training centre, hotel executives were used as technical instructors although untrained as teachers and the emphasis was on multipurpose and practical training. In this way the country managed to train 1,200 staff between 1964 and 1968. Following this first phase, training was upgraded through bilateral assistance; some students were sent abroad for training; the training centres were upgraded to hotel schools and started to train middle level staff; and multipurpose training was dropped and replaced by specialisation. The experiences gained from these two phases enabled the Tunisian National Office of Tourism and Thermal Springs to draw up plans, since implemented, for permanent training schools, etc.

Self-sufficiency

The establishment of training schools is a prerequisite to self-sufficiency in manpower training. It involves high expenditure because foreign teachers will almost certainly be required during the early years. However, the schools' own graduates can eventually take over the teaching, and WTO's workshops are fulfilling the important function of training the trainers so the drain in foreign exchange need not extend over too long a period. The alternative to aiming for self-sufficiency in tourism training is continuing dependence on bilateral or aid schemes (which cannot be relied upon) or sending staff overseas (which is far more costly in the long term than establishing own training schemes).

Funding

The imposition of a training tax on hotel bills, etc, and a levy on foreign hotel chains, tour operators and so on are suggested so that the tourist and the organisations profiting from tourism foot the bill. It should, however, be stressed that such schemes are highly unpopular with the individuals and organisations being penalised and to be successful need to be adopted by all LDCs within a region. Otherwise the tour operators will discriminate against the country introducing such schemes by directing their promotional support to more liberal countries.

Specialist degree courses

Whilst some overseas experience is essential to enable the staff of LDC tourism administrations to do their work most effectively, we believe that LDCs should aim towards establishing degree courses in tourism studies and hotel and travel management so that prospective NTO staff and tourism enterprise management can gain a comprehensive basic grounding. Foreign teaching staff will almost certainly be required over a lengthy period of time but ultimately there will be sufficient qualified local graduates to take over this function. Clearly the establishment of such courses is most appropriate in LDCs which have a fairly well developed tourism sector; a regional approach may prove best.

Turkey is one of few LDCs which has established (1976) a Department of Tourism and Hotel Management at a university (Bosphorus). This offers a two year course in hotel and travel management for 50 students per year. The aim is to provide medium and top level management staff for the tourism sector. The course is not highly specialised; it covers economics, law and management as primary subjects, plus tourism marketing, planning and development, and hotel and travel industry management.

Secondary schools

The purpose of suggesting the introduction of general tourism courses in secondary schools in LDCs is the hope that explaining the tourism phenomenon at an early age will reduce the possibility of social friction between tourist and host.

Upward mobility

It is important for LDCs to encourage the upward mobility of their tourism sector staff. Low season spare time can be used for extra training, thereby both improving the capabilities of staff and keeping them occupied. The Turkish Ministry of Tourism, for example, operates one month programmes in its tourism training schools starting in October. These cater for three groups - front desk, floor service and kitchen staff. The courses are free, as is accommodation for those attending their first course. To reduce costs (both in establishment terms and for participants) mobile teaching units can be provided, for example for training kitchen or floor staff. Turkey is one LDC which does this.

Seasonal unemployment

The seasonal problem can be overcome by training hotel staff in other tourist related skills such as handicrafts. Hotel staff can thus work in the handicraft field during the low season and generate a second form of income. As noted on page 192 such a scheme operates in Turkey where it is already possible to obtain credit for raw materials, equipment and so on for the manufacture of handicrafts, the money being repaid as the goods are sold during the high season.

IMPORT SUBSTITUTION

Support for sectors where self-sufficiency can be achieved

As noted earlier, one of the principal factors leading to the substantial leakage of gross tourism earnings from LDCs is the lack of backward linkages between tourism and other sectors in the economy, i e the economies of LDCs are not geared to supplying the quality of goods and services or the requisite factors of production in sufficient quantity to satisfy the demand created by tourism. The problem is exacerbated by the preference of certain foreign enterprises operating in LDCs (see page 173) for importing supplies rather than seeking local sources. Government action should be designed to increase self-sufficiency, thereby maximising foreign exchange earnings and income. The following procedure is recommended.

1. Assessment of the economic feasibility (human and natural resources, finance, etc) of local development in sectors such as: cement, steel, furniture, fibre glass, glassware, cutlery, linen, air conditioning equipment, water cleaning systems, ceramics (all required in hotel construction, furnishing and fitting), vehicles, vegetables and fruit, beverages, handicrafts and souvenirs.

2. Support for the sectors selected from those itemised above through:

   i.   subsidies, grants, etc, to local investors/developers (e g market gardening, fruit and vegetable processing units, fish processing plants, wooden furniture manufacture);

   ii.   bans, quotas, tariffs, licences or price level limits for imports of goods in these sectors, for example as practised in Turkey where directly substitutable goods are subject to a special licensing regulation (in drawing up such policy close attention must be paid to the danger of initiating any form of trade war).

3. Through the medium of the feasibility scheme for tourism developments (see below, page 229) encouragement of the use of indigenous architecture and design and materials.

INCENTIVES

Too many concessions can be given

One favoured method of creating the conditions to achieve a given objective is to encourage foreign (and domestic) investors through incentives. As noted earlier, however, the tendency in the tourism sector has too often been to offer tax exemptions, grants, credit facilities and so on on an unresearched, blanket basis because the neighbouring country does so. There is little evidence as to the efficiency of such concessions. We, therefore, recommend that, whilst incentives should be considered, the following procedure should be adopted to ensure that incentives are geared to attracting the necessary investment with the minimum loss of revenue to the LDC.

1. Examine the performance of other countries' incentive schemes in the light of their resources and development objectives.

2. Research the actual needs of potential investors.

3. Design codes of investment concessions related to specific development objectives, with precise requirements of the investors (e g in terms of job creation).

4. Establish targets of achievement and periodically monitor and assess the level of realisation of such targets.

LIAISON WITH FOREIGN TRAVEL TRADE

Foreign owned or operated tourism products

If LDCs adopt the "hands on" approach to tourism development (which this report recommends if economic benefits are to be maximised and deleterious social and cultural impacts minimised), then top priority must be given to ensuring that all developments, whether proposed by foreign or local concerns, fit within the country's tourism plan. To this end, a strict vetting process, such as recommended in the UN Ecosoc/IUOTO report (49), is required. This envisages a three step scrutiny.

1. The proposer should submit a full, long term feasibility study, as a pre-requisite to the granting of planning permission.

2. The calculations of this study should be subjected to full social cost benefit analysis to avoid the allocation of government support to projects which are not in accord with the tourism master plan or which are poorly researched.

3. The proposer should provide full details of the organisation to be responsible for the management and operation of the proposed development in order that its experience and competence for such a venture may be checked.

Action in this area is of crucial importance since the type and number of tourists attracted and resultant earnings are a direct function of the type and availability of accommodation and tourism infrastructure. It is also the area where LDCs can best regulate their tourism sectors, i e at the planning stage rather than through the operating practices of tour operators, airlines, etc.

One way in which LDCs may obtain the evidence to prove (or disprove) the widely held belief amongst LDCs (reported in the UN Ecosoc/IUOTO report - 49) that foreign hotel chains engage in transfer pricing, overstatement of costs and under-statement of earnings would be to pass legislation requiring greater detail in books of account presented to fiscal authorities. It should, however, also be noted that there would be an increased cost to LDCs (in the form of additional trained staff) to operate such a scheme.

Distribution and marketing of LDC tourism product

LDC tourism administrations are going to have to deal increasingly with foreign tour operators in the coming decades. This report's already promulgated view is that LDCs should concentrate first and foremost on regulating the volume and type of tourism they permit in order to achieve maximum social and economic benefits. However, in LDCs where local interests can be shown to be still well served even with large scale tourism or where control has long since passed in the main out of the hands of locals and institutionalised tourism is firmly established, package tourism is likely to be the dominant medium. The special problems associated with foreign tour operators have been discussed in detail earlier, pages 178 to 181. Basically the interests of tourist receiving countries (whether or not developing nations) and foreign tour operators are not in alignment. The destination country's interest is in low fares so that more tourists may be attracted and a greater proportion of tourists' spending accrues to the host nation. On the other hand, the tour operator's interest is served by the lowest possible cost for the total package (transportation and accommodation/land element). The result, as noted earlier, is a delicate balance of the supply/demand equation with tour operators trading off destinations against one another according to the accommodation/land rates they offer.

One obvious way for LDCs to try to tilt the balance more in their favour is to enter directly the tour operating market themselves and the implications of this possibility are discussed below (page 232). In suggesting ways in which LDCs might be able to exercise more control over, or at least influence, the activities of foreign tour operators, it must be recognised that the laws of supply and demand are paramount. By adopting the suggested measures and, particularly, by grouping together on a regional basis, LDCs can help to reduce the problems associated with tour operators, but the fact remains that if there are more hotel beds than tourists, then no firm control over foreign tour operators is going to be feasible. The suggested measures are as follows.

1. Introduction of an annual licence. Foreign tour operators will have to deal directly with LDC tourism departments, thus giving the latter the opportunity to influence the type of tourist attracted, the itineraries/programmes featured and the codes of conduct followed with respect to contractual arrangements and payment methods.

2. Establishment of a standard hotel booking contract form. This can have a double advantage: it can benefit LDCs by requiring foreign tour operators to enter into fixed contracts for their hotel beds rather than loose, volume related arrange-ments; and, at the same time, it can ensure that the foreign tour operator gets his beds by eliminating the increasing problem caused by destination hoteliers double letting their accommodation as a safeguard against late cancellations.

3. Introduction of legislation to require foreign tour operators to base a significant proportion of their planned departures on the LDC's charter airline (if it has one); or, requirement for a royalty payment from an approved list of foreign charter airlines.

Legislation of this type is most unlikely to succeed if introduced unilaterally. Close liaison with neighbouring countries on a regional basis is essential (see Regional Cooperation, page 235); even international collaboration may prove necessary (see page 239). It will also be highly desirable for a cooperative approach to the formulation of specific measures with the foreign tour operators themselves. The closer alliance of LDC tourism administrations and foreign tour operators may be achieved in various ways.

Joint conferences to debate tourism policy and legislation. One of the UN Ecosoc/ IUOTO study tour operator respondents put this suggestion: "As a first step for working more efficiently with the developing countries I would recommend a programme of meetings with the policy makers in the respective countries (authorities from civil aviation, tourism and finance, both governmental and private sector) in order to exchange ideas and experience in the vital area of mass tourism. This could be part of the educational phase, after which would follow the practical application of the ideas and policies developed by the respective governments."

Joint programme design and promotion. A tour operator will concentrate his tours programmes on the areas he believes will sell in his marketplace. It is the responsibility of the destination country (through its overseas promotional offices) to create sufficient interest to persuade the tour organiser to design and market a package tour that includes the country. The role of overseas tourism promotion offices is thus twofold: media advertising and information dissemination to the public; liaison with the travel trade. Concentration on only one of these functions means that the job is merely half accomplished. However, there are strong grounds for suggesting that, if budgetary limitations restrict the ideal scope of activities, emphasis should be given to working with the travel trade. The provision of up to date information on facilities and amenities, assistance in organising inspection trips (for tour operators) or familiarisation visits (for travel agency staff), suggested tour itineraries (particularly those involving a number of countries which have been devised by the regional tourist bodies (see page 238) and jointly financed advertising and promotion programmes are all methods by which the overseas tourism promotion offices can forge a close link with, and thereby influence upon, foreign tourist organisations.

STATE'S DIRECT EXECUTIVE INVOLVEMENT

Local control is of major importance

Maximum retention of decision making and ownership of LDCs' tourism products at the local level is, in our view, a key objective for LDCs seeking to maximise the economic benefits to be gained from tourism at the same time as minimising the social and cultural problems. The consequence of pursuing such a policy is that the onus for providing facilities and amenities in sufficient quantity and to acceptable standards rests upon the state. Where local private sector participation is insufficient or inadequate, the state is required to make direct intervention. The blend of local private sector and state participation is, of course, a matter for resolution by each country based on its political system. For LDCs which are keen to maximise the involvement of the local private sector, the restructuring of incentives schemes, as suggested above, in favour of local as opposed to foreign investors is one means of implementing such a policy. Another approach is the provision of a clause in the deeds of foreign owned hotels giving the state the right to take over the hotel (on commercially fair terms) after a specified period. The UN Ecosoc/IUOTO report states: "The terms of such a contract should be geared to providing the foreign investor with specific returns over the period preceding the right to exercise the option, together with a guaranteed purchase price (based on an agreed price plus an allowance for inflation) for his part of the investment". (49)

Greater state involvement in the distribution and marketing of LDCs' tourism products is extremely problematical to resolve satisfactorily. The preceding subsection suggested a number of measures to improve state liaison with foreign tourist operators in the distribution and marketing of LDCs' tourism products. The logical next step is for LDCs to move into direct executive involvement in this function. The idea is that the overseas tourist promotion offices would have their role extended to embrace the design and sale of tour operating programmes.

It is almost certainly the case that LDCs can only effectively control their tourism development in the long term, by entering the market at each level of distribution. The extremist view is that the state's role in the marketing of its tourism product must cover each aspect, i e distribution channels, advertising, public relations, personnel, advertising and sales promotion. However, whilst LDCs should formulate a long term strategy which embraces all of these aspects, it is difficult to see how, for at least a decade, direct sale operations would provide significant benefits to LDCs in the light of the supply/demand balance and the LDCs' lack of knowledge of the characteristics of tourism demand in major generating markets. The costs of establishment would be high; operations limited to a single destination are extremely susceptible to demand fluctuations resulting from actual or reported problems which affect tourists (e g strikes of hotel staff, instances of conflict between locals and tourists, political disturbances) and there exists the possibility of retaliatory action on the part of the foreign tour operators (e g through the exclusion of the country from their own tours programmes). The optimal short (and, probably, mid) term solution lies in closer cooperation between LDC tourism administrations and foreign tour operators. A joint venture, hybrid operation, utilising LDC capital (providing title and ownership) with foreign expertise (to design and market the programmes in generating markets) may be the most sensible bridging operation to a fully owned and operated LDC tour operator. Even for this type of operation, a regional approach may prove to be the most economically viable.

FOREIGN EXCHANGE

Measures to ensure the maximum inflow of foreign currency

LDCs are already active in respect of the operation of measures to ensure maximum foreign exchange earnings. Many countries limit the amount of their own currency which a tourist may bring in/take out to ensure that foreign currency is exchanged in the country; many, troubled by a currency black market, require foreign tourists to pay hotel bills in foreign currency or with local currency for which proof is available that the exchange was made at a bank or an official bureau de change. Some try to prevent, or reduce, the funding of tourists' visits by local residents by stipulating a minimum daily expenditure of foreign currency or, more frequently, check upon entry that the incoming tourist has sufficient funds for his proposed stay.

At the level of dealings between commercial organisations in LDCs and foreign countries, a number of countries seek to eliminate barter arrangements by requiring the whole (or bulk) of foreign tourist operators' commitments in LDCs to be paid for in foreign currencies. Some, in an attempt to preclude abuses of the voucher system of payment by tourists for services provided (a system widely used by West German tour operators) insist that the vouchers are cashed by local hoteliers, etc, inside the country.

All of these measures help to improve foreign exchange earnings. Another measure which has been mooted at various times in recent years, but as yet not acted upon by any individual LDC (or group of LDCs), is the establishment of a credit card/travellers cheque scheme by LDCs (most realistically on a regional basis).

STATISTICS (SECOND GENERATION)

Data compilation must be improved

There are many examples of cost benefit appraisals of specific resort or infrastructural (e g airports) developments, but the task of devising an accurate and comprehensive methodology for undertaking an assessment of the economic and social impact of international tourism on a national or even regional basis has defeated tourism administrations. The efforts which have been made are isolated ones with no follow up (e g Mitchell in East Africa in the late 1960s) or are based on weakly supported claims and counterclaims (particularly applicable to social/cultural impact analysis).

As noted in Section 3, pages 142 to 145 the ignorance of administrators and the poor quality of the data base are closely related. Until the data base is improved, the awareness amongst tourism officials of the impact of tourism will not materially advance. Statistics required for the measurement and assessment of tourism fit into two categories: first generation dealing with direct tourist flows; and second generation covering the impact areas of tourism. The following list of information (and usual sources) represents the minimum second generation data which LDCs should compile on a regular basis.

1. Employment (Central Statistical Office) broken down by: sex, age groups; job type (either SIC or MLH); permanent/temporary, full time/part time; seasons; regions; skilled/unskilled; local expatriate.

2. Census of population (Central Statistical Office).

3. Household budget survey or consumer expenditure survey of domestic population (needed for input/output analysis) including a measure of the amount spent abroad.

4. Domestic savings (usually shown as a residual which is inadequate).

5. Breakdown of tourist businesses' costs according to: electricity, light, water, sewerage, etc; supplies; labour; administration and marketing. The split between local produce and imports is essential. The Tourism Department can assist tne Central Statistical Office in collecting this information through a regular (say, annual) survey.

6. Balance of payments data.

7. Tourist expenditure analysis (Ministry of Finance data to serve as a crosscheck on Tourism Department survey information) showing tourist spending as a percentage of total movement on goods and services. Required for primary, secondary and tertiary sectors.

8. Government revenue showing all categories including customs duties by item and land tax by source. A list of establishments is needed for each category of customs duty, e g if £1 mn is spent on porcelain objects it is essential to know the proportions which are attributable to shops and to hotels. This acts as a check on what the businesses say in the costs survey.

Items 1 to 5 are normally provided by the Central Statistical Office though a good and often ignored source of employment data is the National Insurance Board or equivalent. The Ministry of Finance would usually be responsible for items 6 to 8.

SOCIAL COST BENEFIT AND STRUCTURAL ANALYSIS

Assessing tourism's social and cultural impact

Waters states the case for better understanding of tourism's impacts: "Understanding tourism's impact on employment, energy usage, the environment and political relations requires greatly increased research and educational efforts on the part of political and economic scientists. Government structures need overhauling to permit rational policy-making that recognises an educated public's interest in tourism as a high priority expenditure...as tourism continues to grow, its negative aspects in each particular region must be identified and steps taken to protect the legitimate interests of local residents. Government and private interests have a responsibility to plan and manage tourism in a manner that assures maximum social and economic benefits with minimum cultural disruption or environmental damage." (53)

There are four facets to improving LDCs' assessment of the costs and benefits of international tourism: awareness of the issues to be considered; cost benefit appraisal methodology; individual country analysis; iterative analysis. The full range of economic, social, cultural and environment impact areas of tourism have already been discussed. Any assessment of tourism's effects must cover each of these aspects. We have also demonstrated that the inadequacies of alternative methods (including the multiplier because of the danger of it overstating the benefits accruing from tourism) make a social cost benefit analysis approach the only (partly) effective means currently available of assessing the impacts of the multifaceted tourism sector. We make the following recommendations.

1. LDC tourism departments should establish the machinery (manpower, data

collection, etc) to undertake social cost benefit analysis both of the tourism sector as a whole and of each important proposed new tourism development.

2. The methodology needs to be tailored to each country's particular situation but the Little and Mirrlees methods discussed in Appendix 9 would certainly form a sound basis. (This is a particular area where further investigation is called for, in order to ascertain the exact merits for specific countries, of the differing methodologies proposed by Little and Mirrlees - 25 -, Squire and van der Tak - 45 - and Unido -10).

3. The assessment of tourism's total impact on the nation must be on an iterative, regular (say, annual) basis rather than as a once off, ad hoc study. In this way the analysis can be taken account of in each phase of the planned programme (perspective plan, master development plan and annual programme) suggested on page 223.

4. Research needs to be undertaken (although the initiator of, and body responsible for coordinating, such work should ideally be the WTO) into the patterns of development on an inter-country basis to determine the usefulness of structural analysis of tourism.

5. Environmental impact studies (either based on Burmeister's matrix - see page 208 or some other technique) should be undertaken as part of the social cost benefit analysis for each important proposed new development.

REGIONAL COOPERATION

Areas for regional collaboration -

The WTO/IUOTO regional studies have already indicated the possible ways of collaboration between LDCs on a regional basis. Every aspect of tourism development is suitable, to varying degrees, to a regional approach. Indeed, some of the measures suggested earlier in this section are probably achievable to a significant degree only through collective action by countries within a region. The WTO/IUOTO study on the Middle East region spells out a series of recommendations which should form the basis for discussion by the countries in each region in drawing up systems of collaboration.

'Marketing and promotion...that a joint marketing panel is formed by the member countries to apply, as far is both acceptable and practicable, all the basic principles of marketing to the area.

Tourist facilitation...that a joint commission should examine and implement the possible ways in which all aspects of facilitation could be improved for the tourist...

Gathering of tourist statistics...that the purpose, method and processing techniques of data gathering should be jointly agreed and applied so as to ensure fulfilment and compatibility of desired results.

Investment incentives and regulations...that a joint commission should be formed to examine and agree the basis, terms and conditions of nationally-sponsored investment programmes and inducements so as to limit or control the competition for limited resources which might otherwise be faced by individual member countries.

Standard regional classifications for local tourist industries...that uniform standards for accommodation and other related public amenities such as restaurants, bars, night clubs, cinemas, should be jointly agreed, rated and supervised.

Communications...that a joint commission should constantly review and make recommendations on all forms of communications insofar as they affect the development of tourism; and to ensure that the requirements of tourism are adequately debated and assessed in the formulation of national and international communications plans.

Training...that a joint training enterprise should be established to meet the overall requirements of the Study Area, and that jointly agreed policies and procedures should be formulated for the selection and eventual employment of its graduates.

International representation...that the area should be jointly represented on international bodies and at international congresses, whilst not in any way interfering with the individual countries' rights to membership and attendance."(56z)

Certain of these categories of potential regional cooperation between LDCs may be elucidated and developed further in the light of the analysis made, and conclusions presented, earlier in this report.

- marketing and promotion -

The UN Ecosoc/IUOTO report suggests the pooling of individually small, but collectively substantial, financial resources in order to promote a regional "image" which, in some way, might correct the incomplete and misleading picture put across in the advertising and promotion of foreign tourist operators. In practice, such an approach can have only limited application since there can be no truly effective substitute for individual country (resort and facility) advertising and promotion. Advertising on a regional basis can complement and supplement but not replace that undertaken by individual countries. For example the European Travel Commission is spending $600,000 in the USA in 1979 to bolster the $35 mn that individual member countries are planning to spend in aggregate.

For regional cooperation to be truly successful, the full range of marketing activities should be included and emphasis given to those aspects, such as the commissioning of original research, which lend themselves best to a collective approach. It is also important that the regional marketing effort should involve the cooperation and financial involvement of commercial interests in LDC tourism sectors as well as the NTOs. Clearly the task of drawing up a comprehensive, systematic and coordinated regional marketing programme is a daunting one and few regional bodies have been fully successful. The European Travel Commission is a good model for LDC regions to study. It consults regularly with its membership through conferences and other means and issues each year an action plan which spells out its strategy and advertising and promotional activities for the forthcoming year, along with tourist flow forecasts and the assumed conditions on which these are based. This serves to put commercial interests both in the generating and receiving markets fully in the picture, thereby signficantly increasing its credibility and cohesion.

236

- statistics -

Many of the earlier recommendations on the types of, methods of compiling, and treatment of, tourism statistics lend themselves to regional action. In particular it would be mutually beneficial for neighbouring LDCs to compile tourism statistics to comparable classifications (it is the ambition of WTO that this will apply universally within the medium term) and to conduct joint research programmes into tourism flows and impacts. Regional cooperation on tourism statistics compilation and treatment can materially aid those LDCs with the least experienced manpower at the tourism administration level. With assistance from their more advanced neighbours, the least developed countries will be able rapidly to develop their planning procedures by setting targets and measuring their achievements according to specific examples from other countries which have passed through a comparable stage in their tourism development.

- tourism facility classification -

In its quest eventually to achieve universal grading of tourism facilities, the WTO is currently working on regional standard classifications. In order to control the development of their tourism sectors more effectively, destination countries are beginning to establish codes of conduct which WTO hopes will also ultimately be adopted internationally. Effective examples include the following.

1. Establishing minima and maxima levels for hoteliers and local tour operators to charge to foreign tour operators (the system established successfully in Greece, where such rates are related to grades, is a good example).

2. Drawing up a standard facility booking contract form for use between LDC facility owners and foreign tourist operators. Jointly agreed terms (i e level of group booking discount, cancellation period and forfeit) would help to stop tour operators playing off one country against another.

3. Establishing standard regulations governing the operations of foreign tourist operators (e g feasibility plan process for proposed new developments, licensing of tour operators, control of the content of tour operators' programmes, requirement for fuller accounting to government in order to prevent any foreign currency abuse or transfer pricing).

- incentives -

In implementing the procedure outlined earlier in respect of the appraisal, establishment and monitoring of investment concession schemes, LDCs will benefit collectively from cooperating on a regional basis to avoid damaging and unproductive competition in offering such concessions.

- communications and distribution -

As detailed earlier, LDC tourist receiving countries lose a large proportion of apparent gross earnings (i e tourists' total expenditure). The obvious solution is for LDCs to increase their stake in the distribution of their tourism product. This could be achieved through the establishment of charter airlines and tour operating organisations and the introduction of legislation to protect them. Such action, in the short term at least, would serve to increase supply, affording foreign tour operators the opportunity to play destinations off against each other, and its practicability is, thus, limited. Coupled with the high establishment costs of such operations, this suggests that the best means for LDCs to achieve more direct control of the distribution of their tourism product will be to act on a regional basis, i e forming a regional charter airline and/or tour operating organisation.

If LDCs in a region are to launch their own tour operating company, it is highly desirable that its tour programme should, in some respects at least, be original. The obvious area would be in devising circuit tours[1] of countries in the region. Foreign tour operators are wary of this type of tour because of the organisational difficulties involved. With each country having a stake in the regional tour operator, these problems should be minimised. Circuit tours can also serve to meet regional integration or development objectives (for example by providing some tourism income for the less economically developed countries in the region through combining them with the region's "magnet" countries). There is little evidence to suggest that any individual countries suffer from circuit tourism. Most tourists have a clear idea of how long they wish to spend in any country, so combining two or more countries may well serve to extend the length of time spent in, and increase the foreign exchange income earned by, the region concerned. There will undoubtedly also be instances where a tourist will consider a three or four day trip to one country not to be worthwhile from the point of view of travelling time and cost related to time spent in the chosen destination, whereas if a seven day package to two countries were available the trip would be acceptable.

- training -

There are already many examples where a hotel training school has attracted participants from throughout a region rather than simply from the country in which it is based. Now regional coordination is required at the more senior level of tourism managers and administrators. This report has stressed the need for LDCs to equip themselves with many more and better qualified staff in the areas of administration, marketing and development. To achieve self-sufficiency in all aspects of training, universities and colleges offering degree courses in tourism studies are needed in LDCs. In the short and mid term, at least, the limited availability in LDCs of qualified teachers for such courses means that foreign experts will be required and, therefore, the most effective approach will be to set up such programmes on the basis of one per region.

- multilateral, bilateral agreements

These suggested regional cooperative actions can be implemented either through formal agreements or informally. In the former respect it is encouraging to note that the numbers of such agreements have grown significantly in the past few years. Tourism International Airletter (46a May 1978) records that there are four types

---

1   A circuit tour is a pleasure trip which includes two or more countries taken by a resident of a third country.

of agreement: multilateral agreements concerning tourism (9 in effect to date); bilateral agreements related to cooperation (98 in effect to date); bilateral agreements on facilitation (41 in effect to date); bilateral agreements regarding technical assistance (4 in effect to date)

ROLE OF WTO AND INTERNATIONAL AGENCIES

The WTO -

The World Tourism Organisation (WTO) is a technical agency affiliated to the UN. Its brief is principally one of research (rather than operations) and its constitution prohibits it from taking a direct role in financing developments. Until its 1976 affiliation to the UN, WTO was the International Union of Official Travel Organisations (IUOTO) and its membership has not changed significantly during the transition, consisting largely of LDCs. WTO's mantle of authority in tourism has not yet been recognised by many developed countries with significant tourism sectors, e g the UK, Italy, Japan and Canada. Whilst WTO is actively seeking to broaden its international membership, its current responsibility is to its LDC members.

Adopting the requisite UN procedure, WTO has to submit its programme to the General Assembly for approval biennially. The 1977-78 programme was approved but implementation funds were extremely limited, so that the research and aid programmes in the regions had to be largely funded by the host governments themselves.

- its plans for the next few years -

The new directions and aspirations for the WTO's programme of work over the next few years are as follows.

1. The aid programmes of the UN and other international agencies (ILO, Unesco, maybe even IBRD which is cutting down its direct support for tourism-only projects in its future programme of work), and the funds for inter-governmental assistance will be channelled increasingly through the WTO. The subject will be predetermined by the donor but the WTO will influence the direction and extent of the work required.

2. The specialist tourism training institutes will be expanded and given greater financial support (e g the advanced technical studies institute - CIEST - is located in Mexico and a world hotel training institute has been established in Caracas, Venezuela).

3. The operations side will be expanded through field visits and operational missions (WTO will form a team of experts to visit specific countries or regions). Current attention is on statistics, their method of collection and utilisation. WTO is undertaking workshops in four or five regions, sometimes producing handbooks (such as its Forecasting and Sampling Methods), and then will conduct operational missions to the weakest countries.

4. WTO is currently researching the training needs of LDCs. This has two purposes: the drawing up of comprehensive training programmes; and the submission of these to the General Assembly for funds.

5. WTO considers the optimum approach to its research and operational programmes is a regional one - through its six regional committees. This is not because a global approach is inappropriate ultimately but that, in the short to medium term, regional differences make it more practicable to tackle the problem by groups of countries of similar development, tourism resources, cultural affinity, etc.

6. The emphasis will be on workshops and operational missions rather than seminars, WTO's belief being that the former attract the participants who are actively involved in solving problems and dealing with statistics, etc. Furthermore, missions will increasingly be to, and for, individual countries rather than conducted at a capital city in one country for delegates from throughout a region (because of the lack of foreign currency to enable tourism department staff from many LDCs to travel outside their own countries).

- and areas where it might take action

The research programme for this report has identified a number of subjects on which WTO should fittingly take responsibility for providing guidance and training:

i. statistics (methods and applicability, i e guidelines for domestic tourism in statistics, tourism saturation levels, social cost benefit analysis, environmental impact, structural analysis, tourism data bank);

ii. training (at all levels, i e tourism department, NTO staff, hotels, other tourism facility operations);

iii. standardised hotel contract scheme for use with tour operators;

iv. standardised hotel classification scheme;

v. review of the impact and applicability of incentives.

WTO's emphasis on regional and individual country programmes is clearly more likely to produce positive results than global programmes, likewise, the stated future emphasis on operations (as well as research) and field missions rather than seminars. The key to future success of WTO programmes is global accept- ance of the stature of WTO as the UN agency for tourism (and this means increas- ing membership amongst developed countries) and increased funds voted by the General Assembly. These are, of course, interlinked. It is also important for WTO to encourage (and liaise with the protagonists of) original research programmes conducted by other agencies such as universities and consultancies. This is par- ticularly important in the field of social and economic impact.

WTO's function must, therefore, be to take on a dynamic role in developing the guidance, control and understanding of the impacts of the international tourism industry.

Appendices

Appendix 1 Exchange Rate Adjusted Consumer Price Indices in Main Origin or Destination Countries
(1963=100)

	1964	1965	1966	1967	1968	1969	1970	1971	1972	1973	1974	1975	1976	1977
Australia	102.4	106.4	109.6	113.1	116.1	119.5	124.2	133.7	136.9	162.7	188.1	195.0	217.6	218.5
Austria	103.8	109.4	111.7	116.2	119.4	123.1	128.5	139.7	148.2	171.3	194.9	224.7	246.0	278.5
Belgium/Luxemburg	104.2	108.4	112.9	116.2	119.4	123.8	128.7	137.0	148.1	162.3	182.4	215.2	235.4	268.5
Canada	102.3	104.9	107.9	112.0	117.4	121.8	129.3	137.6	135.8	131.6	148.2	156.7	182.0	180.6
Denmark	103.5	109.2	117.6	125.1	125.8	131.2	139.6	149.0	155.8	179.1	202.9	233.7	255.0	281.7
Finland	110.3	115.6	120.2	118.8	104.9	107.9	110.8	117.8	117.5	130.2	154.1	183.2	210.5	297.0
France	103.4	106.0	108.9	111.9	116.9	118.1	116.6	122.8	131.8	146.0	152.5	189.9	195.6	205.9
West Germany	102.4	105.8	109.4	111.3	113.0	116.0	131.7	144.7	154.8	179.4	196.4	217.0	233.1	260.0
Greece	100.8	103.8	109.1	110.9	111.3	114.0	117.3	120.4	115.9	123.7	153.5	160.3	168.7	185.8
Hong Kong	103.3	102.0	105.0	109.8	107.4	111.2	119.7	122.9	129.2	157.8	180.9	179.9	208.1	218.8
Ireland	106.7	112.1	115.4	117.7	106.8	114.7	123.5	136.0	140.4	139.7	154.8	175.8	176.9	192.3
Italy	105.9	110.6	113.3	117.4	119.0	122.2	128.2	135.1	140.2	141.8	150.0	172.9	166.5	183.9
Jamaica	102.0	104.7	106.8	108.0	99.8	106.0	116.4	123.9	123.8	116.7	147.4	171.3	197.6	217.4
Japan	103.9	110.7	110.4	121.0	127.5	134.1	144.3	156.4	171.9	198.8	228.8	248.8	285.3	336.9
Mexico	102.2	105.9	110.5	113.8	116.4	119.8	126.0	132.4	128.5	131.0	160.8	183.1	180.5	156.3
Netherlands	106.0	109.7	117.4	121.4	126.0	135.3	140.2	155.4	168.6	190.8	215.8	250.1	273.8	310.5
Norway	105.7	110.2	113.8	118.8	123.0	126.8	140.3	150.7	159.6	178.5	201.6	235.9	259.6	300.5
Portugal	103.4	107.0	112.4	118.6	125.8	136.9	145.6	165.1	177.0	199.2	240.0	294.2	292.9	283.2
Spain	107.0	121.1	128.7	134.5	123.1	125.8	133.0	144.6	156.4	175.2	203.0	236.0	250.5	271.8
Sweden	103.4	108.6	115.5	120.5	122.8	126.1	135.0	146.2	153.6	162.7	174.4	203.0	224.4	240.2
Switzerland	103.1	106.6	111.6	116.2	118.9	121.9	126.3	130.9	148.8	178.0	205.8	251.2	276.8	288.5
UK	103.3	108.2	112.5	114.0	103.3	108.9	115.8	128.3	130.4	127.1	139.7	163.2	162.2	179.8
USA	101.3	102.9	106.1	109.1	113.6	119.7	126.8	131.9	125.8	121.7	133.9	144.7	161.0	169.4
Yugoslavia	112.0	117.5	110.4	118.2	124.2	136.8	151.3	145.8	138.2	158.1	193.1	220.7	244.0	278.0

Note: This shows local consumer prices expressed in SDR terms. Divide destination country index x 100 by origin country index to get index of relative prices between two countries.

Sources for basic data: UN Monthly Statistical Bulletin; IMF International Financial Statistics.

Appendix 2 UK Data

	No. of visits abroad by UK residents ('000)	Expenditure by UK residents travelling abroad (£ mn)		UK discretionary incomes at 1970 prices[b] (£ mn)	Relative cost of travel abroad from UK[c] (1963=100)
		Current prices	1970 prices[a]		
1963	5,383	188.0	256.5	4,714	100.0
1964	5,897	190.0	251.0	4,977	101.7
1965	6,472	290.4	364.4	5,118	103.6
1966	6,918	297.4	357.5	5,237	103.6
1967	7,202	273.8	319.1	5,295	105.7
1968	7,269	270.5	301.9	5,382	113.4
1969	8,083	324.1	349.2	5,410	111.5
1970	8,482	381.7	381.7	5,694	110.4
1971	9,426	439.2	397.8	5,906	107.1
1972	10,553	526.2	433.0	6,589	112.0
1973	11,522	682.4	518.9	7,140	126.9
1974	10,489	683.4	422.9	7,270	126.8
1975	11,607	877.6	441.2	7,276	126.1
1976	11,134	1,008.2	445.5	7,213	133.2
1977	...	1,102.0	433.7	7,066	130.6

% increases pa in three year moving averages	Visits abroad by UK residents	Expenditure abroad by UK residents at 1970 prices[a]	Discretionary incomes at 1970 prices	Relative cost of travel from UK[c]
1964-66	8.6	11.6	3.5	1.2
1965-67	6.8	7.0	2.1	1.3
1966-68	3.9	-6.0	1.7	3.1
1967-69	5.4	-0.8	1.1	2.4
1968-70	5.7	6.5	2.5	1.4
1969-71	9.1	5.7	3.2	-1.4
1970-72	9.5	9.3	6.9	0.2
1971-73	10.7	7.6	7.9	5.0
1972-74	3.4	11.3	6.9	5.7
1973-75	3.2	3.3	3.3	3.9
1974-76	-1.2	0.6	0.3	1.7
1975-77	...	-5.2	-0.9	1.0

a GDP deflator used to adjust to 1970 prices. b Total personal disposable incomes, less expenditure on food, housing, fuel and light, all at 1970 prices. c Exchange rate adjusted consumer price indices for ten main destination countries divided by exchange rate adjusted consumer price index for UK and weighted according to UK travel expenditure in each in 1970.

Sources: For travel data – Digest of Tourist Statistics, British Tourist Authority; for discretionary incomes – derived from NIESR data; for relative costs – derived from data published by UN and IMF.

Mn days spent by UK travellers in W Europe & in other destinations[a]

		W Europe	Other[c]	
	Total	Total	% share	Increase in % share (points)
1969	88.40[b]	32.04	26.60	...
1970	93.00[b]	32.53	25.91	-0.69
1971	98.51[b]	35.34	26.40	0.49
1972	107.29[b]	39.40	26.86	0.46
1973	111.25	48.91	30.54	3.68
1974	99.88	40.67	28.94	-1.60
1975	112.12	46.90	29.49	0.55
1976	104.53	48.01	31.47	1.98
1977	...	...	...	...

Seven main W European destinations

	Spain	Irish Republic	Italy	France	West Germany	Austria	Switzerland
1968	23.49	17.43[b]	11.17	9.10	6.83	3.17	4.02
1969	23.59	15.32[b]	11.95	10.38	6.82	4.45	4.28
1970	29.87	14.11[b]	10.66	12.51	5.71	4.53	4.30
1971	32.73	11.57[b]	13.68	14.00	6.95	4.92	4.55
1972	34.97	13.24	12.55	18.45	6.80	4.87	4.37
1973	28.64	13.13	9.49	13.46	7.18	2.84	3.44
1974	33.28	12.84	10.31	17.41	7.69	2.77	3.11
1975	28.64	12.78	9.94	16.08	7.20	2.15	2.85
1976	...	...	...	...	...	...	...
1977	...	...	...	...	...	...	...

Relative cost of travel from UK by destination[d] (1963=100)

	Long haul[e]	All European destinations	Spain	Irish Republic	Italy	France	West Germany	Austria	Switzerland
1969	110.4	111.6	115.5	105.3	112.2	108.4	106.5	113.0	111.9
1970	109.7	110.4	114.9	106.6	110.7	100.7	113.7	111.0	109.1
1971	104.3	107.4	112.7	106.0	105.3	95.7	112.8	108.9	102.0
1972	100.6	112.8	119.9	107.7	105.3	101.1	118.7	113.7	114.1
1973	112.5	127.8	137.8	109.9	111.6	114.9	141.1	134.8	140.0
1974	107.8	128.4	145.3	110.8	107.4	109.2	140.6	139.5	147.3
1975	98.1	128.1	144.6	107.7	105.9	116.4	133.0	137.7	153.9
1976	111.2	134.9	154.4	109.1	102.7	120.6	143.7	151.7	170.7
1977	102.5	132.5	151.2	107.0	102.0	114.5	144.6	154.9	160.5

a Source: BTA. b Assumed average length of stay in Irish Republic, 10 days. c 1976 breakdown (mn days): USA 9.20, Canada 6.14, British West Indies 2.44, Australia/New Zealand 4.45, Middle East 4.45, Eastern Europe 2.27, other 17. d Excludes air fares. e Weighted average of USA, Canada, and Australia.

Index of UK air fares

	1968	1969	1970	1971	1972	1973	1974	1975	1976
Total UK airline revenues, scheduled and non-scheduled, per revenue passenger-km performed (new pence)	1.585	1.608	1.494	1.433	1.447	1.614	2.176	2.396	2.918
Index of revenue per passenger-km relative to UK consumer prices (1968=100)	100.0	96.3	84.1	72.8	72.3	82.8	101.6	95.7	117.3

Note: These figures, based on CAA data, include relatively minor amounts of revenue from excess baggage, mail and freight, and from domestic services, but the effect on the overall index figures is small. A rise in the index indicates that air fares have risen relative to consumer prices.

US travel abroad, expenditure, incomes, costs

	US travel abroad ('000 visits)		US expenditure on travel abroad ($ mn)				Discretionary incomes at 1958 prices ($ bn)[c]	Relative cost of travel abroad from USA (1963=100)[d]		Index of US international air fares relative to US consumer prices (1963=100)[e]
			Current prices		1970 prices[b]					
	Total	Overseas & cruise only	Total	Overseas & cruise only	Total	Overseas & cruise only		Total	Overseas & cruise only	
1963	...	2,312	2,114	1,120	2,649	1,404	224.2	100.0	100.0	100.0
1964	15,659	2,515	2,211	1,171	2,727	1,444	242.3	101.7	102.2	98.1
1965	16,936	2,956	2,438	1,298	2,952	1,571	258.3	103.4	104.2	96.0
1966	18,440	3,312	2,657	1,404	3,130	1,654	279.2	103.7	104.5	89.9
1967	20,137	3,775	3,207	1,535	3,661	1,752	294.9	103.7	104.0	84.5
1968	17,377	4,265	3,030	1,572	3,333	1,729	310.4	100.3	98.0	80.4
1969	19,350	5,153	3,373	1,815	3,539	1,905	317.6	98.3	96.0	75.2
1970	21,511	5,817	3,980	2,184	3,980	2,184	329.0	98.9	97.3	66.5
1971	22,906	6,296	4,373	2,335	4,189	2,237	349.5	101.5	100.5	65.3
1972	23,807	7,447	5,042	2,870	4,673	2,660	363.9	108.2	110.4	59.2
1973	23,762	7,683	5,526	3,104	4,847	2,723	394.1	115.6	122.0	58.1
1974	24,754	7,168	5,980	3,146	4,716	2,481	378.0	120.2	124.7	63.5
1975	22,863	7,109	6,417	3,474	4,613	2,497	372.8	125.1	132.5	65.6
1976	22,372	7,473	6,856	3,762	4,686	2,571	360.7	120.9	127.3	61.8
1977	...	...	...	...	...	...	404.4	118.6	133.5	61.2

a Source: Department of Commerce. b Deflator: GDP price index. c Disposable personal incomes at 1958 prices less expenditure on food, beverages, housing and household operations (source: Survey of Current Business). d Exchange rate adjusted consumer price indices for ten main destination countries, divided by exchange rate adjusted consumer price index for USA, and weighted to reflect the pattern of travel expenditure in 1970. Excludes fare component. e Operating revenues on international operations divided by international revenue passenger miles performed, the resulting index being set against the US consumer price index (source for data: Survey of Current Business).

Percentage shares of US travel by main area[a]

	Canada	Mexico	W Indies & Central America	Europe & Mediterranean	Other overseas
1967	33.6[d]	18.6	9.6	31.5	6.7
1968	26.2	20.5	12.2	33.1	8.0
1969	24.7	20.1	12.3	35.2	7.8
1970	24.7	19.4	10.5	36.6	8.7
1971	23.9	22.1	10.1	35.6	8.3
1972	20.6	23.8	10.9	35.9	8.9
1973	22.1	24.3	12.3	33.8	7.5
1974	24.6	24.6	12.4	30.0	8.4
1975	23.5	25.2	12.9	28.5	9.9
1976	23.2	27.7	11.5	28.1	9.5
1977	...				

Percentage shares of US travel for five European destinations[b]

	France	West Germany	Italy	Switzerland	UK
1967	16.5	22.6	19.8	8.0	33.2
1968	14.3	24.6	18.8	9.6	32.7
1969	18.4	21.6	20.7	9.9	29.4
1970	16.3	20.8	19.7	9.8	33.5
1971	16.7	18.9	18.4	9.7	36.3
1972	16.4	19.5	18.0	10.4	35.7
1973	19.3	19.5	19.1	8.4	33.6
1974	17.6	16.9	17.2	10.3	37.9
1975	17.8	19.7	17.5	6.9	38.1
1976	17.3	18.8	17.0	8.7	38.3
1977	...	...	...	...	...

a Based on percentage breakdowns of total expenditure at 1963 relative prices. b Percentages of five country total, based on visitor days spent in each – source: US Dept of Commerce c Jamaica is taken as representative of West Indies and Central America; the five European countries appearing in this table as representative of Europe and Mediterranean; and Japan, Hong Kong and Australia as representative of other areas. d Inflated by international exposition in Montreal.

Relative cost of travel abroad from USA — Changes above or below all country total (%)

	Canada	Mexico	W Indies & Central America	Europe & Mediterranean	Overseas[c]
1967	1.0	0.2	-1.7	-0.6	0.8
1968	3.9	1.6	-7.9	-2.0	0.7
1969	0.5	-0.3	2.8	-1.3	2.0
1970	-0.4	-1.3	3.0	0.2	0.4
1971	-0.3	-1.6	-0.4	1.0	–
1972	-3.1	-4.9	-1.8	3.4	6.8
1973	-6.6	-1.4	-9.3	3.8	14.7
1974	-1.6	7.6	10.8	-5.4	0.9
1975	-6.3	0.8	3.4	4.9	-7.0
1976	7.7	-8.0	7.0	-4.4	6.4
1977	-3.8	-15.8	6.5	5.1	8.9

Changes above or below five country total in W Europe (%)

	France	West Germany	Italy	Switzerland	UK
1967	0.5	-0.6	1.2	1.7	-0.9
1968	5.6	2.8	2.7	3.6	-7.7
1969	-0.7	0.8	-5.2	-0.6	3.5
1970	-7.7	6.3	4.6	-3.1	-0.6
1971	-2.5	1.9	-2.4	-4.1	2.8
1972	2.6	2.2	-1.2	9.3	2.8
1973	3.9	9.1	-6.0	13.1	-3.3
1974	-3.7	0.9	-2.5	6.5	-9.9
1975	6.2	-6.8	-2.3	3.9	1.3
1976	0.5	4.4	-5.6	6.9	-0.9
1977	-3.2	2.8	1.8	-4.1	2.2

245

Appendix 4 West German Data

	International tourism expenditure by W Germans		% breakdown			No.of visits abroad by W German holidaymakers[c] ('000)	Discretionary incomes at 1970 prices[d] (DM mn)	Relative cost of travel abroad from W Germany[e] (1963=100)		
	Total (DM mn)		European OECD countries	USA/ Canada	Other countries			All destinations	W Europe & Yugoslavia	USA/Canada
	Current prices[a]	1970 prices[b]								
1963	...	...	...	...	...	6,258	176.51	100.0	100.0	100.0
1964	4,553	5,573	...	...	...	...	194.01	102.4	102.7	99.0
1965	5,480	6,470	87.4	7.9	4.7	...	214.44	104.1	104.6	97.5
1966	6,292	7,174	86.6	7.6	5.8	8,462	217.63	103.8	104.3	97.2
1967	6,086	6,854	83.5	8.7	7.8	...	213.93	106.0	106.6	98.3
1968	6,320	7,007	82.4	8.5	9.1	...	232.98	105.6	106.0	100.8
1969	7,600	8,137	82.4	8.2	9.4	10,362	250.21	106.9	107.2	103.4
1970	10,230	10,230	84.7	6.8	8.5	12,122	279.27	98.6	98.8	96.5
1971	12,320	11,418	85.4	5.6	9.0	14,274	288.57	95.3	95.6	91.5
1972	15,615	13,673	84.9	5.3	9.8	...	301.74	93.9	94.8	81.9
1973	17,346	15,488	85.9	4.1	10.0	...	299.30	90.2	91.9	68.3
1974	18,234	14,146	84.8	4.7	10.5	...	298.58	91.8	93.5	68.9
1975	20,940	15,163	84.6	4.6	10.8	18,795	310.13	97.1	99.4	67.2
1976	22,541	15,807	84.7	5.2	10.1	...	318.67	96.4	98.5	69.9
1977	...	...	...	...	...	...	326.00	95.0	97.2	65.6

a Source: OECD; 1964-72 data converted from $ figures at period average conversion rates; 1964 estimate linking old data series to new.
b Deflated by GDP price index (source OECD). c Not continuous series, source OECD. d Derived from OECD national accounts data; disposable personal incomes adjusted to constant prices, less expenditure on food, housing, and related items; 1976 and 1977 are estimates. e Exchange rate adjusted consumer price indices for eleven main destination countries, divided by exchange rate adjusted consumer price index for West Germany and weighted according to estimated expenditure in each in 1970.

Percentage shares of W German travel expenditure at constant 1963 relative prices

	All European OECD countries	USA plus Canada[a]	Austria[b]	France	Italy[b]	Netherlands[b]	Switzerland[b]
1970	92.4	7.6	32.0	11.1	28.0	10.5	18.5
1971	93.6	6.4	32.2	11.6	27.1	10.5	18.6
1972	93.3	6.7	30.2	11.3	30.9	10.9	16.8
1973	94.0	6.0	32.2	12.5	29.7	11.5	14.2
1974	93.0	7.0	31.1	14.2	30.0	10.9	13.9
1975	92.6	7.4	31.4	15.0	31.7	9.6	12.4
1976	92.0	8.0	30.0	14.5	35.3	8.7	11.5

a Share of European OECD plus USA/Canada total. b Share of combined total for these five countries. c Compared with changes in relative prices for West German travellers to Western Europe (and Yugoslavia).

Percentage increases p a in relative prices for W German travellers in country/ area concerned compared with changes in total relative prices for W German travellers

	All European OECD countries	USA and Canada	Austria[c]	France[c]	Italy[c]	Netherlands	Switzerland
1970-72	0.2	-3.1	0.6	-2.0	-0.9	1.8	1.0
1971-73	0.5	-7.6	1.7	-0.3	-4.1	2.4	3.6
1972-74	0.5	-8.1	1.6	-2.2	-5.8	1.5	5.7
1973-75	0.4	-7.9	1.1	-0.6	-6.1	0.4	5.0
1974-76	0.1	-1.4	1.1	-1.3	-5.5	1.0	3.8
1975-77	0.2	-2.7	1.2	-0.7	-3.8	1.6	0.5

Sources for original data: Travel expenditure - World Tourist Organisation; relative prices - UN and IMF.

Appendix 5 French Data

	Summer trips abroad by French holidaymakers ('000)	International tourist expenditure by French travellers (mn francs)		Discretionary incomes at 1970 prices[d] (bn francs)	Relative cost of travel from France[e] (1963=100)
		Current prices[b]	1970 prices[c]		
1963	...	3,235	4,290	178.05	100.0
1964	...	4,184	5,337	178.62	100.9
1965	3,726[a]	4,930	6,132	200.82	104.4
1966	3,918[a]	5,226	6,319	212.97	106.1
1967	3,997[a]	5,451	6,405	227.82	106.8
1968	3,918[a]	5,755	6,474	238.63	100.3
1969	3,500	5,718	6,032	252.92	102.6
1970	4,000	6,218	6,218	274.38	108.9
1971	4,100	7,014	6,642	294.13	111.7
1972	4,400	7,909	7,068	315.23	109.4
1973	5,000	9,627	8,023	336.70	106.4
1974	4,500	11,445	8,397	352.06	114.1
1975	5,200	13,140	8,662	361.42	105.7
1976	4,900	16,417	9,784	377.55	108.6

a Estimate from old data series on number of summer holidaymakers (some of whom made more than one trip); source OECD. b 1963–1972 data converted back to francs from $ data (source OECD) with adjustments to compensate for the exclusion of travel to other franc zone countries from the original data. c Deflated by GDP price index. d Disposable personal incomes adjusted to constant prices, less expenditure on food, housing and related items; 1976 and 1977 are estimates. e Exchange rate adjusted consumer price indices for seven main destination countries, divided by exchange rate adjusted consumer price index for France, and weighted according to estimated 1972 expenditures in each.

Appendix 6 Japanese Data

	No of Japanese travelling abroad ('000)	International tourist expenditure		Discretionary incomes at 1970 prices[b] (bn yen)	Relative cost of travel from Japan (1963=100)
		Current prices ($ mn)	1970 prices[a] ($ mn)		
1963	99.3	65	91	13,411	100.0
1964	127.7	78	105	14,777	99.1
1965	158.8	88	113	16,034	94.3
1966	212.4	118	144	17,318	92.5
1967	267.5	145	169	19,984	91.8
1968	343.5	167	186	22,727	87.0
1969	492.9	241	257	25,000	87.0
1970	663.5	315	315	27,612	85.8
1971	961.1	509	476	30,315	82.6
1972	1,392.0	774	705	34,262	77.0
1973	2,289.0	1,252	923	39,923	72.8
1974	2,335.5	1,358	895	40,723	70.3
1975	2,466.3	1,367	863	42,484	70.2
1976	2,852.6	1,663	940	43,695	67.0
1977	...	...	...	45,115	60.4

a Adjusted to constant exchange rate basis (Y360=$1) and deflated by Japanese implicit GDP price index.
b Disposable personal incomes adjusted to constant prices, less expenditure on food, housing and related items; 1975–77 data are partial estimates.

Sources: Tourism data – OECD annual tourist reports; macroeconomic data – OECD national accounts statistics; price data – UN and IMF monthly statistics.

Appendix 7

Definition of LDC (Less Developed Countries)

The definitions used in the UN statistical series are adopted for this Special Report.

DEVELOPING COUNTRIES (OR DEVELOPING MARKET ECONOMIES)

Africa
North Africa – Algeria, Egypt, Libya, Morocco, Sudan, Tunisia
Other Africa – Territories in Africa not listed elsewhere

America
Latin American Free Trade Association (Lafta) – Argentina, Bolivia, Brazil,
              Chile, Colombia, Ecuador, Mexico, Paraguay, Peru, Uruguay,
              Venezuela
Central American Common Market (CACM) – Costa Rica, El Salvador,
              Guatemala, Honduras, Nicaragua
Other developing America – all countries in America (North, Central and South)
              not listed elsewhere. NB this includes whole of Caribbean

Asia
Middle East (Western Asia) – Bahrain, Cyprus, South Yemen, Iran, Iraq,
              Jordan, Kuwait, Lebanon, Oman, Neutral Zone, Qatar, Saudi
              Arabia, Syria, Turkey, United Arab Emirates, Yemen
Other Asia (Southern and Eastern Asia) – all countries in Asia not listed else-
              where

Oceania
All countries in Oceania not listed elsewhere.

DEVELOPED COUNTRIES (OR DEVELOPED MARKET ECONOMIES)

    Africa   – Customs Union of Southern Africa – Botswana, Lesotho,
                      Namibia, South Africa, Swaziland

    North America – Canada, USA

    Asia   – Israel, Japan

```
Europe    - EEC:    Belgium, Denmark, France, West Germany, Ireland,
                    Italy, Luxemburg, Netherlands, UK
            Efta:   Austria, Faeroe Islands, Finland, Iceland, Norway,
                    Portugal, Sweden, Switzerland
            Others: Andorra, Gibraltar, Greece, Malta, Spain, Yugoslavia

Oceania   - Australia, New Zealand.
```

CENTRALLY PLANNED ECONOMIES

```
Asia    - China, Mongolia, North Korea, Vietnam

Europe - Albania, Bulgaria, Czechoslovakia, East Germany, Hungary, Poland,
         Rumania.
```

Opec

Algeria, Ecuador, Gabon, Indonesia, Iran, Iraq, Kuwait (incl Neutral Zone),
Libya, Nigeria, Qatar, Saudi Arabia, United Arab Emirates, Venezuela.

Appendix 8

Definitions, Abbreviations and Acronyms

<u>Visitor, tourist, excursionist</u>

The application of the terms "visitor", "tourist" and "excursionist" to international travel has been carried out in accordance with the definition of these terms adopted by the UN Conference on International Travel and Tourism in Rome in 1963.

The conference accepted a definition for the term "visitor" which, for statistical purposes, describes any person visiting a country other than that in which he has his usual place of residence, for any reason other than following an occupation remunerated from within the country visited. This definition covered two classes of visitors, "tourists" and "excursionists", which were defined as follows.

<u>Tourists</u>: temporary visitors staying at least 24 hours in the country visited and the purpose of whose journey can be classified under one of the following heads:

    i. leisure (recreation, holiday, health, study, religion and sport);

    ii. business, family, mission, meeting.

<u>Excursionists</u>: temporary visitors staying less than 24 hours in the country visited (including travellers on cruises but excluding travellers in transit).

<u>International tourism receipts</u>

These are defined as the receipts of a country in the form of consumption expenditures, i e payments for goods and services made by foreign tourists out of foreign currency resources. They may, in practice, also include receipts from foreign excursionists or day visitors, except in cases where these are so important as to justify separate classification. They exclude all forms of remuneration resulting from employment, as well as international fare receipts. This category corresponds to "travel credits" in the standard reporting form of the IMF.

<u>Inclusive package tour</u>

An arrangement whereby a traveller purchases transportation and accommodation at a single price from a tours wholesaler. The tour arrangement may also include meals and/or excursions.

<u>Transnational corporation</u>

An enterprise which owns or controls assets in two or more countries.

Abbreviations and acronyms

ARI	–	Accounting rate of interest
Asta	–	American Society of Travel Agents
ATR	–	Annals of Tourism Research
B of P	–	Balance of payments
CBA	–	Cost benefit analysis
CRI	–	Consumption rate of interest
ECE	–	Economic Commission for Europe
EEC	–	European Economic Community
Ecosoc	–	Economic and Social Council
Esomar	–	European Society of Market Research
FE	–	Foreign exchange
IIT	–	Individual inclusive tour
GIT	–	Group inclusive tour
Iata	–	International Air Transport Association
IMF	–	International Monetary Fund
IRR	–	Internal social rate of return
IS	–	Import substitution
IT	–	Inclusive tour
ITC	–	Inclusive tour on charter flight
ITX	–	Inclusive tour on scheduled service flight
LDC	–	Less developed or developing country
NPV	–	Net present value
NTA(O)	–	National tourism administration (organisation)
OECD	–	Organisation for Economic Cooperation and Development
Opec	–	Organisation of Petroleum Exporting Countries
OTC	–	One stop charter inclusive tour
SW(R)	–	Shadow wage (rate)
TEA	–	Transnational economic agent
TNC	–	Transnational corporation
UN	–	United Nations
Unctad	–	UN Conference on Trade and Development
UNDP	–	UN Development Programme
Unesco	–	UN Educational, Scientific and Cultural Organisation
Unido	–	UN Industrial Development Organisation
Uscab	–	US Civil Aeronautics Board
WTO/IUOTO	–	World Tourism Organisation/International Union of Official Travel Organisations

Appendix 9

Methodology for Tourism Multiplier and Social Cost Benefit Analysis

This appendix contains the basic principles and formulae of specific methodologies for tourism multiplier and social cost benefit analysis which are considered likely to produce the most useful results given the current availability and reliability of data inputs. For detailed explanation of the workings of these models, reference should be made to Archer (2b & c), Bryden (5), Little and Mirrlees (25) and Sadler (42) on whose writings this technical appendix has been based.

Multiplier

As noted in the text on page 33, a tourism income multiplier is a coefficient which measures the amount of income generated by a unit of tourism expenditure. Although the theory demands the measure to relate to an <u>additional</u> unit of tourism expenditure, data difficulties generally result in an analysis drawn up according to an <u>average</u> unit of spending.

In designing a model, it is important to gauge tourism's impact on both national income (including that of government) and personal sector disposable income. Archer's model is designed to measure the direct, indirect and induced local value added contribution by tourism to each sector. <u>Direct</u> is defined in the slightly restricted sense as wages, salaries, rent, interest and profits. Government income is excluded but the household income generated by the respending of this public sector revenue is included in indirect value added. <u>Indirect</u> is defined as the additional value added created by local purchases made by businesses using its tourism revenue to finance them and the chain reaction this creates. <u>Induced</u> is defined as the additional income created by the respending of personal sector disposable income. All payments made to foreign based individuals or companies are excluded.

The basic income model is:

$$Y = C + I + G + T_i + X - M \tag{1}$$

where Y represents income, C consumer expenditure, I investment, G government expenditure, T_i indirect tax, X exports and M imports.

Archer then derives a simple income multiplier via the operations described below.

$$C = \overline{C} + c\,(Y - T_d + B) - c_j\,(Y - T_d + B) \tag{2}$$

where c represents the propensity to consume, c_j the proportion of that propensity which is spent abroad, T_d the value of direct deductions from gross income such as income tax, national insurance, etc, and B the level of government benefits (e g social security payments).

$$I = \bar{I} \qquad (3)$$
$$G = \bar{G} \qquad (4)$$
$$T_i = t_i(c) \qquad (5)$$
$$X = \bar{X} \qquad (6)$$
$$M = \bar{M} + mY \qquad (7)$$
$$B = \bar{B} - bY \qquad (8)$$
$$T_d = \bar{T}_d + t_d(Y) \qquad (9)$$

One benefit of this model is that it allows for import leakages in the form of consumers' remittances abroad and the commercial sector's import purchases.

By substituting equations 2 to 9 into equation 1 and injecting an additional unit of tourist spending, ΔE, an equation assessing the impact of this extra unit on the economy is obtained:

$$\Delta Y = c\Delta(Y - t_d Y - bY) - c_j\Delta(Y - t_d Y - bY) - t_i c\Delta(Y - t_d Y - bY) - m\Delta Y + \Delta E \qquad (10)$$

Dividing by ΔY gives

$$1 = c(1 - t_d - b) - c_j(1 - t_d - b) - t_i c(1 - t_d - b) - m + \frac{\Delta E}{\Delta Y} \qquad (11)$$

Simplification produces

$$1 = (c - c_j - t_i c)(1 - t_d - b) - m + \frac{\Delta E}{\Delta Y} \qquad (12)$$

therefore

$$\frac{\Delta Y}{\Delta E} = \frac{1}{1 - (c - c_j - t_i c)(1 - t_d - b) + m} \qquad (13)$$

This produces an instantaneous multiplier, k, which, because it omits any measure of the effect of possible additional exports to those countries which have benefited from extra sales to the country concerned or any possible investment in the country arising from increased output, is only usable in countries with relatively small economies.

A final modification eliminates that amount of tourism expenditure which leaks out of the economy immediately without generating any value added. L represents these direct first round leakages producing

$$k = \frac{1 - L}{1 - (c - c_j - t_i c)(1 - t_d - b) + m} \qquad (14)$$

This simplistic model will provide useful guidelines for the governments of LDCs but its value is limited because of its assumption that each form of external injection of income has the same general effects on the recipient economy. For practical purposes, therefore, it is necessary to:

i. break down the initial round of expenditure into the component parts and analyse the impact of each separately;

ii. disaggregate the internal structure of the economy.

253

Input-output analysis is required. However, since the data needs for such an analysis are likely to be too demanding for LDCs, a modified approach has to be adopted. Archer has used the following modified form of input-output on various studies in both developed and developing countries.

His first step is to disaggregate the simple income model of equation 14 into two main parts:

    i.   the direct and indirect income generated by an additional unit of tourism expenditure;

    ii. the additional income generated by the respending of factor-earnings by population.

The direct and indirect income created is expressed as

$$\sum_{j=1}^{N} \sum_{i=1}^{n} Q_j K_{ji} Y_i \tag{15}$$

where j represents each tourist category by source country, $j = 1$ to N; i each type of business establishment, $i = 1$ to n; Q_j the proportion of total tourism expenditure accounted for by the jth type of tourist; K_{ji} the proportion spent by the jth type of tourist in each ith type of business; and Y_i is the aggregated direct and indirect income generated from each unit of turnover by the ith type of business receiving tourism income.

Direct and indirect income generated can be separated, as in the two following equations

$$\sum_{j=1}^{N} \sum_{i=1}^{n} Q_j K_{ji} Y_{di} \tag{16}$$

where Y_{di} represents the factor incomes produced by each unit of turnover exclusively within the ith type of business which directly receives tourism income.

$$\sum_{j=1}^{N} \sum_{i=1}^{n} Q_j K_{ji} Y_i - Y_{di} \tag{17}$$

where Y_i represents the income generated from each unit of turnover by the ith type of business.

The additional income generated by the respending of factor earnings by the population is found by applying a multiplier expression to the sum of equations 16 and 17

$$\sum_{j=1}^{N} \sum_{i=1}^{n} Q_j K_{ji} Y_i \frac{1}{1 - c \sum_{i=1}^{n} X_i Z_i Y_i} \tag{18}$$

where X_i represents the pattern of consumer spending in the country, i e the proportion of total consumer spending in the ith type of business and Z_i the proportion of consumer spending which takes place within the country.

Archer then advocates the use of separate formulae for each of the principal categories of business activity, dividing these into two broad categories:

    i.   businesses dependent on tourism activity - equation 19;

    ii. businesses capable of surviving without an active tourism sector - equation 20.

$$Y_a = \frac{W(1 - h) + P + F + \sum_{i = 1}^{n} M_{ai} Y_i}{D} \qquad (19)$$

where Y_a represents the income generated coefficient for this type of business, W gross wages and salaries paid to local residents, h statutory deductions made from these wages and salaries, P profits realised within the country, F rent and interest payments made locally, M_{ai} cost payments made by this type of business to the ith business and D the total turnover.

$$Y_b = \frac{\triangle W (1 - h) + \triangle P + \triangle F + \triangle \sum_{i = 1}^{n} M_{bi} Y_i}{\triangle D} \qquad (20)$$

where Y_b is the income generated coefficient for this type of business.

Social cost benefit analysis

Because tourism multipliers assume a widespread unemployment of resources, ignoring any opportunity cost, they overstate the benefits of tourism. To get around this, the income obtained from tourism should be offset against the possible income which could be earned from the alternative use of these resources.

As noted by Bryden (5), this could be achieved through a programming approach if (and in respect of LDCs it is a big if) sufficient, accurate, data on inter-industry transactions and resource use by industry as well as resource availabilities and other constraints can be obtained. The programme would give a dual solution thereby enabling correct valuation of the various resources available to the economy and computation of the appropriate prices (shadow or accounting prices) to be attached to the inputs/outputs of any activity. However Bryden concludes that the data collection problems and doubts about certain of the linear programming assumptions make a programming approach unfeasible in the Caribbean, a finding which still applies to the majority of LDCs.

The social cost benefit analysis approach therefore recommends itself as the most appropriate. It is particularly attractive because it calculates the social justification for tourism development rather than simply the private profitability arising from it. The three principal decisions to be made in undertaking a cost benefit analysis are:

  i. the welfare function to be maximised;

  ii. the choice of an appropriate discount rate (since projects differ in the time profiles of costs and benefits);

  iii. The means of calculating accounting or shadow prices.

The debate on these issues is complex and contentions and reference should be made to the suggested bibliography (2b & c, 5, 25 and 42) for details.

Little and Mirrlees use a simple rule to overcome the problems of weighting the costs and benefits between regions and income groups. They treat government income as one, that of profit earners zero and that of workers unity or less depending on the value the government puts on earnings versus immediate consumption. Beyond this, distributional objectives are assumed to be met by the tax system. Bryden stresses, however, that a distinction between nationals and non-nationals should be made because income accruing to non-nationals resident in the economy does not normally form part of the welfare function which the government is seeking to maximise.

Of the various approaches to the selection of an appropriate discount rate, the one favoured by a large core of researchers takes account both of the social time preference rate and the opportunity cost rate expressed in social terms. In the Little and Mirrlees method, the social time preference rate is termed the consumption rate of interest (CRI) and is used in conjunction with the accounting rate of interest (ARI). The CRI revalues consumption in terms of savings for each time period. The resultant benefits are discounted back to the present using the ARI which is set at a level such that, if all investment was under public sector control, there would be just sufficient projects, with positive present social value, to add to the total amount investment will permit, whereas in a mixed economy, Little and Mirrlees state than planners should seek to spread the marginal social yield evenly in both sectors.

Accounting or shadow prices are determined by adjusting market prices to correct for the distortions which are significant in such a way that they reflect real scarcity and needs in the economy. This is one area where Bryden is at odds with the approach adopted by Little and Mirrlees. Bryden points out that adjustments have to be made to the total wages and salaries bill before any shadow pricing takes place because non-nationals are employed in all LDCs' tourism sectors and shadow pricing of wages and salaries refers solely to national labour resources. After deducting taxes, the wages and salaries of non-nationals should be treated as a real cost in FE terms. Bryden also considers it desirable to allow for different levels of skill in devising the shadow wage rate whereas Little and Mirrlees regard the charging of actual salary payments to the project as likely to provide sufficiently accurate results. A further point of contention is the treatment of unskilled labour which Little and Mirrlees assume to come from the subsistence agricultural sector, where, they contend, the consumption of the worker may be above his marginal product owing to the operation of a "sharing mechanism". Bryden disagrees, claiming instead that it is likely to be the younger, more active, members of the rural community who migrate and their marginal product may well be higher than the average. The shadow wage rate should, according to Bryden, reflect the effect of employment generated both on production elsewhere and on the commitment to consumption.

To be able to recast on a common basis the attributes of a series of alternative investments, it is necessary to determine a maximand to which the contribution of all the attributes can be identified and a numeraire according to which the relative contribution of each to the maximand can be measured. The method deemed by Little and Mirrlees integrates as many variables as possible via a single numeraire into a consistent relationship with a maximand. Growth (including health, education, infrastructural, etc, improvements as well as physical output) is presumed to be the aim of the country concerned. Investable funds accruing to government can be used to achieve that growth and so constitute a convenient numeraire quantity. All other allocations of output from a project can be given a comparative evaluation in terms of this numeraire.

Adjustments are necessary to some of the inputs, e g the tariff element of the cost of imported goods must be eliminated in the social accounts as this accrues to government, increasing the funds available; not all of the money wages may be included as costs in the accounts if government's aim is to enable the low paid to increase their consumption as part of the development process. The Little and Mirrlees method values everything at world prices thus balancing out the effect of currencies being maintained at artificially high levels. All costs are thus reduced to a common opportunity cost by showing precisely what a country forgoes in using individual resources and what it can earn in potential output.

Sadler suggests a model which takes account of the problem of the impact of the project on changes in income and the patterns of personal consumption. The point is that, if workers change their consumption to imported goods, the results of the analysis will be invalid. Sadler puts forward the following system:

Vector $X = (X_1, X_2 \ldots X_n)$ Changes in level of activity in each of n sectors

Vector $Y = (Y_1, Y_2 \ldots Y_n)$ Changes in created surplus in each of n sectors

$$\begin{bmatrix} a_{11} & a_{12} & \cdots & a_{1n} \\ a_{21} & a_{22} & \cdots & a_{2n} \\ & & & \\ a_{n1} & a_{n2} & \cdots & a_{nn} \end{bmatrix} = A = \text{Matrix of input/output coefficients}$$

$$\begin{bmatrix} b_{1h} & o & \cdots & o \\ o & b_{2h} & & \\ & & & \\ o & o & \cdots & b_{nh} \end{bmatrix} = B_h \begin{array}{l} \text{Income creation coefficients for each of the h} \\ \text{receiving sectors} \\ (h = n + 1 \ldots p) \end{array}$$

$$\begin{bmatrix} c_{1h} & c_{1h} & \cdots & c_{1h} \\ c_{2h} & c_{2h} & \cdots & c_{2h} \\ & & & \\ c_{nh} & c_{nh} & \cdots & c_{nh} \end{bmatrix} = C_h = \begin{array}{l} \text{Marginal propensities to consume of each of} \\ \text{the h sectors} \end{array}$$

which yields

$$X - AX - c_{n+1} (1 - A) B_{n+1} X \ldots C_p (1 - A) B_p X = Y$$

257

Factorising:

$$X = (1 - A)^{-1} \left[1 - \sum_{n+1}^{p} C_h (1 - A) B_h (1 - A)^{-1} \right]^{-1} Y$$

The changes in created surplus represent that part of an increase in total output which is not consumed, i e balance of payments surplus and increases in taxation and savings. It should also be noted that there are both international (producing exportable outputs) and domestic (e g electricity, construction) sectors. The way in which the model operates can be demonstrated by postulating an increase in created surplus in one international sector (i) with output in the remaining international sectors (j) holding constant. To achieve this the i sector requires more inputs which results in reduced exports (increased imports) in the j sectors and increased output in the domestic sector (d). The resultant income increases in sectors i and d will further reduce exports (increase imports) in the j sectors and increase outputs in sectors i and d.

Logically then the net change in created surplus would be the increase postulated in sector i minus the reductions in the surpluses in sector j, i e

$$\sum_{1}^{n} Y$$

To arrive at the social benefit it is essential to add to this reinvestable surplus an allowance for extra consumption (the excess of the actual wage over the shadow wage). Assuming that the worker consumes all his income, the extra consumption can be calculated as follows:

$$C^o \left(\frac{w - sw}{w} \right)$$

where C^o represents the increase in income, w the actual wage and sw the shadow wage.

Total social benefits will therefore be

$$\sum_{1}^{n} Y + C^o \left(\frac{w - sw}{w} \right)$$

Since these benefits accrue over time they must be treated by an appropriate discount factor (r). Total social benefits over time will therefore be:

$$\sum_{1}^{t} \left[\frac{\sum Y_t + C^o \left(\frac{w - sw}{w} \right)}{(1 + r)^t} \right]$$

where t represents the life of capital invested in sector i.

258

It is now necessary to calculate the cost of capital incurred in creating these net benefits in terms of the amount of investable surplus which will be needed. By multiplying the increase in output in sector i and the consequent decline in output in the j sectors by their appropriate capital output ratios (k), there results the amount of investable surplus needed to create the required capital $X_i K_i + \sum_j X_j K_j$.

The <u>cost-benefit ratio</u> for each sector is thus

$$\frac{\displaystyle\sum_{1}^{t} \left[\frac{\sum_t Y_t + C^o \left(\dfrac{w - sw}{w} \right)}{(1 + r)^t} \right]}{X_i K_i + \sum_j X_j K_j}$$

The sector producing the highest ratio will be the one with the highest social return to the use of capital resources.

Appendix 10

Tourism Vocational Training
Responsibilities of National Tourist Organisations

TOURISM VOCATIONAL TRAINING

	I	II	III	IV	V	VI
Afghanistan	*	*				
Algeria	*		*			
Argentina	*	*	*	*	*	
Bahamas		*	*			
Bangladesh	*	*	*	*	*	*
Bolivia		*	*	*	*	*
Botswana	*					
Brazil	*	*	*	*		*
Bulgaria	*	*	*	*	*	*
Burundi	*	*	*			*
Cameroon	*	*	*	*	*	*
Central African Republic	*		*	*		*
Chad	*				*	
Chile			*			
Colombia	*	*	*	*	*	
Cuba	*		*	*	*	
Czechoslovakia						*
Dahomey	*	*				
Ecuador				*		*
Egypt		*	*	*	*	*
Ethiopia	*		*	*	*	*
Gabon		*				*
Ghana	*		*	*		
Greece	*	*	*	*	*	*
Hungary	*		*	*		
Iran	*	*	*	*	*	*
Iraq	*	*	*	*	*	*
Israel	*	*	*	*	*	*
Ivory Coast	*	*	*	*	*	*
Jamaica	*	*				*
Jordan	*	*	*	*	*	*
Kenya	*	*	*	*	*	
Khmer Republic	*		*	*		
Korea	*		*	*		
Lebanon	*	*				*
Libya	*	*			*	*
Malawi	*		*	*	*	
Malaysia	*	*	*	*		
Mali	*	*	*	*	*	*

(continued)

	I	II	III	IV	V	VI
Malta	*		*			
Mauritania	*	*	*	*	*	*
Mexico	*	*	*	*	*	*
Morocco	*	*	*	*	*	*
Nepal	*	*	*	*	*	
Nigeria	*	*		*	*	*
Pakistan	*	*	*			
Peru	*					
Portugal	*	*	*	*	*	*
Rumania	*	*	*	*	*	*
Senegal	*	*	*	*	*	*
Singapore	*		*	*		*
Spain		*	*	*	*	*
Sri Lanka		*	*	*	*	*
Syria	*					
Tanzania	*		*	*		
Thailand			*	*		
Togo	*	*	*		*	*
Tunisia	*	*	*	*	*	*
Turkey	*	*	*	*	*	*
Uganda	*		*	*		*
Upper Volta	*	*	*	*	*	*
Venezuela	*	*	*	*	*	
Vietnam	*		*	*		
Zaire	*	*	*	*	*	*
Zambia	*			*		*

I Determination of manpower and training requirements.
II Granting of fellowships. III Formulation of training programmes for hotel and catering staff, guides, etc.
IV Organisation of vocational training courses, seminars,
and study cycles. V Establishment of hotel and tourism
schools. VI Reception of trainees.

Source: Aims, Activities and Fields of Competence of
National Tourist Organisations, WTO, 1975.

Appendix 11

OECD Recommendations
and UN Guidelines on Tourism Statistics

OECD COMMON DATA

To be collected within the framework of the visitors sample survey, July 1975
(at frontiers and/or in accommodation establishments)

A. <u>Foreign visitors</u>

1. Month of arrival and/or departure
2. Country of usual residence or, failing that, nationality
3. Type of visitor (tourist or excursionist)
4. Sex
5. Age
6. Number and composition of party travelling together[a]
7. Means of transport used and point of entry or departure
8. Main purpose of visit
9. Socio-economic status
10. Actual or intended length of stay
11. Type of accommodation mainly used
12. Region mainly visited
13. Type of resort (destination) mainly visited
14. Payments for international transport made to carriers of the compiling country
15. Other consumption expenditure in the country visited
16. Main categories of consumption expenditure in the country[b]

B. <u>Residents</u>

Same questions as above, A14, A15 and A16 being adapted as follows:

B14 Payments for international transport made to foreign carriers
B15 Other consumption expenditure abroad
B16 Main categories of consumption expenditure abroad

Add the following supplementary question:

B17 Principal country or countries visited.

---

a Including identification of inclusive tour travellers. b Items A16 and B16 can be broken down into specific categories to meet the requirements of each country.

Source: OECD Tourism Policy and International Tourism in OECD Member Countries, 1977.

UN GUIDELINES ON TOURISM STATISTICS, 1977

As presented by BarOn at an Esomar seminar (3).

These guidelines were based on previous work by IUOTO (now WTO), Unctad and
OECD and by countries with advanced tourism statistical systems, and coordinated
with other international recommendations - especially on migration statistics, the
system of national accounts and balance of payments, the system of social and
demographic statistics and various international classifications. The draft guidelines (UN 1975) were distributed to national statistical offices and tourism administrations and were discussed by the Conference of European Statisticians (April
1976), the UN Statistical Commission (November 1976) and by the East Caribbean
Common Market Seminar (ECCM, May 1977), and were then reissued by the UN
after revision.

Definitions

The following basic definitions are of most relevance.

1. International visitors: persons visiting a country other than that of their usual
residence for a period not exceeding one year, for purposes other than employment
remunerated from within the country. Visitors are classified into:

1.1   tourists (or stay-over visitors): staying at least one night in land accommoda-
      tion;
1.2   excursionists: cruise visitors and other day excursionists by land, air or sea
      who do not use land accommodation.

Note that visitors should include nationals resident abroad and visiting, business
visitors, foreign crew on layover, etc, but exclude diplomats and military personnel
stationed in the country, transit passengers not leaving the airport (or other ter-
minal), short or long term immigrants (those taking up employment or residence
for more than one year and their dependants).

2. Persons visiting abroad: residents of the country (including non-nationals) departing or returning from visiting other countries, defined similarly to 1 to exclude
emigrants, etc.

The most important statistics of international visitors relate to:

i.   arrivals, and

ii.   departures at frontiers measured by frontier control forms or sample surveys;

iii. the stay of a tourist in the country (nights between the date of arrival and the
      date of departure); in parallel

iv.   stay abroad, for residents visiting abroad.

Note that one trip may involve two or more arrivals to a particular country (and
departures from it), travelling to and from the most distant destination or taking
side trips. National statistics usually count total arrivals and departures, though

it is desirable to distinguish first arrivals in the country on a trip according to port of embarkation to distinguish the total trips to the country or region and in order to reconcile with departure statistics (e g of Americans visiting Europe). An individual may make several trips during a year; this can be studied only by household surveys or in-depth frontier surveys.

3. Accommodation:

3.1 hotels and related establishments: there may be a national definition of a "tourist hotel" or a grading system distinguishing hotels from guesthouses, etc;

3.2 supplementary accommodation establishments: youth hostels, camping sites, etc;

3.3 other accommodation: second homes, rented apartments, health establishments, staying with relatives and friends, camping out other than at an organised site, etc.

The most important statistics relate to:

i. arrivals at accommodation establishments providing data. These arrivals may be classified by the principal countries of nationality (or of residence), and provide for some destinations the only adequate statistics on arrivals. Many tourists are not covered at all by these accommodation records, while some tourists may arrive in more than one accommodation establishment during their trip (indications of first arrival in the country are difficult to collect and unreliable). Note that the extent of stay outside accommodation establishments reporting and patterns of stay at more than one establishment during the trip will affect the reliability of the measures of level of tourism flows, while changes in tourism patterns will result in the year to year trends in arrivals at accommodation differing from those of arrivals in the country;

ii. person nights spent in accommodation recording: these data can be related to the number of beds to provide bed occupancy data;

iii. room nights, relating to number of rooms to provide room-occupancy;

iv. revenue of the accommodation establishments, which can be related to the number of rooms, room nights and person nights.

Accommodation statistics can be compiled for each of the destination resorts and regions of the country, in relation to the international tourists (by principal country) and residents (domestic tourists, etc) using such accommodation.

Classifications

The UN guidelines propose standard classifications for all the important topics including:

1. Age groups: 0-14, 15-24, 25-44, 45-64, 65 and over, in order to link with population statistics of the source country; further detail may be required of youth tourism (possibly distinguishing age groups for which reduced prices are available) and for "golden age tourism".

2. Occupation: based on the International Standard Classification of Occupations.

3. Purpose of visit: the minimum recommended classification is into:

3.1 holiday (including visits to family and friends);
3.2 business and professional, including conferences;
3.3 other purposes, including study and health;
3.4 crew duty (if covered in the statistics).

Specific purposes which are important to the country should be distinguished, e g winter sports or shopping holidays, pilgrimages, health treatment, etc.

4. Consumption expenditures of visitors, distinguishing outlays on:

4.1 accommodation (including meals, etc), preferably distinguishing between expenditures in accommodation establishments, current expenditures related to second homes, etc;
4.2 other meals and drinks;
4.3 shopping;
4.4 internal transport;
4.5 entertainment and other consumption expenditures in the country;
4.6 international transport;
4.7 package tour expenditures: the individual cannot usually split these down into appropriate categories, but the statistician should make the best estimates possible into the appropriate categories.

5. Regions of the world: international statistics have until now been compiled primarily in terms of the countries reporting, aggregated according to WTO regional commissions (the Commission for Europe includes Cyprus, Israel and Turkey). A classification has now been prepared of the source and destination regions.

THE SCOPE OF TOURISM STATISTICS

Subject	Related fields of statistics and methodology
TOURISM MOVEMENTS AND ACTIVITIES	
International tourism flows[a]	Migration statistics
	Transport statistics
Domestic tourism	Sampling of flows and records
	Surveys of activities, attitudes, intentions
	Time series analysis
	Geostatistics
Use of accommodation[a]	System of social and demographic
Touring	statistics
Cultural	Social indicators
Sport	Sociology, sociometry
Shopping	Use of time, leisure and
Gambling	recreation
	Ecology statistics

(continued)

265

Subject	Related fields of statistics and methodology
TOURISM MARKETING	
Production and image development	Market and motivation research
Promotion	Design of experiments
Pricing policies	
TOURISM SERVICES	
Accommodation[a]	Business statistics
Restaurants	Labour statistics
Shops	Price statistics
Entertainment	Investment and building
Banks	statistics
Travel operators and agents	Foreign trade
Transport: international	Government services
and internal	Economic indicators
Health	Transport branch statistics
TOURISM OUTLAYS	
Consumption expenditures:	National accounts
non-resident visitors[a]	Balance of payments
residents touring abroad[a]	Taxation and subsidies:
domestic tourism	national, local
	Flow of funds
Other expenditures in the	Visitor and household
country related to tourism	expenditure surveys
	Distribution of income
International travel expenditures[a]	Input-output tables
TOURISM PLANNING	
Physical planning	Forecasting
Economic planning	Economics, econometrics
Policies: national, regional,	Management science
industry, enterprise	Operations research
Training	Education statistics
Benefits of tourism (net)	

a Basic System of Tourism Statistics, in UN Guidelines.

FIGURE 4

MANAGEMENT INFORMATION SYSTEM
FOR TOURISM

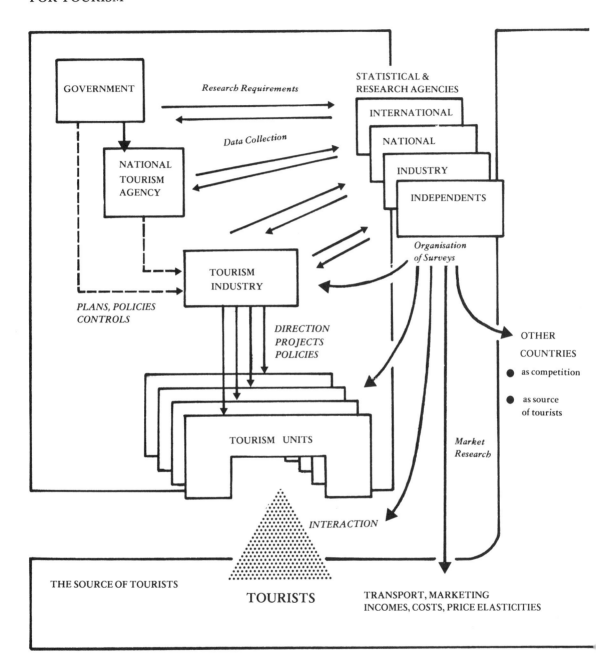

TOURISM STATISTICS REQUIRED FOR ANALYSIS, MONITORING AND PLANNING

PAST DEVELOPMENT	Present	Potential	Plans
Historic data: systematic (monthly, annual) and occasional surveys	Current data	Future oriented data	Forecasts of demand & supply, prices & costs

Demand statistics
Tourism to a country/region/resort
World tourism departures and
  arrivals (especially to
        competitors)
	Current trends	Markets:
		future potential,
		trends
		scenarios
			Possible,
			desirable,
			optimal.
			Financing,
			timetable of
			development

Supply of tourism services (especially accommodation) Quantity, quality, prices, utilisation	Status, being built & plans	Potential development of resources	

Bibliography

1. Annals of Tourism Research (ATR) Department of Habitational Resources -
Tourism University of Wisconsin - Stout

    a.   Britton, Robert A. Making Tourism more supportive of small state
          development - the case of St Vincent Vol IV No 5 May/Sept 1977
    b.   Evans, Nancy H. Tourism and Cross Cultural Communication
          Vol III No 4 Mar/Apr 1976
    c.   Hills, Theo L. & Lundgren, Jan The Impact of Tourism in the Caribbean
          Vol IV No 5 May/Sept 1977
    d.   Sessa, Prof Alberto The Tourism Policy Vol III No 5 May/Aug 1976
    e.   Unesco The Effects of Tourism on Socio-cultural Values Vol III No 6
          Nov/Dec 1976
    f.   Wenkam, Robert The Pacific Tourist Blight Vol III No 2 Nov/Dec 1975

2. Archer, Brian

    a.   The Impact of Domestic Tourism Bangor Occasional Papers in Economics
          University of Wales Press 1973
    b.   Tourism Multipliers: the State of the Art Bangor Occasional Papers in
          Economics University of Wales Press 1977
    c.   Tourism in the Bahamas and Bermuda: two case studies Bangor
          Occasional Papers in Economics University of Wales Press 1977
    d.   Welcome The Crown Agents' Quarterly Review 1978

3. BarOn, Raphael Raymond Tourism Statistics - the Current Situation,
Problems and Needs Esomar October 1977

4. Bond, M.E. & Ladman, Jerry R. International Tourism and Economic
Development: a special case for Latin America Mississippi Valley Journal
of Business and Economics Vol III No 1 1972

5. Bryden, J. M. Tourism and Development a case study of the Commonwealth
Caribbean Cambridge University Press 1973

6. Chenery, H. & Syrquin, M. Patterns of Development 1950-1970, World
Bank Oxford University Press 1975

7. Chen-Young, Paul Transnationals and Tourism in the Caribbean (unpublished)
Commonwealth Secretariat, London 1977

8. Chib, S. N. Organisation of Tourism Paper presented at IUOTO/WTO
conference 1973.

9. Cohen, Erik Toward a Sociology of International Tourism Social Research Vol 39 No 1 1972

10. Dasgupta, P. , Sen, A. & Marglin, S. Guidelines for Project Evaluation Unido Vienna 1972

11. Diamond, J. Tourism and Development Policy: a quantitative appraisal Bulletin of Economic Research Vol 28 No 1 May 1976

12. Doxey, G. V.

    a.   The Tourist Industry in Barbados - a socio-economic assessment Dusco Graphics Kitchener, Ontario 1971

    b.   Paper presented at seminar entitled Recent Methodological Developments in Travel Research at Sixth Annual TTRA conference, San Diego, California 1975

    c.   Caribbean Tourism: tourism impact Vol 1 The Economic Impact of Tourism. Paper on tourism as a tool of development. Caribbean Tourism Research Centre, Barbados 1977

13. Elkan, W. The Relation between Tourism and Employment in Kenya and Tanzania Journal of Development Studies Vol II No 2 Jan 1975

14. Erbes, Robert International Tourism and the Economy of Developing Countries OECD June 1973

15. Esh, T. & Rosenblum, I. Tourism in Developing Countries - trick or treat? A Report from the Gambia Scandinavian Institute of African Studies Uppsala 1975

16. Forbes, A. M. The Trinidad Hilton: a cost benefit analysis of a luxury hotel in I. M. D. Little and M. F. G. Scott (eds) Using Shadow Prices Heinemann 1976

17. Goulet, Denis What kind of tourism? Or, poison in a luxury package Working Paper Series No 2 - Tourism Research Dept of Geography, McGill University, Montreal, June 1977

18. Gray, H. Peter International Travel - International Trade Heath Lexington Books 1970

19. Haites, Erik F. Paper on levels of tourism at which adverse social impact occurs University of Western Ontario 1974

20. Hilton International Management Path to Profit

21. International Tourism Quarterly Economist Intelligence Unit passim but particularly:

    a.   Tourism in Developing Countries No 2 1977

    b.   Economic Development - The Role of Tourism in Economic Development: is it a benefit or a burden? No 2 1973

    c.   The Role and Functions of an NTO Abroad No 3 1976

    d.   Tourism and National Development in Tanzania No 3 1974

f. International Tourism Development Special - Forecasts to 1990 Edwards, A. April 1979

g. Air Inclusive Tour Marketing Yacoumis, J Nov 1975

h. Indian Ocean Islands No 1 1972

22. Jafari, J. Role of Tourism on Socio-Economic Transformation of Developing Countries Cornell University 1973

23. Lal, D. Appraising Foreign Investment in Developing Countries Heinemann 1975

24. Lasry, J. Le Tourisme en Maroc Institut Supérieur de Commerce Paris 1965

25. Little, I.M.D. & Mirrlees, J.A.

a. Manual of Industrial Project Analysis in Developing Countries OECD Paris 1968

b. Project Appraisal and Planning for Developing Countries HEB Paperback

26. Lundberg, David Caribbean Tourism - Social and Racial Tensions Cornell H.R.A. Quarterly Feb and May 1974

27. MacLuhan, Marshall & Fiore, Quentin The Medium is the Message Random House New York 1967

28. Mathematica The Visitor Industry and Hawaii's Economy: a cost-benefit analysis Mathematica Princeton, New Jersey 1970

29. McGrevy, Noel L. The Polynesian Cultural Centre: a model for cultural conservation 1975

30. Mitchell, Francis H.

a. The Value of Tourism in East Africa East African Economic Review 1970

b. The Economic Value of Tourism in Kenya University of California 1971

31. Mozoomdar, Dr Ajit Tourism and the Balance of Payments in a Developing Country Paper given at WTO/BTA Seminar on Tourism Forecasts and Tourism and the Balance of Payments September 1974

32. Myers, Norman The Tourist as an Agent for Development and Wildlife Conservation: the case of Kenya International Journal of Social Economics Vol 2 No 1 1975

33. Nettekoven, L. Mass Tourism in Tunisia: sociological investigations of tourists from highly industrialised societies Starnberg 1973

34. O'Loughlin, C. Tourism in the Tropics: lessons from the West Indies Insight and Opinion 5, 2 1970

35. Patterson, Wm. D. Can Culture Survive Tourism? Paper given at the 25th Anniversary Anniversary Conference of PATA in April 1976

36. Rake, Alan The Economics of Tanzania Tourism African Development Economic Survey Dec 1970

37. Renaud, B.M. The Influence of Tourism Growth on the Production Structures of Island Economies Review of Regional Studies, Vol 2 No 3 1972

38. Rivers, Patrick, Ash, John & Tuckwell, Sue Misguided Tours New Internationalist No 12 Feb 1974

39. Rosenblatt, J. Current Problems of Tourism as a Component of International Trade Paper given at WTO/BTA Seminar on Tourism Forecasts and Tourism and the Balance of Payments September 1974

40. Ruiz, Abel Garrido Efectos del Turismo en la Economía Nacional Departamento de Turismo, Mexico 1969

41. Sadler, P. G. & Archer, Brian The Economic Impact of Tourism in Developing Countries Tourist Research Paper University College of North Wales July 1974

42. Sadler, P.G. Integration of Sector and Project Analysis New Essays in Economics, ed. Parkin Longmans 1973

43. Schawinsky, R. The Socio-Economic Effects of Tourists' Travel in Developing Countries St Gallen Beitrage zum Fremdenverkehrsund zur Verkehrwirtschaft Berne 1973

44. Sessa, A. Tourism in the Third World, Ed. Sarda Fossaturom Cagliari 1972

45. Squire, Lyn & van der Tak, Herman Economic Analysis of Projects Johns Hopkins University Press 1975

46. Tourism International Press Publications:

   a. Tourism International Airletter Twice monthly
   b. Tourism International Policy Quarterly
   c. Tourism International Research Quarterly
   d. Tourism Marketing Wahab, Crampon & Rothfield 1976
   e. Tourism Promotion Schmoll 1977

47. Turner, Louis

   a. The Golden Hordes: International Tourism and the Pleasure Periphery Constable 1975 (with Ash, J.)
   b. The International Division of Leisure: Tourism in the Third World ATR Vol 4 No 1 1977

48. UNCTAD

    a. Invisibles: Tourism, Elements of Tourism Policy in Developing Countries
       1971

    b. The Development of Tourism in Yugoslavia, 1958-1967 1971

    c. The Development of Tourism in Israel, 1958-1966 1971

    d. Developing Island Countries 1974

49. UN Ecosoc Study by the then IUOTO (now WTO) on the Impact of International
Tourism on the Economic Development of Developing Countries May 1975

50. Unesco/IBRD Seminar on the Social and Cultural Impacts of Tourism -
Policy Recommendations Dec 1976

51. UN

    a. Planning and Development of the Tourist Industry in the ECE Region
       Seminar Proceedings Oct 1975

    b. Tourism Development in Developing Countries

    c. Guidelines on Tourism Statistics 1977

52. Varley, R. C. G. Tourism in Fiji: some Economic and Social Problems
University of Wales Press June 1978

53. Waters, Somerset The Big Picture Annual Review of Tourism published
by ASTA Travel News

54. World Bank (IBRD)

    a. Tourism Sector Working Paper June 1972

    b. Calvo, D. Caribbean Regional Study Vol VI 1974

    c. Noronha, R. Social and Cultural Dimensions of Tourism: a review of
       the literature in English (to be issued as World Bank Working Paper in
       1979)

55. Wright, D. Air Inclusive Tour Holiday Industry Article in British Business
Policy: a casebook eds. Channon, D. F., Norburn, D., & Stopford, J. M.
Macmillan 1975

56. WTO/IUOTO Publications:

    a. Technical Bulletin Bi-monthly

    b. Information Press Releases Monthly

    c. World Travel Bi-monthly

    d. Travel Research Journal Annual/biannual

    e. Tourism Compendium, 1975

    f. World Travel Statistics, 1976

    g. Tourism Vocational Training in Africa Sept 1972

    h. Physical Planning and Area Development for Tourism March 1973

    i. Organisation of Tourism 1973

    j. National Parks and Wildlife Areas as Tourist Resources 1973

    k. Protection of Tourist Resources and Perpetuation of Cultural Traditions
       1973

l. International Organisations Directly or Indirectly Concerned with Tourism 1973
m. Presentation and Financing of Tourism Development Projects 1973
n. Systems of State Aid to the Hotel and Tourist Industries
o. Study on Present and Potential Distribution Channels
p. The Marketing of Tourist Products of the Developing Countries Aug 1973
q. Aims, Activities and Fields of Competence of National Tourist Organisations 1975
r. Compilation and Preliminary Analysis of Information on Educational and Vocational Training Programmes
s. The Role of Tourist Administration with respect to the Environment and Folklore Sept 1974
t. State Incentives for Private Investment 1976
u. Africa's Tourist Image 1977
v. Distribution Channels March 1977
w. Factors Influencing Travel Demand and Leading to the Redistribution of Tourist Movements March 1977
x. Inventory of Tourism Development Plans 1978
y. Sources and Conditions of Financing for Tourist Development Projects 1971
z. Study of the Prospects for Tourism Development in the Middle East Region

57. Young, Sir George Tourism - Blessing or Blight? Pelican 1973.